the
astrological
book of baby names

the astrological

book of baby names

Catherine Osbond

VERMILION
LONDON

To Wayne, for your constant love and support. Also to Matthew, Luke, Adam and Clare, for providing me with the inspiration.

357908642

Text © Catherine Osbond 2001

Catherine Osbond has asserted her right to be
identified as the author of this work under the Copyright, Designs
and Patents Act 1988.

First published in the United Kingdom in 2001 by Vermilion
an imprint of Ebury Press
Random House
20 Vauxhall Bridge Road · London SW1V 2SA

Random House Australia (Pty) Limited
20 Alfred Street · Milsons Point · Sydney · New South Wales 2061 · Australia

Random House New Zealand Limited
18 Poland Road · Glenfield · Auckland 10 · New Zealand

Random House South Africa (Pty) Limited
Endulini, 5A Jubilee Road · Parktown 2193 · South Africa
Random House UK Limited Reg. No. 954009

Papers used by Vermilion are natural, recyclable products made from wood
grown in sustainable forests.

A CIP catalogue record for this book is available from the British Library.

ISBN 0 09 1882206

Cover design by Vivid Design

Design by Lovelock & Co.

Printed and bound in Great Britain by Mackays of Chatham plc, Chatham, Kent

Contents

Introduction

Choosing a name is one of the most important things a parent does for their child and there are many things to consider when doing so. Naturally you will choose a name which you like and which you feel that your child may enjoy owning. You may also wish to give your child a name which you feel 'suits' them. Whether a name 'suits' your child is usually determined by the sound of your baby's name, but you may also wish to consider the meaning behind your chosen name.

THE ASTROLOGICAL BOOK OF BABY NAMES is a baby name book with a difference. It gives you the opportunity of choosing a name which is directly related to your baby's astrological star sign.

In astrology the personality of a person is said to be influenced by the position of the sun, moon and planets at the time of his or her birth. All these planets exert an influence on your baby's personality, to a greater or lesser degree. To get a truly accurate astrological reading of your baby's personality a complete birthchart should be drawn up.

However the sun exerts the strongest influence on your baby's personality and it is your baby's sun sign to which I will primarily refer in this book.

Finding Your Baby's Sun Sign

There are twelve signs of the zodiac. In astrology, the sky, as viewed from earth, is divided into twelve equal sections and a name from the zodiac given to each one. As the earth moves around the sun, the sun appears to move from one zodiac sign to the next. For example, if your baby was born on the first of June, the sun would be in the zodiac sign of Gemini. Your baby's sun sign would therefore be Gemini. Here are the approximate dates of each sign:

SIGN	DATES
Aries	21 March – 19 April
Taurus	20 April – 20 May
Gemini	21 May – 20 June
Cancer	21 June – 22 July
Leo	23 July – 22 August
Virgo	23 August – 22 September
Libra	23 September – 22 October
Scorpio	23 October – 21 November
Sagittarius	22 November – 21 December
Capricorn	22 December – 19 January
Aquarius	20 January – 18 February
Pisces	19 February – 20 March

These dates are correct for babies born in 2001. The exact dates for different years can vary slightly from year to year, and may change by one day. Therefore if your child was born right at the end of one sign, or the beginning of another (the 'cusp'), you may be unsure as to which is his or her sun sign. The only way to be really sure is to have their astrological chart drawn up by an astrologer.

Personality and Your Baby's Sun Sign

In astrology your baby's personality is said to be influenced by his or her sun sign. A baby born under the sign of Libra, for example, is said to be peaceful, companionable and co-operative. So if you wish to provide your Libran baby with a name which 'suits' their sun sign, and therefore their personality, simply look under the sign of Libra and you will find a list of relevant names from which to choose.

Most of the names in this book have been selected because the meaning attached to the name is directly linked to characteristics of a particular astrological zodiac sign. Taking Libra again as our example, a

peaceful disposition is a particular characteristic of a Libran personality. If you wish to choose a name with this connection, you could choose Eiran, which is an Irish boy's name meaning 'peace', or Serena which is a Latin girl's name meaning 'peaceful'.

Names have also been included under each zodiac sign because their meaning may relate directly or indirectly to the ruling planet, or planets, of that astrological sun sign. For example, the ruling planet of Cancer is the Moon. Lucius is a Latin boy's name meaning 'light'. Lewanna is a Hebrew girl's name meaning 'as clear as the moon'.

Some of the names have been chosen because they are alternative names connected to mythological characters related to that sign. For example, the ruling planet of Taurus is Venus, the goddess of love in Greek mythology. So you may find a name such as Ishtar, which is the Babylonian goddess of love.

A few names have been selected because of other connections, such as the names of stars in the relevant constellation, lucky elements, or plants related to your baby's star sign. Other names are related to the time or season of the year of your baby's birth.

Names that relate to one of the four elements connected to your baby's sun sign have also been included. Each one of these – Earth, Water, Fire and Air – has certain characteristics. For example, Aries, Leo and Sagittarius are all linked to the element of Fire, and people born under any of these three signs are said to be energetic, fiery and warm. You may therefore wish to name your 'firesign' baby Ethne, which is an Irish girl's name meaning 'little fire' or Brendan, which is a Gaelic boy's name meaning 'fiery one'.

Finally, good luck in choosing that perfect name for your very special baby!

Aries

THE RAM
21 March – 19 April

RULING PLANET   Mars – The roman god of war. In astrology Mars is the planet of energy and creative action.

ELEMENT   Fire

General characteristics
- Self-assertive, active, daring, adventurous, aggressive.
- Creative, self-directive, persistent.
- Like to be in control. Strong leaders.
- Competitive, like to be first.
- Courageous. Defends the vulnerable.
- Honest, noble, open.

Characteristics of young Ariens
- Strong and active in both mind and body.
- Very strong willed.
- Early walkers and talkers.
- Very generous with possessions.
- Often very affectionate.
- Curious and imaginative.

Arien lucky connections
Gemstones: ruby, diamond
Colours: red, black, white
Plant: tiger lily
Metal: iron
Animals: ram and lamb
Tarot card: the magician

ARIES is the first sign of the zodiac and Ariens always want to be first. They are natural born leaders and are very competitive. Determined and decisive with bright, alert minds, Ariens are always interested in new challenges. They also tend to be impulsive individuals with bundles of energy and a courageous spirit. This side of their character will doubtless lead to tumbles and tussles but Ariens have a resilience that will see them bouncing back. They usually possess strong, active bodies and are constantly on the move, thereby exhausting both their parents and themselves. Even as babies they will want to be up and about as quickly as possible and may well crawl and walk earlier than usual.

Life with an Arien toddler can be exhausting. A definite "No" can often produce wild tantrums, so try to provide options as often as possible, such as: "Do you want to go to the park before or after shopping?" Having a choice in the matter will give your child the feeling of having some control over the situation. Positive reinforcement also works well with Arien children when you wish

them to do something. So give lots of encouragement, smiles and hugs when they do the right thing.

Ariens also love a challenge, so when you wish them to do something, for example, tidying up, try telling them that it's not their fault that they're not very good at clearing away their toys. They will probably rush to prove you wrong! Ariens also love to be first, so initiating a race to the bathroom or a competition as to who can get dressed first will soon have your child rushing to be the winner.

As they mature continue to give your Arien child outlets for all that energy. Competitive sports and games will fulfil this need and are best encouraged.

As Ariens are also very creative try also to foster this side of their personality as an alternative outlet for that unceasing energy.

As Ariens are not the best team players – they always want to be in charge – try to encourage your child to co-operate with others by providing activities or tasks which can only be successfully accomplished by co-operation. For example, working on a large wall painting or collage that requires him to plan and work with others in order to produce a finished product.

Coupled with their boundless energy of body and spirit, Ariens also possess an openness and an engaging child-like innocence that will stay with them well into adulthood. This quality gives them, as adults, a sense of honesty and integrity that will remain with them all their lives.

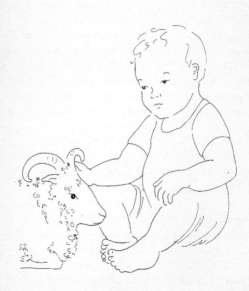

Aries ~ Boys

AIDAN, AIDEN (Irish Gaelic) 'Fiery one'. The name was borne by several early Irish saints including a famous Irish 7th century monk. The name enjoyed a revival in the early 19th century and remains in regular use today.

ALARIC (Old German) 'Ruler of all'. A famous bearer of this name was Alaric I, a Visigoth king who was a conqueror of Rome in the 5th century.

ALBAN (Latin) 'White'. White is a lucky colour for Aries. St. Alban was the first British martyr. The name was revived in the 19th century and has been in occasional use since then.

ALBANY Form of Alban.

ALBIN Form of Alban.

ALPIN (Latin) 'White'. White is a lucky colour for Aries.

ALEXANDER (Greek) 'Defender of men'. Alexander the Great (4th century BC) was the most famous bearer of the name. The Egyptian city of Alexandria was named after him. The name is also found in the New Testament and was borne by a few early Christian saints. The name has been in regular use in Britain since the Middle Ages.

ALEX Shortened form of Alexander.

ALEXIS (Greek) 'Helper, defender'. Originally a Russian masculine name. The name became popular in Britain and the USA and is now regarded as either a boys' or girls' name.

ALASDAIR Original Scottish Gaelic form of Alistair.

ALISTAIR Gaelic form of Alexander.

ALISTER, ALASTER Alternative spellings of Alistair.

ALOYSIUS (Old German) 'Famous warrior'. A Provençal form of Louis. the name has been in use in Britain since the 16th century. It is the name of an Italian saint Aloysius of Gonzaga (1568-91).

ALVA (Irish Gaelic) 'White'. In medieval times the name was used as a boys' name but in its revival it is used mainly as a girls' name.

ANDOR Form of Andrew.

ANDRÉ French form of Andrew.

ANDREAS (Greek) 'Courageous man', 'warrior'. The original form of Andrew found in the New Testament. It is becoming increasingly popular in English-speaking countries.

ANDREW English form of the Greek name Andreas. St Andrew, an apostle of Jesus Christ and patron saint of Scotland, was one of the earliest and famous bearers of the name. The name has been popular in Scotland for hundreds of years and was in regular use in Britain in the Middle Ages. Its use spread to the USA where it was borne by two presidents, Andrew Jackson and Andrew Carnegie. The name became particularly popular in the latter half of the 20th century

after the birth of Queen Elizabeth II's son Prince Andrew.

ARABIA Name given to the large, heavily cratered circular area of Mars.

ARCHIBALD (Old German) 'Noble, bold'. The name was introduced into Britain at the time of the Norman Conquest. The name has been most frequently in use in Scotland.

ARDEN (Latin) 'Enthusiastic'.

ARES Name of the Greek god of War.

ARIES Name given to astrological sun sign.

ARIETIS Latin possessive of the constellation of Aries.

ARNAUD Form of Arnold.

ARNOLD (German) 'Ruler. Strong as an eagle'. The name was introduced into Britain at the time of the Norman Conquest and was in frequent use until the 13th century. It was revived in the 19th century and remains in occasional use today.

AUBIN (Latin) 'White'. White is a lucky colour for Aries.

BAIN (Gaelic) 'White'.

BALDRIC (Old German) 'Brave and noble ruler'.

BALDWIN (Old German) 'Bold friend'. The name was in frequent use in Britain during medieval times but is little used as a first name today.

BARNARD, BERNHARD Forms of Bernard.

BARNET Form of Barnard.

BERNARD (Old German) 'Bold as a bear'. The name was borne by several saints, the most famous being St Bernard of Menthon, patron saint of mountaineers. The name was introduced into Britain at the time of the Norman conquest. It was in regular use until the 17th century and was revived in the 19th century and has been in occasional use since then.

BILL, BILLY Shortened forms of William.

BIRCH (Old English) From the tree name meaning 'white'. White is a lucky colour for Aries.

BLAKE (Old English) From two origins, both from Old English. One meaning is 'white', one meaning is 'black.' Both white and black are lucky colours for Aries.

BRADY (Gaelic) 'Spirited one' or 'one from the broad island'.

BRENDAN (Gaelic) 'Fiery one' or 'prince'. The name was borne by two 6th century Irish saints. Legend has it that one, Brendan the Voyager, was the first European to set foot on North American soil.

BRIAN (Celtic) 'High, noble' or 'strong'. Originally an Irish name which is now in regular use throughout English-speaking countries.

CARL (Old German) Derivative of Charles.

CARLOS (Old German) Spanish derivative of Charles.

CATHAL (Irish Gaelic) 'Battle' and 'rule'. A traditional Irish Gaelic name which was borne by a 7th-century saint.

CHARLES (Old German) 'Strong, virile man'. The name became popular in the 9th century due to Charles the Great who became the first ruler of the Holy Roman Empire. The name has been borne by several European monarchs. The name was introduced into Britain at the time of the Norman Conquest although it was rarely found until the 17th century when it became popularized by the reigns of King Charles I and II. In the mid-19th century it had become one of the most popular boys' names in English-speaking countries.

CHU-JUNG Name given to the spirit of fire in Chinese mythology.

CHUCK (Old German) Derivative of Charles.

CIARÁN (Irish Gaelic) 'Black'. Black is a lucky colour for Aries. The name was borne by two Irish saints of the 5th and 6th centuries.

CLAIRMOND (Old German) 'Famous protector'.

CLANCY 'Red warrior'. Transferred use of Irish surname. The name is mainly found in the USA.

COLBRAN (Old German) 'Man of fire'.

COLE A name of uncertain origin. It may be a derivative of Nicholas – 'Victorious leader', or it may be from Old English meaning 'coal-black'. Both meanings are appropriate for Aries.

CONALL (Irish and Scottish Gaelic) 'Strong'. The name was borne by several early chieftains and warriors of Ireland.

CONN (Irish Gaelic) 'Chief'.

CONRAD (Old German) 'Brave counsel'. The name was borne by four German kings of the Middle Ages. The name has been in occasional use in the English-speaking countries since the 15th century.

DEIMOS Name of one of Mars' moons. Named after one of the two mythical horses that drew the chariot of the Greek god of war, Mars. Means 'panic'.

DEREK, DERRICK, DERYCK, DERYK Forms of Theodoric (Old German) 'people's ruler'. The name was introduced into Britain in the 15th century. It was revived in the early 20th century and has been in regular use since then.

DIRK (Old German) 'People's ruler'. Dutch form of Derek.

DUANE, DWAYNE (Irish) 'Black'. Black is a lucky colour for Aries. It has been in regular use in English-speaking countries since the mid-20th century.

DUKE (Latin) 'Leader'. From a surname originally borne by members of a duke's family, or from the title itself.

DWIGHT (Old English) 'White, fair'. White is a lucky colour for Aries. The name is originally from a surname. Its use as a first name is more frequently found in the USA, possibly due to the popularity of Timothy Dwight (1752-1817) an early president of Yale University, and of the 20th-century US president Dwight D Eisenhower.

EASTMAN (Old English) 'Protector of grace'.

EDAN (Celtic) 'Flame'. Scottish and Irish form of Aidan. The name was borne by St Edan, an Irish disciple of St David of Wales.

EGAN (Celtic) 'Formidable', 'fiery'.

EDSEL (German) 'Noble'. In German mythology the name is a form of Etzal. In modern times the most famous bearer of the name was Edsel Ford, son of the founder of Ford Motor Corporation.

EGBERT (Old English) 'Bright, famous'. The name was borne by two English 8th-century saints and also by a 9th-century king of Wessex. It enjoyed a brief revival in the 19th century.

EINAR (Norse) 'Warrior leader'.

EMERY (Old German) 'Powerful ruler'. The name was introduced into Britain after the Norman Conquest but is found mainly as a surname in modern times.

ERIC (Old Norse) 'Honourable or all powerful ruler'. The name was introduced into Britain from Scandinavia before the Norman Conquest, but was seldom used until the early part of the 20th century when it spread to the USA.

ESMOND (Old English) Means a combination of 'grace' and 'protection'. The name was little used as a first name after the end of the Middle Ages but enjoyed a brief revival in the latter half of the 20th century.

EVERARD (Old English) 'Hardy, brave, strong'. The name was introduced into Britain at the time of the Norman Conquest and was fairly common in the Middle Ages. It enjoyed a brief revival in the 19th century.

FAGAN, FAGIN (Gaelic) 'Little fiery one'.

FARAMOND (Old German) Means a combination of 'journey' and 'protection'.

FARRELL (Celtic) 'Of great valour'.

FERDINAND (Old German) 'Courageous peacemaker' or 'adventurous'. The name was used traditionally in Spanish royal families from an early date. It spread to Britain in the 16th century but has never been common.

FERNANDO Form of Ferdinand.

FARON, FARRAN, FARREN Forms of Ferdinand.

FERGAL (Irish) 'Man', 'valour'.

FERGUS (Scottish and Irish) 'Vigorous man'. The name was borne by a 8th-century king of Ireland

FERRANT (Old French) 'Iron grey'. Iron is a lucky metal for Aries.

FERRIS (Latin) 'Iron'. Iron is a lucky metal for Aries.

FINBAR (Irish) 'White, fair'. White is a lucky colour for Aries.

FINGAL, FINGALL (Scottish) 'White, fair'.

FINLAY (Scottish) 'White or fair hero'. The name was borne by the father of Macbeth. The name has been popular in Scotland for centuries, used both as a first name and surname, and remains in use today.

FINN (Irish) 'White, fair'.

FIONN Modern Gaelic form of Finn.

FINNIAN (Irish) 'White', 'fair'.

FINTAN (Irish) 'White', 'fire'.

FINDLAY (Gaelic) 'Fair hero'.

FLANN (Gaelic) 'Lad with red hair'. Red is a lucky colour for Aries. The name is a traditional Irish name which was borne by several early Irish heroes.

FLINN , FLYNN (Gaelic) 'Son of the red-haired one'.

FREEMONT (Old German) 'Protector of freedom'.

GARNER (Old German) 'Noble protector'.

GARRET, GARRETT Forms of Gerard.

GAVA (Sanskrit) 'Swift'.

GAVAN, GAVEN Forms of Gavin.

GAVIN (Celtic) 'Battle hawk'. A form of Gawain. The name Gavin was little used outside Scotland from the 17th century until the 20th century when it began to spread to other English-speaking countries.

GAWAIN (Welsh) 'Battle hawk' or 'white hawk'. The name was borne by one of the legendary knights of the Round Table, a nephew of King Arthur. The name is seldom found today.

GAWAINE, GAWEN Forms of Gawain.

GAYLORD (Old French) 'Brave' or 'high-spirited'. More frequently used as a surname than as a first name.

GEAROID Irish Gaelic form of Gerald.

GED Short form of Gerald or Gerard.

GERALD (Old French) 'Spear' and 'rule'. The name was introduced into Britain by the Normans. It was little used in England after the 13th century but it continued to be used in Ireland. The name was revived in England in the 19th century and remains in use today.

GERARD (Old French) 'Spear' and 'brave, strong'. The name was introduced into Britain by the Normans and was popular in the Middle Ages. It was revived in the 19th century and remains in use today.

GERRARD Variant spelling of Gerard, borne by an early saint. It was introduced into Britain by the Normans and is still infrequently used today.

GERVAIS, GERVAS (Old German) 'Alert warrior'. The name was borne by an early saint. It was introduced into Britain by the Normans and is still in occasional use in modern times.

GORDON (Greek) 'Bold'. Originally a Scottish surname and place name. Its usage as a first name in the 19th century has been attributed to Charles George Gordon, the 19th-century British general who died at Khartoum.

GORDAŃ Variant spelling of Gordon.

GORDEN Variant spelling of Gordon.

GRIFFITH (Celtic) 'Fierce, red-haired warrior'. The name was borne by several medieval Welsh monarchs. As a first name it remains in occasional use in Wales but is found more frequently as a surname in other parts of Britain.

GRIFFIN Form of Griffith.

GRUFFYDD Welsh form of Griffith

GUILLYM (Old German) Welsh derivative of William – 'Resolute defender'.

GUNTER, GUNTAR (Old German) 'War' or 'battle'. The name was introduced into Britain at the time of the Norman Conquest. It remained in regular use until the 15th century. It is now regarded as a German name.

GUNTHER, GUNTHAR (Old German) 'Bold warrior'. The name was introduced into Britain at the time of the Norman Conquest but is little used today.

GUNNAR, GUNNER, GUNAR Forms of Gunther.

GUTHRIE (Celtic) 'Hero'.

GWILYM, GWYLIM (Old German) 'Resolute protector'. Welsh forms of William.

GWYN (Welsh) 'White'. White is a lucky colour for Aries.

HAL Pet form of Henry, sometimes used as an independent name.

HAMEL 'The Ram'. The brightest star in the constellation of Aries.

HANK Dutch pet form of Henry, often used as a name in its own right.

HARDY (Middle English) 'Brave'. The name has been in occasional use as both a first name and a surname since the 19th century. It is more common in the USA.

HAROLD (Old English) 'Ruler' or 'powerful army'. The name was borne by two 11th-century kings of England, notably Harold II who was killed at the Battle of Hastings. The name died out during the Middle Ages but it enjoyed a revival in the 19th century until the 1930s.

HARRY Pet form of Henry. 'Home ruler'. Often used as a name in its own right.

HENRY (Old French) 'Home ruler'. The name was introduced into Britain by the Normans and was borne by eight kings of England. The name remained in frequent use throughout English-speaking countries until the 20th century when its popularity began to decline.

HERBERT (Old German) 'Bright or famous army'. The name was introduced into Britain at the time of the Norman Conquest. It was revived in the 19th century.

HEREWARD (Old English) 'Army' and 'defence'. The name is associated with the 11th-century Anglo-Saxon hero Hereward the Wake who led a revolt against William the Conqueror.

HEW, HUW Welsh spelling of Hugh, derived from a Celtic word for 'fire' or 'inspiration'.

HUMBERT (Old German) 'Bright or famous warrior'. It was introduced into Britain at the time of the Norman Conquest.

HUMPHREY (Norman) 'Strength' and 'peace'. The Old German form of the name was introduced into Britain by the Normans and gradually absorbed the Old English form of the name, resulting in the name Humphrey. The name has been in occasional use throughout the English-speaking countries since.

HUNT (Old English) 'To search or hunt'.

HUNTER (Old English) 'Hunter'. Transferred use of surname, in origin an occupational name.

IDRIS (Welsh) 'Fiery lord' or 'impulsive'. The name was borne by a character in Welsh mythology. The mountain Cader Idris in Gwynedd is named after him.

IGNATIUS (Latin) 'Fire'. The name was borne by St Ignatius of Antioch, a 2nd-century martyr, and also by St Ignatius of Loyola, the founder of the Jesuits (1491-1556).

IGNACE, IGNATE, IGNACIO Forms of Ignatius.

INIGO 'Fire'. Spanish form of Ignatius.

IRA (Hebrew) 'Watchful' and also from Latin 'anger'. The name was adopted by the Puritans possibly because of its Latin origin 'anger', which refers to the wrath of God against sinners. The name is more commonly found in the USA.

JAEGER (German) 'Hunter'.

JAI (Sanskrit) 'Hail, praise, victory'.

JARETH (Old German) 'Strong fighter'.

JARRATT (Old German) 'Strong ruler'.

JARVIS (Old German) Derivative of Gervais. 'Alert warrior'.

JASON (Greek) 'Healer'. The name is borne by an important character in the mythological story of the creation of the constellation of Aries.

KANE Of uncertain origin. It may be from Celtic, meaning 'warrior' or from a French place Caen, meaning 'field of combat'. Either meaning is appropriate for Aries.

KELSEY (Old English) 'Victory'. Originally a surname used occasionally as a first name.

KEMP (Middle English) 'Warrior, champion'. Transferred use of a surname which originated from the Middle Ages.

KENELM (Old English) 'Brave helmet' or 'brave protection'. The name was popular in the Middle Ages when a 9th-century Prince of Mercia of this name was revered as a saint and martyr. The name is rarely found today.

KENWARD (Old English) 'Brave guard'.

KENWYN (Cornish) 'White chief or white ridge'.

KERRIN Form of Kieran.

KERRY Form of Kieran.

KERWIN (Irish) 'Dark, black'. Black is a lucky colour for Aries.

KEYE (Gaelic) 'Son of the fiery one'.

KIERAN (Irish) 'Black.' Black is a lucky colour for Aries. The name was borne by two Irish saints of the 5th and 6th centuries. Kieran was rarely found outside Ireland until the mid-20th century, when it began to spread to other parts of the English-speaking world.

KIERON Alternative spelling of Kieran.

KIM Shortened form of Kimball.

KIMBALL Of uncertain origin. It may be from Old English, meaning 'bold family' or Welsh, meaning 'chief' and 'war'. Both meanings are appropriate for Aries.

KUAN TI Name given to the god of war in Chinese mythology.

KYRAN Form of Kieran.

LABAN (Hebrew) 'White'. White is a lucky colour for Aries. The name was used in the 17th century by the Puritans but is rarely found today.

LACHLAN (Celtic) 'Famous warrior'. The name has been used in Scotland for centuries but is little used elsewhere.

LEOPOLD (Old German) 'Bold man'. The name became popular in Britain in the 19th century after the uncle of Queen Victoria and Prince Albert, the Belgian king Leopold I. Queen Victoria also gave the name to her youngest son.

LEWIS English form of the French name Louis. 'Famous warrior'.

LIAM Irish form of William. 'Resolute protector'.

LOIC (Old German) Celtic derivative of Lewis. 'Famous warrior'.

LOUIE Form of Louis.

LOUIS (French of Germanic origin) 'Famous warrior'. The name was used by the Fench royal family for centuries and was given to eighteen kings. It was introduced into Britain at the time of the Norman Conquest and altered forms such as Lewis were produced. The French form was revived in the 19th century and has remained in use since then.

LORCAN (Irish) 'Fierce'. The name was borne by St Lorcán Ó Tuathail in the 12th century, the archbishop of Dublin.

LUDOVIC Form of Louis. Occasionally the name is used in Scotland.

LUTHER (German) 'People's army'. Originally from a German surname. The name was popularised in the 20th century by Martin Luther King, the civil rights leader who was assassinated in 1968.

LYULF, LYULPH (Old English) 'Flame' and 'wolf'.

MADISON, MADDISON (Old German) 'Great and heroic'. Mainly found in the USA, used both as a boys' and girls' name. Madison was originally used as a surname. Its use as a first name appears to have been influenced by the president James Madison (1751-1836). The name has recently been popular as a girls' name.

MALDWYN (Welsh) 'Bold friend'.

MARC See 'Mark'.

MARCEL French form of Marcellus.

MARCELLUS Latin pet form of Marcus. In ancient Rome the name was used as a family name. The name has been borne by several minor saints and two popes.

MARCIUS (Latin) Linked to Marcus and ultimately to Mars.

MARCUS (Latin) Connected with Mars, the Roman god of war. Also means male, virile. The name was popular in ancient Rome, a famous bearer of the name being Marcus Antonius, better known as Mark Antony. Marcus was little used in English-speaking countries until the 19th century and was particularly popular in the latter half of the 20th century.

MAREK (Latin) Derivative of Marcius.

MARIO (Latin) Italian derivative of Marcius.

MARIUS (Latin) Connected with Mars. Also means 'virile'. The name was used as a Roman clan name. It is occasionally found in English-speaking countries.

MARK (Latin) English form of Marcus. Connected with Mars, the Roman god of war. The name is found in the New Testament, St Mark was the author of the second Gospel. The name was little used in English-speaking countries until the latter half of the 20th century when it became very popular.

MARKUS See 'Marcus'.

MAYNARD (Norman French) 'Strength, brave'. The name was introduced into Britain by the Normans. It is more frequently found today as a surname than as a first name.

MARTIN, MARTYN English form of the Latin name Martinus. Derived from Mars, Roman god of war. The name was borne by St Martin, a 4th-century soldier who was converted to Christianity. His fame led to the name being very popular in the Middle Ages. It enjoyed a further revival in the latter half of the 20th century.

MARTY Short form of Martin.

MAX Short form of Maximillian.

MAXIMILIAN (Latin) 'Greatest'. The name was borne by a 3rd-century martyr St Maximilian. The name is seldom found in this form in English-speaking countries.

MAXWELL An extension of Max.

MEILYR (Welsh) 'Chief ruler'. A traditional Welsh name.

MERELLO (Latin) Derivative of Maricus.

MILES, MYLES (Norman) 'Generous' or possibly from Latin meaning 'soldier'. Both meanings are appropriate to Aries. The name has been in fairly regular use in English-speaking countries since the Middle Ages.

NARA (Sanskrit) 'Hero'.

NEIL, NEILL, NEAL, NIALL (Irish) 'Champion' or 'passionate'. The name was borne by the Irish King Niall of the Nine Hostages, who died in the early 5th century. Neil was introduced into Britain from France and Scandinavia during the Middle Ages.

NICHOLAS (Latin) 'Victorious little one'. A famous early bearer of the name was a 4th-century bishop St Nicholas on whom Father Christmas or Santa Claus is based. The name was popular in the latter half of the Middle Ages and has been in regular use since then. It became particularly popular in the the mid-20th century and remains in regular use today.

NICO Modern short form of Nicholas.

NICOL Medieval form of Nicholas.

NICOLAS, NICKOLAS Alternative spellings of Nicholas.

NIGEL Form of Neil. The name has been used in Britain for centuries and was particularly popular in Britain in the mid-20th century.

NILES Shortened form of Nicholas.

NOLAN (Gaelic) 'Champion', 'famous' or 'noble'. All meanings are appropriate to Aries. The name was originally an Irish surname, occasionally found as a first name in recent times.

OSWALD (Old English) 'Rule' or 'power'. The name was borne by two saints in the 7th and 10th century. The name was rarely found after the Middle Ages but was modestly revived in the 19th century.

PASCAL (Hebrew) 'Born at Eastertime'. The name has been in use in Britain since the Middle Ages and underwent a modest revival in the latter half of the 20th century.

PASCOE (Latin) Connected with Easter. A form of Pascal. The name has been in occasional use in Cornwall since the 16th century but is little used elsewhere.

PASQUALE Italian derivative of Pascal.

PHOBOS Name of one of Mars' moons. Named after one of the mythical horses that drew the chariot of the Roman god of war, Mars. Means 'fear'.

QUINN (Irish) 'Leader, chief'. Originally an Irish surname, occasionally found as a first name.

RABBIE, RABBY, RAB (Scottish) Pet form of Robert. 'Famous'.

RADCLIFFE, RADCLIFF (Old English) 'Red cliff'. Red is a lucky colour for Aries.

RAGHNALL (Irish Gaelic) 'Decisive ruler'.

RAMAN Spanish form of Raymond. 'Wise protection'.

RAMON Spanish form of Raymond.

RAMSDEN (Old English) 'Valley with rams'. The ram is the symbol and lucky animal for Aries

RAMSAY, RAMSEY (Old English) 'Ram's island'. The ram is the symbol and lucky animal for Aries. Ramsey is originally from a surname and place name and is still in occasional use today.

RANALD (Scottish) Anglicized form of Raghnall. 'Decisive ruler'.

RANDALL Medieval form of Raghnall. 'Decisive ruler'.

RAYMOND (Old German) 'Wise protector'. The name was introduced into Britain by the Normans. It fell out of use but was revived in the mid-19th century.

RAYMUND (Old German) 'Wise protector'.

REED (Old English) 'Red-haired'. Red is a lucky colour for Aries.

REMUS One of the twin sons of Mars, Roman god of war.

REYNARD (Old French) 'Advice' and 'hardy, brave, strong'. The name was introduced into Britain by the Normans. It is rarely found today.

REYNER, RAYNOR (Old German) 'Counsel' and 'army'. The name was introduced into Britain at the time of the Norman Conquest. It was in regular use until the 14th century and then revived in the 19th century.

REYNOLD (Old French) 'Decisive ruler or strong counsel'. French form of Norman name introduced by them into Britain. The name was in regular use until the 15th century but is found mainly as a surname today.

ROB, ROBBIE, ROBBY Pet forms of Robert.

ROBERT (German) 'Famous'. The name was introduced into Britain by the Normans. It was borne by three kings of Scotland, notably Robert the Bruce (1274-1329) who freed Scotland from English rule. Robert has been a popular name throughout English-speaking countries for several centuries and remains in regular use today.

ROBERTO Form of Robert.

ROBIN Originally a medieval pet form of Robert. 'Famous'. Now used as a name in its own right. In recent times it has also been used as a girls' name.

ROD, RODDY Shortened forms of Roderick.

RODERICK (German) 'Fame, power'. The name was introduced into Britain by Scandinavian settlers and later by the Normans. The name is found throughout English-speaking countries but has never been common.

RODRICK, RODRIC, RODERIC Forms of Roderick.

RODGER, RODGE Forms of Roger.

ROGAN (Gaelic) 'Red-haired one'. Red is a lucky colour for Aries.

ROGER (Old French) 'Fame' and 'spear'. The name was introduced into Britain by the Normans and became very popular. Its use declined in the 16th century but was revived in the 19th century increasing in popularity in the mid-20th century.

ROLAND (Old French) 'Fame', 'land, territory'. The name was introduced into Britain at the time of the Norman Conquest. Until the 19th century Rowland was the usual spelling of the name. The French form Roland gradually became more frequently found and by the 20th century was in regular use throughout English-speaking countries.

ROMULUS One of the twin sons of Mars, god of war.

RORY, RORIE (Gaelic) 'Red'. Red is a lucky colour for Aries. The name was borne by a 12th-century Irish king Rory O'Connor. Rory has been frequently in use in Scotland and Ireland for centuries but is seldom found elsewhere.

ROWLAND Variant of Roland.

ROY (Gaelic) 'Red'. Red is a lucky colour for Aries. The name Roy was originally a Scottish name. Its spread to other English-speaking countries has been attributed to its reanalysis of the Old French *roy*, meaning king.

RUDGE (Old French) 'Red-haired'. Red is a lucky colour for Aries.

RUFUS (Latin) 'Red'. Red is a lucky colour for Aries. Rufus was given as a nickname to King William II of England. The name is occasionally found in English-speaking countries.

RUPERT Modern German form of Robert. 'Famous'.

RUPRECHT Form of Rupert.

RUSSELL, RUSSEL (Old French) 'Red'. Red is a lucky colour for Aries. The name has been used as a first name since the 19th century and became particularly popular in the latter half of the 20th century.

SAYER (Old German) 'Victory'.

SEARLE (Old German) 'Warrior with armour'.

SEBERT (Old English) 'Bright victory'.

SIEGFRIED (Old German) 'Peaceful victory'. The name has been in occasional use since the late-19th century.

SIGBERT (Old German) 'Famous victory'.

SIGISMUND Form of Sigmund. The name was borne by a 15th-century Holy Roman emperor and three Polish kings but has never been used regularly in English-speaking countries.

SIGMOND, SIGMUND (Old German) 'Victory, shield'. The name has been in use in English-speaking countries since the latter half of the 19th century.

SKIPPER Originally a nickname from the word skipper, to mean 'boss'. It is sometimes used as a name in its own right in the USA.

SORLE (Old German) 'Armoured one'.

TARANIS Name borne in Gallic mythology by the god of thunder.

TESMOND (Old German) 'Protector'.

TEUTATES Name borne in Gallic mythology by a god of war whom the Romans connected with Mars, The Roman god of war and ruling planet of Aries.

THEOBALD (Old German) 'People, bold'.

THERON (Greek) 'Hunter'.

THOR (Scandinavian) 'Of thundery nature'. Norse god of thunder.

TORQUIL (Scan) 'Belonging to Thor'.

TRAHERN (Welsh) 'Strong as iron'. Traditional Welsh name.

TYR Name given to the Scandinavian god of war.

UILLEARN Scottish Gaelic form of William.

UILLIAM Irish form of William.

VALENCE (Latin) 'Vigorous'.

VALENTINE (Latin) 'Vigorous'. The name came into general use in Britain during the Middle Ages but has never achieved widespread popularity.

VALERE (Old German) 'To be strong'.

VALERIAN (Latin) 'To be strong'.

VALMOND (Old German) 'Strong protection'.

VICTOR (Latin) 'Victory'. The name was borne by three popes and several minor saints. It was used as a first name in medieval Britain but was not in regular use in English-speaking countries until the mid-19th century.

VIJAY (Sanskrit) 'Victory'.

VINCE Pet form of Vincent.

VINCENT (Latin) 'Conquering'. The name was borne by several saints and was fairly common in medieval Britain. It was revived in the 19th century and has been in use throughout English-speaking countries since then.

WALDO (Old German) 'Power' and 'rule'. A famous bearer of the name was the 19th-century US philosopher Ralph Waldo Emerson.

WALT Pet form of Walter. Probably the most well-known bearer of this name is Walt Disney.

WALTER (Old French from Germanic origin) 'Ruling people'. The name was introduced into Britain at the time of the Norman Conquest. It was in regular use in English-speaking countries until the mid-20th century.

WARNER (Old German) 'Protective warrior'. Originally used as a surname, Warner was introduced into Britain at the time of the Norman Conquest.

WARWICK (Welsh) 'Hero'. Originally used as a surname and place name it has been in occasional use as a first name since the 19th century.

WAT Pet form of Walter, used mainly in Medieval times. The name was borne by Wat Tyler, a leader of the Peasants Revolt in 1381.

WATKIN Medieval form of Walter.

WHITE Lucky colour for Aries.

WILEY Form of William.

WILKIE, WILKES Forms of William.

WILHELM Form of William.

WILL, WILLIE, WILLY Shortened forms of William.

WILLARD (Old English) 'Bold resolve'. The name is more common in the USA than other English-speaking countries.

WILLET Form of William.

WILLIAM (Old German) 'Resolute defender'. The name was introduced into Britain by William the Conqueror in the 11th century. The name has also been borne by three other British kings and several saints. After the Norman Conquest the name rapidly became one of the most popular boys' names in English-speaking countries, a position it retained until the early 20th century. In modern times a famous bearer of the name is Prince William, elder son of the Prince and the late Princess of Wales.

WILLIAMSON Form of William.

WILLIS From a surname with the meaning 'son of Will'. Introduced as a first name in the 19th century.

WILMER (Old German) 'Will' and 'fame'. The name died out as a first name in the Middle Ages, but was still found as a surname. It is seldom found in modern times.

WILMOT Medieval form of William.

WILSON Form of William.

WIM (Old French) 'Victory'.

WINGATE (Old English) 'Victory gate'.

WITTER, WITT (Old German) 'Wise warrior'.

WREN (Celtic) 'The chief'.

WODEN In Norse mythology Woden is the god of war.

WYMAN (Old English) 'Protector', 'the warrior'.

WYNFORD, WENFORD From a surname and place name meaning 'white stream'. White is a lucky colour for Aries.

WYNNE, WYNN (Welsh) 'White, pure'. From a Welsh surname.

WYSTAN (Old English) 'Battle, stone'. The name was borne by the British poet W.H. Auden.

ZEVAN (Slavonic) 'Lively'.

Aries ~ Girls

ACACIA (Greek) 'Innocent'.

ADAR (Hebrew) 'Fire'.

AIDEEN (Gaelic) 'Fire'. Feminine form of Aidan.

AINE (Gaelic) 'Fire'. Feminine form of Aidan.

AITHNE (Irish) 'Little fire'. The name has been popular in Ireland for centuries.

ALBINA (Latin) 'White'. White is a lucky colour for Aries. The name was popular during the 17th and 18th centuries.

ALBINIA (Latin) 'White'. Feminine form of Albin The name was introduced from Italy into Britain during the early-17th century.

ALEXA (Greek) 'Protector of men'. Variant of Alexandra.

ALEXANDRA (Greek) Feminine form of Alexander.

ALEXANDRIA Variant of Alexandra.

ALEXANDRINA Variant of Alexandra.

ALEXIA, ALEXIE, ALEXINA Shortened versions of Alexandra.

ALEXIS (Greek) 'Helper, defender'. The name was borne by St Alexius, a 5th-century saint of Edessa. Alexis was originally a Russian boys' name but is now more commonly given as a girls' name.

ALOISIA, ALOYSIA (Old German) 'Famous warrior'. Feminine forms of Aloysius. Form of Louis

ALVA (Irish Gaelic) 'White'. In medieval times the name was used as a boys' name but in its revival it is used mainly as a girls' name.

ALVITA (Latin) 'Vivacious'.

ALWEN (Welsh) 'White path'.

ANDREA Feminine of Andrew. 'Courageous'. The name dates back to 17th century.

APRIL (Latin) From the name of the month.

ARDELIA (Latin) 'Zealous'.

ARDELLE (Latin) Feminine form of Arden. 'Enthusiastic'.

ATHENA Greek goddess of war.

AUDREY (Old English) 'Noble, strength'. An altered form of Etheldreda which was the name of a 6th-century saint who was popular in the Middle Ages. The name was revived in the first half of the 20th century when it came particularly popular, partly due to the fame of the actress Audrey Hepburn.

AUDRENE Variation of Audrey.

AVRIL (French) 'April'. The month during which many Ariens are born.

BEDELIA Form of Bridget.

BEIBHINN (Irish Gaelic) 'White lady', 'fair lady'. Pronounced 'bay-vin'.

BERENICE (Greek) 'Bringer of victory'. The name was introduced into the Egyptian royal house by the second wife of King Ptolemy I of Egypt. It has been in occasional use in English-speaking countries since the Reformation.

BERNADETTE (Old German) 'Bold as a bear'. Feminine form of Bernard. The name became popular in English-speaking countries due to the fame of St Bernadette, a 19th-century French peasant girl whose visions of the Virgin Mary and uncovering of a spring led to the establishment of the shrine at Lourdes.

BERNADINE, BERNADINA, BERNETTA, BERNETTE Feminine forms of Bernard.

BERNICE (Greek) 'Bringer of victory'. A more common form of Berenice.

BIANCA (Italian) 'White'. White is a lucky colour for Aries. The name was used in two of Shakespeare's plays, but is little used in English-speaking countries today.

BILLIE (Old German) 'Determined defender'. Diminutive of Wilhelmina.

BIRGITTA Form of Bridget.

BLANCHE, BLANCH (French) 'White'. White is a lucky colour for Aries. The name has been in occasional use in Britain since the 13th century. It was particularly popular in the USA in the late-19th century.

BLODWEN (Welsh) 'White flower'. White is a lucky colour for Aries. The name was fairly common in the Middle Ages and has recently seen a revival.

BOBETTE Pet form of Roberta.

BOBBY, BOBBIE (Old German) 'Bright, shining fame'. Pet forms of Roberta.

BOBINA Pet form of Roberta

BRIANA, BRIANNA (Celtic) 'Strong', 'high' or 'noble'. Feminine form of Brian.

BRIDE Form of Bridget.

BRIDGET, BRIGIT (Celtic) 'Strong and mighty'. The name was borne by a Celtic goddess and two saints. The name has been in regular use throughout Britain, especially Ireland, since the 17th century

BRIGID, BRIGIDA (Celtic) Forms of Bridget.

BRIGITTE, BRIGITTA (Celtic) Forms of Bridget.

BRINA (Slavonic) 'Protector'.

BRONESSA (Welsh) 'White'.

BRONWEN, BRONWYN (Welsh) 'White breast'. White is a lucky colour for Aries. The name has been in regular use throughout the last century.

BRONYA (Russian) 'Armoured'.

BRYNA (Celtic) 'Strong'. Feminine form of Briana.

CANDACE (Greek) 'Fire white'. The name was borne by several Ethiopian queens, one of whom is mentioned in the New Testament. The name has been in occasional use throughout English-speaking countries since the 17th century. In the mid-20th century the name was particularly popular in the USA and Canada.

CANDI, CANDIE, CANDY Shortened versions of Candace.

CANDICE, CANDIS, CANDYCE Forms of Candace.

CANDIDA (Latin) 'White'. The name has been borne by several minor saints.

CARLA (Old German) 'Strong one'. Feminine form of Charles.

CARLETTA (Old German) 'Strong little one'. Feminine form of Charles.

CARRIE (Old German) 'Strong one'. Feminine form of Charles.

CELINE (Latin) Feminine form of Marcius – connected to Mars.

CELOSA (Greek) 'A flame'.

CERIDWEN (Welsh) 'Poetry' and 'white'. White is a lucky colour for Aries. In Celtic mythology it was the name borne by the Welsh god of poetic inspiration.

CHARLENE Feminine form of Charles.

CHARLOTTE French feminine form of Charles. The name was borne by the wife of King George III in the 18th century. The name became popular in Britain from that time until the late-19th century. It then regained popularity in the latter half of the 20th century.

CIARA (Irish) 'Black'. Pronounced kee-a-ra. A feminine form of Ciarán.

CLOTILDA (Old German) 'Famous battle'. The name was borne by a 6th-century French saint. The name has been in occasional use in English-speaking countries but has never been frequently found.

COLETTE (Latin) 'Victorious little one'. Feminine form of Nicholas. The name was originally a medieval pet form of Nicolette. The name was borne by a 15th-century French nun and was made popular by the fame of the French writer Colette in the early part of the 20th century.

DARA (Middle English) 'To dare'.

DIAMOND Lucky gemstone for Aries.

EBREL (Cornish) 'April'. The name of the month in which many Ariens are born.

EDANA (Gaelic) 'Little fiery one'. One of a warm and loving nature. Feminine form of Edan.

EIDANN Form of Edana.

EITHNE Form of Ethne.

ELOISE, ELOISA Possibly a variant of Aloysia, a feminine form of Louis, meaning 'famous warrior'.

ENA Form of Ethne. The name was borne by a granddaughter of Queen Victoria, Princess Ena, who became Queen of Spain in the early-20th century.

ENRICA (Old German) 'Ruler of the home'. Form of Henrietta.

ERLINDA (Hebrew) 'Lively'.

ERICA (Old Norse) 'Honourable ruler'. Feminine form of Eric. The name Erica has been in use in English-speaking countries since the late-19th century.

ERMA (Old German) 'Army maid'.

ERMINIA, ERMINA, ERMINIE Forms of Erma.

ETHNE (Irish) 'Little fire'. The name and its various forms have been popular Irish names for centuries.

EUNICE (Greek) 'Good victory'. The name is found in the New Testament and has been in occasional use in English-speaking countries since the early-17th century.

FARICA (Old German) 'Peace-loving ruler'.

FENELLA (Gaelic) 'White shoulder'. White is a lucky colour for Aries.

FERNANDA (Old German) 'Adventurous'. Feminine form of Fernando.

FINOLA Irish form of Fenella.

FIONA (Gaelic) 'White'. The name was little used outside Scotland until the mid-20th century. Since then it has become popular in the rest of Britain and in Australia and Canada.

FINOLA Irish form of Fenella.

FLANNA (Gaelic) 'Red-haired'.

FLEET (Old Norse) 'Swift'.

FLORA Name of the Roman goddess of flowers and the spring. The name was also borne by a 9th-century martyr St Flora. The name was introduced into Scotland from France and then spread to other English-speaking countries.

GARNET, GARNETTE (English) 'Deep red-haired beauty'. Red is a lucky colour for Aries. The name was originally a surname. It has been used as a boys' first name since the 19th century and as a girls' name since the mid-20th century.

GERDA (Old Norse) 'Protection'. The name occurs in Scandinavian mythology as the name borne by the wife of Frey, the god of peace and fertility. It has occasionally been found in English-speaking countries since the 19th century.

GULIELMA (Old German) 'Resolute protector'. Italian feminine form of William. It has been in occasional use in the English-speaking world since the 17th century.

GENEVIEVE (Celtic) A name of uncertain origin. It could be derived from two Celtic words meaning 'tribal woman' or it could mean 'white wave'. Both meanings are appropriate for Aries. The name was introduced into Britain from France in the 19th century.

GUINEVERE (Celtic) 'White wave'. White is a lucky colour for Aries. The name was borne by the legendary wife of King Arthur. The name is seldom used in modern times but exists in various forms such as Jennifer.

GWEN (Welsh) 'White'. White is a lucky colour for Aries. It is often regarded as a shortened form of

Gwendoline, although it has been in use as an independent name since the late 19th century.

GWENDOLINE, GWENDOLYN, GWENDOLEN, GUENDOLEN (Welsh) 'White circle'. In Arthurian legend the name was borne by the wife of Merlin. The name has been in fairly regular use in English-speaking countries since the latter half of the 19th century.

GWENLLIAN Form of Gwendoline

GWENETH, GWENYTH, GWENITH Welsh forms of Gwen.

GWENIVER Cornish form of Jennifer, meaning 'white wave'.

GWYN (Celtic) 'White'.

GYTHA, GITHA (Anglo-Saxon) 'War-like'.

HALEY, HALLEY, HALLY (Old Norse) 'Hero'.

HARMONIA (Greek) Greek goddess of war. Also means 'unifying'.

HARRIET Feminine pet form of Henry. 'Home ruler'.

HARRIETTE Alternative spelling of Harriet.

HESTIA The Greek goddess of fire.

HAURA (Maori) 'Lively'.

HENDRIKA (Old German) 'Ruler of the home'. Feminine form of Henry.

HENRIETTE (Old German) Feminine form of Henry.

IANESSA (Greek) 'Gentle ruler'.

IDINA, IDONA, IDONEA (Old Norse) Name given to the Norse goddess of spring. The meaning of the name is 'labour'. The name has been in occasional use since the 13th century.

IGNATIA (Latin) 'Fire'. 'Woman of fiery temperament'. Feminine form of Ignatius.

IMOGEN (Latin) 'Innocent'. The name was borne by the heroine in Shakespeare's play *Cymbeline*. The source used for this play spells the name as Innogen, Imogen was thus the result of a printing error. The name Imogen is still in use today.

INNOGEN (Latin) 'Innocent' or (Celtic) 'girl, maiden'. Innogen may be derived from Latin meaning 'innocent' or from Celtic origins meaning 'girl or maiden'.

INA Form of Ena.

INGA (Old Norse) Protection of Inge, god of peace in Norse mythology. Therefore 'Protector of peace'.

IRETA (Latin) 'Little enraged one'.

JAI (Sanskrit) 'Hail, peace, victory'.

JENEFER Alternative spelling of Jennifer.

JENI, JENIA Shortened versions of Jennifer.

JENIFER Alternative spellings of Jennifer.

JENNA, JENA Shortened forms of Jennifer.

JENNI, JENNIE, JENNEY Shortened forms of Jennifer.

JENNIFER (Welsh) 'White wave'. White is a lucky colour for Aries. Jennifer is a Cornish form of Guinevere. The name was seldom found outside Cornwall until early in the 20th century. By the mid-20th century it had become very popular throughout English-speaking countries and remains in regular use today.

JENNY Shortened version of Jennifer.

JENYTH Form of Jennifer.

JOLIE (Middle English) 'High spirits'.

JUNO (Irish) 'Lamb'. Form of Una. The lamb is a lucky animal for Aries. The name is borne by a goddess in Roman mythology.

KAIMANA (Hawaiian) 'Diamond'. The diamond is a lucky precious stone for Aries.

KEELEY, KEELIE, KEELIEGH, KEEGHLEY, Forms of Kelly.

KEELIN (Irish) 'White'.

KELLY, KELLIE (Irish) 'War'.
Originally from an Irish surname. The name has only became popular as a first name since the mid-20th century and was particularly popular in Britain in the 1980s.

KELSEY, KELSIE (Old English) 'Victory'. Originally existed as an Old English surname.

KEYA (Gaelic) 'Daughter of the fiery one'.

KIERA (Irish) 'Black'. Feminine form of Kieran. Black is a lucky colour for Aries.

LAILA Alternative spelling of Leila.

LAVERNE (Latin) Spring-like, verdant.

LAYLA Alternative spelling of Leila.

LEE Shortened form of Leila.

LEELA Form of Leila.

LEILA (Arabic) 'Black as the night'. Black is a lucky colour for Aries. The name came into occasional use in Britain in the 19th century.

LEILIA Form of Leila.

LEILAH Form of Leila.

LENE Form of Lenis.

LELA form of Leila.

LENIS (Latin) 'Smooth and white as the lily'. The lily is a lucky plant for Aries.

LENTA Form of Lenis.

LENITA, LENETA Forms of Lenis.

LENOS Form of Lenis.

LILA, LILAH Forms of Leila.

LILIAN, LILLIAN (Latin) 'Lily'. The tiger lily is a lucky plant for Aries. The name has been used in Britain since the 16th century and was particularly popular at the turn of the 20th century.

LILIAS, LILLIAS Scottish form of Lilian.

LILLA, LILLAH Form of Lily.

LILY, LILLIE The tiger lily is a lucky plant for Ariens.

LOIS Form of Louise.

LOUISA (Old German) 'Famous warrior'. Feminine form of Louis. The name was particularly popular in the 18th and 19th cenuries.

LOUISE Feminine form of Louis. The name has been in use since the 17th century.

LULU Pet form of Louise.

MADISON (Old German) 'Great and heroic'. Mainly found in the USA, used both as a boys' and girls' name. Madison was originally used as a surname. Its use as a first name appears to have been influenced by the president James Madison (1751-1836). The name has recently been popular as a girls' name.

MAIA The Roman goddess of spring.

MARCELLA (Latin) Feminine form of Marcellus, a Latin pet form of Marcus, which in turn is derived from Mars, the Roman god of war.

MARCELLE Feminine form of Marcel.

MARCIA Feminine form of Marcus. The name originates from a Roman clan name Marcius, which is connected to Mars, the Roman god of war. Marcia came into use in English-speaking countries in the 19th century and became particularly popular in the mid-20th century.

MARINER Name of the spacecraft sent to explore Mars, the ruling planet of Aries. The name is from Latin meaning 'of the sea'.

MARSHA Phonetic spelling of Marcia.

MARTI Short form of Martina.

MARTIA Derived from Marcia.

MARTINA Feminine form of Martin. Derived from Mars the Roman god of war, the name of the ruling planet of Aries.

MARTINE French form of Martina.

MAXINE (Latin) 'Greatest'. Feminine form of Max. The name has been in regular use in English-speaking countries since the beginning of the 20th century.

MEDEA (Greek) Name of an important character in the creation of the constellation of Aries.

MEHIRA (Hebrew) 'Energetic'.

MEL Shortened from of Melanie.

MELANIE, MELLONEY (Greek) 'Black'. Black is a lucky colour for Aries. The name was borne by two Roman saints in the 4th and 5th centuries. In the 17th century it was introduced into Britain from France although it was little used outside Devon and Cornwall until the 20th century.

MILLICENT (Old French) 'Strength'. The name was introduced into Britain from France in the Middle Ages. It was fairly popular at the turn of the 20th century and is still occasionally found today.

MINA, MINNA Shortened Scottish forms of Wilhelmina. The name has been in occasional use as a name in its own right since the 19th century.

MINERVA Roman goddess of war, wisdom and arts and crafts. It is occasionally found as a first name in English-speaking countries.

MINNIE Shortened form of Wilhelmina. It was used as an independent name at the turn of the 20th century.

MÓR (Scottish and Irish Gaelic) 'Great'. In late medieval times this was the most popular girls' name in Ireland. It is still in frequent use in Ireland and Scotland today.

MORAG (Scottish) Pet form of Mór. In Scotland this has become a popular independent name.

MOREEN (Irish) A pet form of Mór.

MORRIGAN Irish Celtic goddess of war.

NICKY, NICKIE, NIKKI (Greek) 'Victorious'. A pet form of Nicola.

NICO (Greek) Modern short form of Nicola.

NICOLA (Greek) 'Victorious'. Latinate feminine form of Nicholas.

NICOLE (Greek) French feminine form of Nicholas.

NICOLETTE (Greek) French pet form of Nicole, often used as an independent name.

NIKITA (Greek) 'Unconquerable'. Originally a Russian boys' name. In recent times it has become more common as a girls' name, possibly taken as an elaborated from of Nikki.

NORMA (Latin) 'Rule'. The name has been in use in Britain and other English-speaking countries since the 19th century.

NUALA (Irish) 'White shoulder'. Pet form of Fenella. Nuala is often used as an independent name.

OLWEN, OLWYN (Welsh) 'White track' or 'white footprint'. This meaning refers to the white flowers that grew from the footsteps of Olwen, a character from Welsh legend. White is a lucky colour for Aries.

ORENDA American Indian 'Magic power'. The magician is the Tarot card for Aries.

OSMA (Old English) 'Heroic protector'.

PANACHE (French) 'Confidence'.

PASQUALA (Italian) Feminine derivative of Pascal. Born at Eastertime.

PRIMA (Latin) 'The first'. Aries is the first sign of the zodiac. Ariens also like to be 'first'.

PRIMAVERA (Spanish) 'Child of the spring'.

PRIMROSE (Latin) A flower name meaning 'the first rose'. The name came into use as a first name in the 18th century and increased in popularity in the late-19th century.

PRIMULA (Latin) A flower name meaning 'first'.

PYRENA, PYRENIA (Greek) 'Fiery one'.

RAYMONDE (Old German) 'Wise protector'. Feminine form of Raymond.

RISHONA (Hebrew) 'First'. Aries is the first sign of the zodiac.

ROBERTA Feminine form of Robert.

ROBINA, ROBYN (Old German) 'Bright, shining fame'. Feminine forms of Robin, a form of Robert. Originally a medieval pet form of Robert, now used as a name in its own right. In recent times it has more frequently been used as a girls' name.

ROBINIA, ROBINETTE Elaborated forms of Robina.

ROBERTHA, ROBERTHE Elaborated forms of Roberta.

ROMILDA, ROMILDE, ROMHILDA, ROMHILDE (Old German) 'Glorious warrior maiden'.

ROSAMOND, ROSAMUND (Old German) 'Protector'. The name was introduced into Britain by the Normans and has been in regular use since that time.

RUBERTA Form of Roberta.

RUPERTA Feminine form of Rupert.

RUBETTA, RUBETTE Forms of Ruby.

RUBIA, RUBIE Forms of Ruby.

RUBINA Form of Ruby.

RUBY (Latin) From the name of the gemstone. The ruby is a lucky gemstone for Aries.

SABLE (Old French) 'Black' (in heraldry). Black is a lucky colour for Aries.

SARANA (Sanskrit) 'Protecting guardian'.

SERAPHINA (Hebrew) 'Fiery' or 'winged'. The name was borne by two saints in the 13th and 15th centuries.

SERILDA (Old German) 'Girl of War'.

SIGRID (Old Norse) 'Victory' and 'beautiful'.

SIRI (Norman French) 'Conquering impulse'.

SHUSHANA, SHUSHANNA (Hebrew) 'Lily'. Forms of Susannah The tiger lily is a lucky plant for Aries. The name has been in occasional use in English-speaking countries since the 17th century.

SPRING (Old English) The season name used as a first name. Spring is the season in which Ariens are born.

SPRYNG Alternative spelling of Spring.

SUSAN Form of Susannah. The name has been in regular use since the 18th century. In the mid-20th century it was one of the most well-used girls' names in English-speaking countries.

SUSANNAH, SUSANNA, SUZANNA (Hebrew) 'Lily'. The tiger lily is a lucky plant for Aries. The name is found in both the Old Testament and the New Testament. The name was readopted by the Puritans after the Reformation and has been in use throughout English-speaking countries since that time.

SUSANNE, SUZANNE French form of Susannah. The name has been in frequent use throughout English-speaking countries since the early-20th century.

SUE, SUSIE, SUZY Pet forms of Susan, Susannah or Suzette.

SUZETTE French form of Susannah.

TAIMANA (Maori) 'Diamond'. The diamond is a lucky gem for Aries.

TALI Shortened form of Talia.

TALIA (Aramaic) 'Young lamb'. The lamb is a lucky animal for Aries.

TEGWEN (Welsh) 'Lovely, white, fair'.

THORA (Scandinavian). Derived from Thor, the Norse god of thunder.

THYRA (Scandinavian) Form of Tyr, the Norse god of war.

TREASA (Irish Gaelic) 'Strength, intensity'. A traditional Irish Gaelic name.

TRUDI, TRUDIE, TRUDY (German) 'Strength'.

TYRA Form of Thyra.

UNA, ONA, OONA, OONAGH A name of uncertain origin. It may be from Latin, meaning 'one' or Irish, meaning 'lamb'. Aries is the first sign of the zodiac and its symbol is the ram, so both meanings are appropriate.

UNI (Latin) 'One'.

VALBORGA, VALBURGA (Old German) 'Protecting ruler'.

VALDA (Old German) 'Power' and 'rule'. The name is found occasionally in English-speaking countries.

VALENCIA (Latin) 'Strong and vigorous'.

VALENE Diminutive of Valerie. To be strong.

VALENTIA, VALENCIA (Latin) 'Vigorous'.

VALENTINA Form of Valentine.

VALENTINE (Latin) 'Strong' or 'healthy'. St Valentine's Day is believed to be a pagan custom and has no connection with the Christian saints who bear the name. The name

was used in the Middle Ages but has never been frequently used. The name is occasionally given to girls.

VALERIA, VALERIE 'To be strong'. Feminine forms of Valerian.

VALESKA (Slavonic) 'Glorious ruler'.

VAL Shortened version of Valerie

VALDA (Old German) 'Heroine, power' or 'rule'.

VALORA (Latin) 'To be strong'.

VALORIE See Valerie.

VANORA (Celtic) 'White wave'.

VEGA (Arabic) 'The great one'.

VELDA (Old German) 'Heroine, power or rule'. Form of Valda.

VELMA Of uncertain origin. Possibly a form of Wilhelmina.

VERDA (Old French) 'Green, spring-like'.

VERENA, VERNIS Forms of Verna

VERNA (Latin) 'Spring-like'.

VERNE, VERN (French) 'Spring-like'. Shortened forms of Laverne.

VERNICE Form of Verna.

VERNITA, VERNETA Forms of Verna.

VESTA Goddess of fire in Roman mythology. It is only rarely found as a given name in English-speaking countries.

VICTORIA (Latin) 'Victory'. The name was little used in England until the reign of Queen Victoria, who was named after her German mother. It became a popular name during the mid-20th century and remains in regular use today.

VINCENCIA, VINCENTA Forms of Vincentia

VINCENTIA (Latin) 'The conqueror'. Feminine form of Vincent.

VIRNA, VIRINA Forms of Verna

VITESSE (French) 'Swiftness'.

WALBURGA, WALBORGA (Old German) 'Protecting ruler'

WALESKA (Slavonic) 'Glorious ruler'.

WHITE Lucky colour for Aries.

WILHELMINA (Old German) 'Resolute defender'. A feminine form of William. The name has been in use in English-speaking world since the 18th century.

WILLA Pet form of Wilhelmina.

WILLIAMINA Feminine form of William. Not usually found outside Scotland.

WILMA Form of Wilhelmina. Found mainly in Scotland, the USA and Canada.

WYNN, WYNNE (Welsh) 'White, pure'. Originally used as a surname.

YELENA (Latin) 'Lily blossom'.

ZAVANA (Slavonic) 'Lively'.

ZINEVRA (Celtic) 'White wave'.

Taurus

THE BULL
20 April - 20 May

RULING PLANET   Venus - The god of love. In astrology Venus is the planet of love, affection, sensuality and personal values.

ELEMENT   Earth

General characteristics

- Romantic, sentimental, sensual.
- Materialistic values.
- Love of nature, harmony, love of living things.
- Possessive. Likes security. Depends on others.
- Organised, resourceful, thorough.
- Kind, trustworthy, calm.
- Shy, cautious.
- Appreciates talents, abilities and values.

Characteristics of young Taureans

- Usually quiet, gentle and calm.
- Occasionally stubborn and want their own way.
- Fond of cuddles and affection.
- Outdoor lovers.
- Like music and creative play.
- Slow but steady to move and work.

Taurean lucky connections

Gemstones:	topaz
Colours:	blues and pastel colours
Plant:	mallow
Perfume:	storax
Metal:	copper
Animal:	bull
Tarot Card:	high priest

TAURUS is the sign of the bull and like a bull they can be stubborn individuals. But along with that stubborn streak and their inborn tenacity, their loving and affectionate nature makes them devoted and loyal friends and family members. Indeed, Taurus is ruled by Venus, the goddess of love.

Harsh words are not the best way of getting what you want from a Taurean. Loving words and a warm hug are by far the best way of melting that stubborn streak. Taureans need to feel loved and valued and in return they can be the most trusted caring ally and friend. They possess an unquestioning acceptance of others which can make them magnetic to those who are less secure. They do not get upset easily and are patient with the more volatile nature of others.

Taureans prefer consistency in their everyday lives and dislike change. They can become quite resistant to any change and can be stubborn in their refusal to try new things. Gentle persuasion and warm reassurance is the best way of encouraging Taureans to attempt new things, insistence is likely to increase resistance.

Taurus is also a very physical sign. Individuals born under this sign often enjoy the sense of touch, therefore, and can be quite sensual beings. They love the touch of silk upon their skin or the warm reassurance of a loving hug. 'Feely' books and toys will be popular, as will edible playdough or smearing her food all over her plate.

Being an earth sign Taureans are also very attuned to nature and love the outdoors. They also possess a strong appreciation of beauty in all forms and can often be artistically and musically gifted.

A typical Taurean will often be a peaceful baby. They tend to whimper rather than cry ferociously, but if they do get very upset they are soon soothed by their milk and a warm hug.

All Taureans enjoy eating and a baby Taurean will often eat to a regular pattern at an early age. Indeed, with their sense of order, they may well establish both a sleeping and eating pattern at such a young age that mum and dad may well be the envy of other, less fortunate parents.

A Taurean baby will often be content to sit and watch the world go by rather than be in a hurry to learn to crawl in search of it. This is not to say that your Taurean baby will not be interested in what's going on around her, but a Taurean baby would rather savour each moment of her day with gentle pleasure and a resolute thoroughness.

Once your toddler is walking well she will love to stroll around the garden or the park on a regular basis. It is more likely to be a stroll, as distinct from a run, for she will love to stop and stare, to enjoy the myriad sights and sounds on offer. Try to be patient with your little Taurean. Rushing her will only produce stubbornness. Try to give her plenty of time to stand and stare.

As your child grows older and starts to play with others you will find that your Taurean baby will prefer to play quietly with one or two children rather than in a large noisy group. Indeed your child will probably have one or two special friends rather than groups of playmates. She will make a loyal and affectionate friend to those special chosen few.

Provide your child with the playthings she loves, the security which she needs and the affection which she craves and you will find yourself with a most contented Taurean child.

Taurus ~ Boys

ABSALOM (Hebrew) 'The father is peace' or 'father of peace'. In the Old Testament it was the name borne by the son of King David.

ADAM (Hebrew) 'Of the red earth'. Adam of the Old Testament, the father of the human race, was said to be created from the red earth. The name was particularly popular in the 13th century, the mid-19th century and again in the 1960s.

ADAMNAN 'Little Adam'. The name was borne by St Adamnan, an Irish 7th-century saint.

ADDIS Form of Adam.

ADDISON (Old English) 'Son of Adam'.

AIKEN, AIKIN, AICKIN (Old English) 'Little Adam'.

ALAN (Gaelic) 'Cheerful harmony'. The name entered Britain at the time of the Norman invasion. It was popular in medieval times and remains in regular use.

ALAIN French form of Alan.

ALLAN, ALLEN, ALLYN, Forms of Alan.

ALAND, AILEAN, AILIN Forms of Alan.

ALDEBARAN Name of a star in the constellation of Taurus.

ALDEN Form of Aldwin.

ALDIS, ALDOUS, ALDUS Form of Aldo.

ALDO (Old German) 'Steady and wise'. The name was borne by a 8th-century saint. The name has been popular in Italy for many years and is used in English-speaking countries by families of Italian descent.

ALDWIN, ALDWYN (Old English) 'Old friend'. The name was popular in the Middle Ages and is still occasionally found today.

ALUN Welsh form of Alan.

ALVAN (Old German) 'Old friend'.

ALVIN (Old English) 'Noble friend'. The various forms of the name have been in existence since the Norman Conquest.

ALWYN, ALWIN Forms of Alvin.

AMYAS, AMIAS (Old French) 'Loved'. The name was in use as early as the 12th century.

ANGHUS OG Name of the god of love in Irish Druid mythology. The name is also spelt as Aonghus Og.

ANGUS Anglicised form of Anghus or Aonghus, god of love in Irish mythology.

AURIGA Constellation next to Taurus. The horns of the bull of Taurus go into the Auriga constellation. The name means 'the charioteer'.

AXEL (Old German) 'Father of peace'.

BELLAMY (Greek) 'Fair friend'.

BLUE From the colour name. Occasionally used as a first name. Blue is a lucky colour for Taurus.

BONAMY (French) 'Good friend'. The name originates from a Guernsey surname. It is occasionally found as a first name in English-speaking countries.

BRAN In Welsh Druid mythology the name was borne by a guardian of the land. Bran was also a god of war who defended British lands.

BUDDY, BUD From an informal term of address used in the US, meaning 'friend'. More usually used as a nickname than as a first name.

BULL Lucky animal and name of the symbol of Taurus.

CALLUM, CALUM Forms of Malcolm.

CARADOC (Welsh) 'Love'. The name borne by a British king in the 1st century. The name is still in occasional use in Wales but infrequently found elsewhere.

CARADOCK Form of Caradoc.

CASEY Shortened form of Casimir.

CASIMIR (Polish) 'Proclamation of peace'. Occasionally used in Britain and the USA.

CERI (Welsh) 'Loved one'.

COLM, COLUM Shortened forms of Columba.

COLUMBA (Latin) 'Dove', the symbol of peace. The name was borne by St Columba, a 6th-century Irish abbot and missionary who converted Scotland and Northern England to Christianity.

COLVER Form of Culver.

CONSTANT (Latin) 'Constant'. The name was in use in the 17th century and was revived in the 19th century.

CONSTANTINE (Latin) 'Constant'. The name was borne by several Roman emperors and by two Greek kings of the 20th century. The name is seldom used in English-speaking countries.

COPPER The name of the lucky metal for Taurus.

CORWIN , CORWEN (French) 'Friend of the heart'.

CRADDOCK (Welsh) 'Amiable'.

CRAIG (Scottish) 'Rock'. Originally a Scottish surname, the name was used as a first name in the USA in the mid-20th century and spread to other English-speaking countries.

CULVER (Old English) 'Gentle as the dove, peaceful'. The symbol of peace.

CUPID (Roman) Name of the Roman god of love.

DAFDD Welsh form of David.

DAI Shortened form of David.

DANTE (Latin) 'Enduring'. Form of Durand.

DAREL, DARELL, DARRELL (French) 'Loved one' or 'darling'. The name has been in use as a first name since 1860 and was particularly popular in the mid-20th century.

DARRYL, DARYL (Old English) 'Loved one' or 'darling'.

DARRY Shortened version of Darryl.

DAVE, DAVY Shortened forms of David.

DAVID (Hebrew) 'Beloved' or 'friend'. It was borne by a 6th-century bishop St. David, the patron saint of Wales. It is one of the most popular masculine names in English-speaking countries.

DERWIN (Old German) 'Animal lover'.

DEWI Welsh form of David.

DILLON (Celtic) 'Faithful, loyal'.

DURAND (Latin) 'Enduring', 'one who's friendship is lasting'. The name was introduced into Britain from France at the time of the Norman Conquest. The name was popular in the Middle Ages but is little used today.

DURAN (Latin) 'Enduring'. Form of Durand.

DURRANT (Latin) 'Enduring'.

EARTHAN (Old English) 'Of the earth'.

EDMOND French spelling of Edmund, introduced into Britain in the Middle Ages.

EDMUND (Old English) 'Rich protector'. The name was borne by St Edmunds, a 9th-century martyr who was also King of East Anglia. The Suffolk town of Bury St Edmunds is named in his honour. The name was also borne by two English Kings in the 10th and 11th century and by another saint, Edmund Rich, who was a 13th-century Archbishop of Canterbury.

EDOM Form of Adam.

EDWIN, EDWYN (Old English) 'Rich friend'. The name was borne by King Edwin of Northumbria after whom, it is believed, the city of Edinburgh was named. The name was little used after the 12th century until its revival in the 19th century. It remained in regular use until the mid-20th century.

EIRAN (Irish) 'Peace'.

ELLESWORTH (Old English) 'A farmer', 'lover of the earth'.

ELLIS (Old Welsh) 'Kind and benevolent'.

ERASME Form of Erasmus.

ERASMUS (Greek) 'To love'. The name has been in occasional use since the 17th century but is rarely found today. St Erasmus was the patron saint of sailors.

ERASTUS (Greek) 'The beloved'.

EROS (Greek) Name of the Greek god of love.

ESME (Old French) 'Loved' or 'esteemed'. The name was popular in Scotland in the 16th century and its use spread to England where it was used as both a boys' and girls' name.

ETHAN (Hebrew) 'Steadfast, unwavering'. The name is mentioned in the Old Testament. It has been in use in the USA since the mid-18th century when it was popularised by the soldier Ethan Allen who played a leading role in the American War of Independence.

EUNAN (Irish and Scottish) 'Earth'. Gaelic form of Adam.

EUSTACE (Old French) 'Well, good'. The name was borne by St Eustace, a Roman soldier martyred in the 2nd century. The name was introduced into Britain by the Normans. It was in regular use during the Middle Ages and remains in use today.

EVANDER (Gaelic) 'Good man'. Legend has it that Evander was the name of an Arcadian hero who founded an Italian city where Rome was eventually built.

EZRA (Hebrew) 'The one who helps'. The name was borne by a prophet of Old Testament. It was adopted by the Puritans and used in Britain and the USA until the end of the 19th century.

FARQUHAR (Gaelic) 'Friendly man' or 'very dear one'. The name was borne by an early King of Scotland. The name is still used occasionally in Scotland but is little used elsewhere.

FERDINAND (Old German) 'Courageous peacemaker'. The name has been used in Spanish royal families from an early date. The name spread to Britain in the 16th century where it has been in occasional use ever since.

FIDEL (Latin) 'Faithful'. The name was borne by Fidel Castro, the Cuban revolutionary leader who was born in the early 20th century. The name is still in occasional use in English-speaking countries.

FREY (Old German) 'The lord of peace and prosperity'. From the name of the Norse god.

GAIAN (Greek) 'Child of the earth'.

GARETH (Welsh) 'Gentle'.

GARTH Origin uncertain. It may be from a surname and place name meaning 'garden'. Or it may be a form of Gareth. Both meanings are appropriate for Taurus.

GEOFFREY, JEFFREY (Old German) 'Gift of peace'. The name spread from France into Britain in the 11th century. The name became little used after the 16th century but was revived in the late 19th century and was particularly popular in the mid-20th century.

GEORGE (Old French) 'Earth, farmer'. The name was borne by St George, the patron saint of England. The legend of St George and the Dragon is thought to be a medieval Italian invention. The name became popular in Britain after the accession of King George I in 1714. Its popularity in the USA grew with the initiation of George Washington as the first president of the USA (1732-99). The name remains popular today.

GEORGIE, GEORDIE Pet forms of George.

GLADWIN (Old English) 'Kind friend'.

GODFREY (Old German) 'God's peace'. The name was introduced into Britain at the time of the Norman Conquest. The name was fairly well used in the Middle Ages and is in occasional use today.

GODWIN (Old English) 'God's friend'. The name was popular in the Middle Ages but is little used today.

GOLDWIN (Old German) 'Golden friend'.

GOODWIN (Old English) 'Good friend'. Originally a surname, transferred use to that of a first name.

GLADWYN (Old English) 'Glad friend'. Originally a surname, transferred use to that of a first name.

GRANGER (Old English) 'The farmer'.

HARMAN, HARMOND (Greek) 'Peace, harmony'.

HAMLET Medieval form of Hamo. The name was in regular use in Britain until the end of the 18th century but is rarely found today.

HAMLYN (Old German) 'Home lover'. A medieval form of Hamo.

HAMMOND Of uncertain origin. It may be a form of Hamo or it may mean 'home protector'.

HAMNET Form of Hamo. The name was borne by the son of William Shakespeare and Anne Hathaway.

HAMO (Old German) 'Home'. The name was introduced into Britain at the time of the Norman Conquest. It was in regular use during the Middle Ages but is little used today.

HEDDWYN (Welsh) 'Peace' and 'white'.

HORTON (Latin) 'A garden'.

HOWARD (Old English) 'Guardian of the home'. The name was used by the aristocracy as a family name for hundreds of years. It was adopted as a first name in the 19th century.

HUGH (Old French) 'Heart, mind, spirit'. The name was used by the aristocracy in medieval France, adopted by the Normans who then introduced the name into Britain.

HUMPHREY (Old English) Means both 'strength' and 'peace'. The name existed in Britain before the Norman Conquest but was influenced by the Normans to form the name as we know it today. Humphrey is still in occasional use today, a famous bearer of the name being the US actor Humphrey Bogart.

HYADES Name of a star cluster in the constellation of Taurus.

ING In Norse mythology Ing is the name given to the god of peace.

JARON (Bohemian) 'Firm peace'.

JEDIDIAH (Hebrew) 'Beloved or friend (of the Lord)'. The name was used by the Puritans in the 17th century but is rarely found today.

JONAH (Hebrew) 'Dove'. The symbol of peace. The name was borne by a prophet of the Old Testament. The name was readopted by the Puritans after the Reformation and is still occasionally in use today.

JONAS Form of Jonah. The name was fairly common in medieval Britain.

JORGE 'Earth, farmer'. Variation of George.

KAMA (Sanskrit) 'Love'. Name of the Hindu god of love, equivalent to Cupid in Greek mythology.

LAMBERT (Old German) Name meaning both 'land' and 'bright'. The name was borne by a 7th-century bishop and martyr, St Lambert of Maastricht. It was introduced into Britain during the Middle Ages and was still found occasionally until the early 20th century.

LANDRY (Old English) 'Rough land'.

LELAND (Middle English) 'Fallow land'. Originally a surname now sometimes found as a first name, usually in the USA. It is also the name of a town in Mississippi.

LELIO (Old German) 'Loyal'.

LEWIN (Old English) 'Beloved friend'.

LOYAL Derived from English adjective 'Loyal'.

MALCOLM (Gaelic) 'Servant or disciple of Columba'. Columba means 'dove' the symbol of peace. Malcolm was the name borne by four Scottish Kings. It was used in Scotland from the end of the Middle Ages until the early 20th century when it spread to other English-speaking countries.

MANFRED (Old German) 'Peaceful man'. The name was introduced into Britain by the Normans.

MINGO (Gaelic) 'Amiable'.

MOSTYN (Welsh) 'Settlement'. From Old English. The name appears in its Old English form Mastone in the Doomsday Book.

MUNGA (Scottish) Gaelic form of Mungo. 'Dearest friend'.

MUNGO (Scottish) 'Dearest friend' or 'beloved'. The name is mainly found in Scotland.

NEWTON (Norman) 'New settlement'. The name was originally a surname and place name. It has been in occasional use as a first name since the 19th century.

OLIVER (Latin) 'The olive tree' hence 'the symbol of peace'. The name was fairly well-used in Britain during and after the Middle Ages. The name became less popular in the late-17th century but was revived in the 19th century and remains in use today.

ORWIN (Old German) 'Golden friend'.

OSCAR (Old Irish) 'Friend'. The name was rarely found in Britain from the time of the Norman conquest until the 18th century. The name was borne by two Swedish kings in the 19th century. In more recent times the name has been associated with Oscar Wilde, the Irish poet and dramatist, and with the annual awards for achievement in the film industry made by the American Academy of Motion Picture Arts and Science.

PAICE (Old French) 'Peace'.

PELHAM (Old English) 'Homestead'. Originally a surname used by the aristocracy derived from a Hertfordshire place name.

PETER (Greek) 'Steadfast as a rock'. Peter is the English form of the name Cephas, which was given to the leader of Jesus' disciples. St Peter eventually became the first Bishop of Rome. The name became popular throughout Christian countries during medieval times and has been in regular use since then.

PHILEMON (Greek) 'Affectionate' or 'kiss'. The name is the title of one of the books of the New Testament. The name was adopted by the Puritans but is little used today.

PHILO (Greek) 'Friendly love'.

PLEIADES Name of a star cluster in the constellation of Taurus.

PRESTON (Old English) 'Enclosure'. The name was originally a surname and place name. It has been occasionally used as a first name since the 19th century.

PRYDERI (Welsh) 'Caring for'.

RAS Shortened form of Erasmus or Erastus.

RASMUS (Greek) 'Beloved'. Form of Erasmus.

RASTUS (Greek) 'To love'. The name occurs in the New Testament as a shortened form of the Latin name Erastus.

RODHLANN Form of Roland.

ROLAND, ROWLAND (Old German) 'Fame' and 'land, territory'. The name was introduced into Britain at the time of the Norman Conquest. Rowland was the usual spelling of the name until the 19th century when the French form of the name Roland became more popular.

ROLEY, ROLLIN, ROLLO Forms of Roland.

ROLLAND Form of Roland.

ROWE Shortened form of Rowland.

SELWYN Name of uncertain origin. It may be from Old English meaning 'prosperous friend' or it may be a combination of two Welsh words meaning 'ardour' and 'fair'.

SHERWIN (Old English) 'A true and loyal friend'.

SHEEHAN (Gaelic) 'The peaceful one'.

SIEGFRIED (Old German) 'Peaceful victory'. The name has been in occasional use in the English-speaking world since the late-19th century.

SOLOMON (Hebrew) 'Peace'. King Solomon of the Old Testament was considered one of great wisdom. In the Middle Ages the name was in regular use in Britain. It was revived by the Puritans but is generally used as a Jewish name today.

STACEY (Latin) 'Constant', 'reliable'. A form of Eustace meaning 'well, good'.

STERLING, STIRLING (Old German) 'Reliable, worthy'. Originally used as a surname, now transferred to use as a first name. In the 20th century Stirling Moss, the British racing driver, and Sterling Hayden, the American actor, were famous bearers of the name.

STILLMAN, STILMAN (Old English) 'Quiet and gentle man'.

TAFFY 'Beloved' or 'friend'. Pet form of David.

TAI (Chinese) 'Peace'.

TAURI Latin for 'Taurus'.

TEX Generally used as a nickname for someone from Texas, the name is sometimes given as a first name in the USA. 'Texas' is derived from an Indian name meaning 'Friends'.

THESEUS (Greek) In Greek mythology Theseus was the name of an important character in the formation of the constellation of Taurus.

THU Name given to the god of the earth in Chinese mythology.

TIBON (Hebrew) 'Lover of Nature'.

TIVIAN Derived from Tibon.

TIVON Derived from Tibon.

TREMAINE (Cornish) 'Stone homestead, settlement'. Originally a Cornish surname, transferred use to that of a first name.

TREVELYAN (Cornish) 'Homestead', 'settlement'.

TREVOR (Welsh) 'Large settlement'.

TRIGG (Scandinavian) 'Loyal, faithful'.

TRUMAN (Old English) 'True, trusty man'. Then name is found mainly in the USA. Originally used as a surname, then as a nickname for a trustworthy man. The frequency of its use as a first name was increased by the fame of the president of the US, Harry S. Truman.

URLWIN (Old German) 'Noble friend'.

VERDANT (Latin) 'Green, spring - like'. Taureans are born in the Spring.

WILFRED, WILFRID, WILFRYD (Old English) 'Hope for peace'. The name was borne by St Wilfrid, a 7th-century Bishop of York. The name was revived in the 19th century and was in regular use until the mid-20th century.

WINFRED (Old English) 'Peaceful friend'. The name is rarely found in modern times.

WYNDHAM (Old English) 'Homestead of Wigmund'. Originally a surname and place name. Two 20th-century British writers bore the name as a middle name: Percy Wyndham Lewis and John Wyndham Harris.

YARILO (Slavonic) 'God of love'.

YORICK 'Earth'. Danish form of George.

Taurus ~ Girls

ABRA (Hebrew) 'Earth Mother'.

ADAMINA (Hebrew) A feminine form of Adam.

AIMEE (French) 'Beloved friend'.

AINE (Irish) Pronounced 'ah-na'. Name given to the ancient Irish god of love. The name means 'delight' or 'pleasure'.

ALCINA (Greek) 'Strong-minded one'. Legend has it that the name was borne by a Grecian lady who could turn stardust into gold.

ALVINA (Old English) 'Noble friend'. Feminine form of Alvin.

ALVA Form of Alvina.

ALVINA (Old English) 'Beloved friend'. Also the name given to a 'continent' on the surface of Venus, the ruler of Taurus.

AMABEL (Latin) 'Lovable'. The name

was popular in the Middle Ages and agin in the 19th century.

AMANDA (Latin) 'Lovable'. The name has possibly been in existence since the Middle Ages, although some schools of thought believe that it was invented in the 17th century. The name became increasingly popular in the mid-20th century.

AMATA Form of Amy.

AMECIA (Latin) 'Love'.

AMELINDA (Latin) 'Beloved and pretty'.

AMERA A blend of Amy and Vera. 'Love and faith'.

AMIA (Latin) 'Love'. Form of Amy.

AMICA (Latin) 'Friend'.

AMICE Of uncertain origin. Possibly a form of Amy or a French form of Amica.

AMICIA Form of Amice.

AMINA (Arabic) 'Faithful'.

AMINTA (Latin) 'Loving'.

AMORETTA (Latin) 'Loved one'.

AMY (Old French) Form of Aimee. 'Loved'. The name has been in use since the 13th century. It enjoyed a revival in the 19th century but did not become popular in the USA until the late-20th century.

ANGHARAD (Welsh) 'Much loved'. The name was in use in medieval Welsh folk tales.

ANNABEL, ANNABELLE (Latin) 'Lovable'. A form of Amabel. Annabel has been used as a first name in Scotland since the Middle Ages. It was the name of the mother of King James I of Scotland, Annabel Drummond. The name has become used in other English-speaking countries since the 19th century although the spelling Annabelle has only been in use since the mid-20th century.

ANNABELLA Form of Annabel.

AO (Maori) 'Planet Earth'.

APHRODITE (Greek) In Greek mythology the name is borne by the goddess of love. The name is also given to a 'continent' on the surface of the planet Venus.

APRIL (Latin) Name of the month used as a first name. The name was popular in the 20th century.

ARABELLA Form of Annabel. The name was borne by Lady Arabella Stuart, a cousin of King James VI of Scotland. The name was popular in England in the 18th century.

ARAMINTA (Latin) 'Loving'. Possibly a combination of Arabella and Aminta.

ARIADNE (Greek) In Greek mythology Ariadne is the name of an important character in the mythical story of the formation of the constellation of Taurus.

AROHA (Maori) 'Love'.

AXELLE (Old German) 'Mother of peace'. Feminine form of Axel.

BEL, BELL, BELLE Shortened forms of Annabelle.

BELLA Shortened form of Annabella.

BRANWEN Name borne by a goddess of love and death in Welsh Druid mythology.

CARA, KARA (Italian) 'Dearest friend'. The name has been in use since the the early part of the 20th century and became increasingly fashionable in the 1970s.

CAREL, CARELLA, CARELLE (Old English) 'Dear' or 'carer'.

CARINA, KARINA (Latin) 'Beloved'. Carina is also the name given to a star.

CARINE, KARINE Forms of Carina.

CARITA Form of Carina or Cara.

CARMEL (Hebrew) 'Garden' or 'orchard'. A name of early Christian origin, in reference to the Virgin Mary, 'Our Lady of Carmel'. It is also the name given to a mountain in Israel.

CARMELA Italian form of Carmel. Occasionally used in the USA.

CARMELITA Italian form of Carmel. Occasionally used in the USA.

CARMEN Spanish form of Carmel.

CAROMY (Celtic) 'Friend'.

CARON, CARRON (Welsh) 'To love'.

CARREN Variant of Caron.

CARYL Form of Carys.

CARYS (Welsh) 'Love'.

CERI (Welsh) 'To love' or 'loved one'.

CERIAL Derived from Ceri.

CERYS Derived from Ceri.

CERIA Derived from Ceri.

CHARITY (Latin) 'Affectionate'. The name was adopted by the Puritans but is not so commonly found today.

CHERIDA (Spanish) 'Beloved one'. Form of Querida.

CHERYL Form of Carys.

CHATTIE Pet form of Charity.

CHER, CHERE, CHERIE, CHERRIE, CHERI (French) 'Dear one'.

CHERINE, CHERISE, CHERISSA, CHERITA Variants of Cherie.

CHERITH (Latin) 'Cherish', 'hold dear'.

CHERRY Pet form of Charity, sometimes used as a name in its own right.

COLINE, COLUMBINA, COLUMBINE, COLUMBIA, COLOMBE, COLLY Variations of Columba.

COLUMBA (Latin) 'The dove', 'one of peaceful disposition'.

COPPER Lucky metal for Taureans.

CONSTANCE (Latin) 'Steadfast'.

CORAH (Hindu) 'Constant'.

CYAN (Greek) 'Dark blue'. Blue is a lucky colour for Taureans.

DANU, DANA Name given to the mother goddess of the land in Irish Druid mythology. She is also known as a river goddess.

DARLA (Middle English) 'Loved one'.

DARLENE, DARLEEN (Old English) 'Dearly beloved'. From the English word darling. Used occasionally as a first name, particularly in the USA and Canada, in the mid-20th century.

DARLIN, DARLINE (Old English) 'Loved one'.

DARYN Derived from Darlin.

DARYL, DAREL, DARELLE, DARRELLE Forms of Darlene (Old English) 'Loved one' or 'dearly beloved'.

DAVIDA 'Beloved'. Scottish feminine form of David.

DAVINA Scottish feminine form of David.

DAVINIA Scottish feminine form of David.

DILYS (Welsh) 'Genuine', 'steadfast', 'true'.

EARTHA (Old English) 'From the earth'. The name was made famous by the 20th-century American creole singer Eartha Kitt.

EASTER Form of Ester.

EBREL (Cornish) April.

EDWINA Feminine form of Edwin. (Old English) 'Friend'.

ELVINA (Old English) 'Noble friend'. Feminine form of Elvin.

ELVIRA (Spanish form of German origin) 'True'. The name was popular in Spain during the Middle Ages and spread to English-speaking countries in the 19th century.

ERDA (Old German) 'Child of the earth'.

ESMEE (Old French) 'Loved'.

ESTER, ESTHER (Persian) 'Star', in particular reference to the planet Venus. It is also a form of Ishtar, the name borne by the Babylonian goddess of love. The name was in regular use in English-speaking countries until the mid-20th century.

EVADNE (Greek) 'Well, good'. In Greek mythology Evadne was the name of the wife of Capaneus, a hero in Seven Against Thebes. The name has occasionally been found in English-speaking countries.

FAE, FAY, FAYE Shortened forms of Faith.

FAITH (Old English) 'One who is loyal and true'. The name came into use as a first name in the 16th century and was particularly popular with Puritans in the 17th century. It is still in use today.

FAVO, FAVORA (French) 'The helpful one'.

FEALTY (French) 'Faithful one'.

FIDELA, FIDELE, FIDELIA (Latin) 'Faithful one'.

FONDA (English) 'Affectionate'.

FREDA (Old English) 'Peace'. One who is calm and unhurried.

FRIEDA, FREIDA, FRIDA, FRIEDA, FREDDIE Forms of Freda.

FREYA (Old Norse) Goddess of love in Scandinavian mythology. The name has been in occasional use in English-speaking countries since the beginning of the 20th century.

GAEA (Greek) Name given to the goddess of the earth in Greek mythology.

GAIA Alternative spelling of Gaea.

GAIANE (Greek) 'Child of the earth'.

GALINA (Greek) 'Peace'.

GE (Greek) In Greek mythology Ge was the name of earth goddess who gave birth to the heavens.

GEORGETTE 'Earth'. Feminine diminutive of George.

GEORGIA 'Earth'. Latin feminine form of George .

GEORGIANA Elaborated form of Georgia.

GEORGIE Pet form of Georgia or Georgina.

GEORGINA Latin feminine derivative of George.

GRANIA (Irish) 'Love'. The name was borne by a character of Gaelic legend who eloped with Diarmuid. The name is rarely found outside Ireland.

HATHOR Name of a goddess of love in Egyptian mythology. Hathor was also known as a moon goddess and as a water goddess.

HAVIVA (Hebrew) 'Beloved'.

HERTA (Old German) 'Earth mother'.

HERTHA (Old German) 'Earth Mother'.

HESTER Form of Esther.

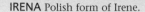

HORTENSE (Latin) 'A garden'. From an old Roman family name. The name has been in use as a first name in English-speaking countries since the 19th century but is seldom found today.

HYACINTH (Greek) A flower-name meaning 'blue gem or sapphire'. In Greek mythology, the Hyacinth flower grew out of the blood of the youth Hyacinthus, who was accidently killed by Apollo. The name Hyacinth was originally used as a boys' name. Its use as a girls' name is a fairly recent adoption.

IDINA, IDONA, IDONEA (Old Norse) Name given to the Norse goddess of spring. The name has occasionally been in use as a first name in Britain since the 13th century.

INARET (Welsh) 'Much loved'.

INGA, INGE (Old Norse) Pet form of Ingeborg 'the protection of Ing'. In Norse mythology Ing is the god of peace.

INGRID Scandinavian form of Inga.

IRANA Form of Irene.

IRENA Polish form of Irene.

IRENE (Greek) 'Peace'. In Greek mythology Irene is the name of a minor goddess of peace. The name was also borne by an early Christian martyr and several Byzantine empresses. The name has been in use in English-speaking countries since the 19th century and became particularly popular in the early-20th century.

IRINA Form of Irene.

ISHTAR (Mesopotamian) Name of the Babylonian goddess of love. Ishtar Terra is also the name of a 'continent' on the surface of the planet Venus.

JEMIE, JEMMIE Pet forms of Jemima.

JEMIMA (Hebrew) 'Dove'. The dove is a symbol of peace. The name is found in the Old Testament, being the name of one of the three beautiful daughters of Job. The name was used by the Puritans in the 17th century and has been in use since that time.

JEMINA (Persian) Form of Jemima. 'Peace'.

JEMIRA Blend of Jemima and Mira. Mira is from the Greek for myrrh, a sweet-smelling oil.

JEMITA A blend of Jemima and Rita. Rita is an Italian or Spanish variation of Margaret, meaning 'pearl'.

JEMMA Form of Jemima.

KALILA (Arabic) 'Beloved'.

KARENZAZA (Cornish) 'Love', 'affection'.

KASHIMA Form of Kasmira.

KASMIRA (Slavonic) 'Commander of peace.'

KERANZA (Cornish) 'Love, affection'.

LAIS (Greek) 'Adored'.

LAVERNA Form of Laverne.

LAVERNE (Latin) 'Spring-like, verdant'.

LEALA (French) 'The true one'. One who is true to home, family and friends.

LEEBA (Yiddish) 'Beloved'.

LENE Form of Lenis.

LENIS (Latin) 'Smooth and white as a lily'. The lily is the symbol of peace, an important attribute of Taurus.

LENTA Form of Lenis.

LENITA, LENETA Form of Lenis.

LENOS Form of Lenis.

LILIAN, LILLIAN (Latin) 'Lily'. The lily is a symbol of peace, an important attribute of Taurus. The name has been used in Britain since the 16th century and was particularly popular at the turn of the 20th century.

LILIAS, LILLIAS Scottish form of Lilian.

LILLA, LILLAH Form of Lily.

LILY, LILLIE The lily is a symbol of peace, an important attribute of Taurus.

LILAC (Persian) A flower name, meaning 'bluish'. The name came into use as a first name in the late-19th century.

LILAH Form of Lilac.

MAHALA, MAHALAH, MAHALIA (Hebrew) 'Tenderness'. The name has been in occasional use in English-speaking countries since the 17th century.

MAIA Roman goddess of spring. Taureans are born in the spring.

MALLOW Name of the lucky plant for Taurus.

MALU (Hawaiian) 'Peace'.

MALVA (Greek) 'Tender'.

MAY Name of month used as a first name. The name was particularly popular in English-speaking countries in the early-20th century.

MEHALA, MEHALAH, MEHALIA Forms of Mahala.

MERNA, MIRNA (Gaelic) 'Beloved'.

MILDRED (Old English) 'Gentle strength'.

MIMA Shortened form of Jemima.

MINA Shortened form of Jemina

MOCARA (Gaelic) 'My friend'.

MOINA, MOYNA Forms of Myrna.

MORNA (Gaelic) 'Beloved', 'gentle'. Anglicized form of Muirne.

MUIRNE (Irish Gaelic) 'Beloved'. Pronounced 'moor-nya'.

MYRNA 'Beloved' Anglicized form of Muirne. This form is more usually found than Morna.

NALANI (Hawaiian) 'Calmness of the heavens'.

OLIFF Form of Olive.

OLIVE (Latin) 'Olive'. A symbol of peace. In medieval times the name occurred in a variety of forms. Olive has been in use as a first name since the 16th century and became particularly popular in the 1920s.

OLIVET Form of Olive. The name was found in medieval times.

OLIVIA An Italian form of Olive. The name became fashionable in English-speaking countries in the 18th century.

OPHELIA (Greek) 'Help'. The name was borne by a heroine in Shakespeare's *Hamlet*. The name has occasionally been found as a first name in English-speaking countries.

PACIFA (Latin) 'Peace-loving'.

PALOMA (Spanish) 'The dove' or 'a gentle, tender girl'.

PALOMETA, PALOMITA Forms of Paloma.

PAMPHILA (Greek) 'All-loving'.

PATIENCE (English) 'Patience'. The name was adopted by the Puritans after the reformation and is still found in English-speaking countries today.

PAZ (Spanish) 'Peace'.

PEACE (English) 'Peace, harmony'. Adopted by the Puritans after the reformation but is rarely found today.

PERONEL Form of Petronilla.

PERPETUA (Latin) 'Constant'.The name was borne by St Perpetua who was martyred in the 3rd century.

PETRINA (Greek) 'Steadfast as a rock'. Feminine form of Peter.

PETRA (Greek) 'Steadfast as a rock'. Feminine form of Peter.

PETRONELLA, PETRONELLE (Greek) 'Steadfast as a rock'. Forms of Petronilla, dating back to the Middle Ages.

PETRONIA (Greek) 'Steadfast as a rock'.

RHIANNON (Welsh) 'Maiden'. The name Rhiannon is borne by a Welsh goddess of the land in Druid mythology. The name is also associated with the moon in Celtic mythology. It has only been given as a first name since the 20th century.

ROLANDA (Old German) 'Land'. Feminine form of Roland.

ROSALIND Name of uncertain origin. It may be from Old French, meaning 'weak, tender, soft', or from Spanish origin, meaning 'pretty rose'.

ROSALINE Form of Rosalind.

ROSALYN, ROSALYNN, ROSALYNNE Altered forms of Rosalind.

ROSELINE, ROSELYN, ROSLYN Forms of Rosaline.

SALEMA (Hebrew) 'Peace'.

SALOME (Hebrew) 'Peace'. The name was borne by the granddaughter of Herod the Great in the New Testament. The name has been in occasional use in English-speaking countries since the 17th century.

SERENA (Latin) 'Calm'. The name has been in occasional use in English-speaking countries since the 18th century.

SHALOM (Hebrew) 'Peace, wholeness'.

SHANTI (Sanskrit) 'Peace'.

SHIMONEL Modern name meaning 'peace of the elves'.

SHUKA Form of Shula.

SHULA, SULA, SHULIE (Arabic) 'Peace'.

SHUNA, SHUNE Forms of Shula.

SHUSHANA, SHUSHANNA Forms of Susannah. These forms have been in use in English-speaking countries since the 17th century.

SIGRID (Old German) 'Victory', 'peace'. Feminine form of Siegfried.

PETRONILLA, PETRONILLE (Greek) 'Steadfast as a rock'. The name Petronilla was fairly popular in Britain during the Middle Ages.

PERRINE (Greek) 'Steadfast as a rock'. Feminine form of Peter.

PETULA (Greek) 'Steadfast as a rock'.

PHILA (Greek) 'Love'.

PHILANA A blend of Phila and Lana. Lana is a Latin name meaning 'wool'.

PHILANTHA A blend of Phila and Samantha. Samantha is an Aramaic name meaning 'listener'.

PHILENA (Greek) 'Lover of Mankind'.

PHILINA (Greek) 'Lover of Mankind'.

PHILOMENA (Latin) 'To love' and 'strength'. The name came more frequently in use in the 19th century after the supposed discovery in 1802 of the relics of St. Philomena in Rome.

PHILOMON (Greek) 'Affectionate'.

PIERETTE, PIERRETTE (Greek) French feminine form of Peter. 'Steadfast as a rock'.

PLACIDA (Latin) 'Peaceful one'.

PLACIDIA Form of Placida.

PLEIADES Name of a star cluster in the constellation of Taurus.

PRIMAVERA (Spanish) 'Child of the spring'.

PRU, PRUE Shortened forms of Prudence.

PRUDENCE (English) 'Prudence'. The name was first used in the 13th century. It was readopted by the Puritans after the Reformation and remains in occasional use today.

QUERIDA (Spanish) 'Beloved one'. A term of endearment.

RATI (Indian) Name of an Indian goddess of love.

RAYA (Hebrew) 'Friend'.

RENE, RENIE Pet forms of Irene.

SPRING The seasonal name used as a first name.

SPRYNG Alternative spelling of Spring.

STORAX Name of the lucky perfume for Taurus.

SUE, SUSIE, SUZY Pet forms of Susan, Susannah or Suzette.

SUSAN Form of Susannah. The name has been in regular use since the 18th century. In the mid-20th century it was one of the most well-used girls' names in English-speaking countries.

SUSANNAH, SUSANNA, SUZANNA (Hebrew) 'Lily'. The lily is the symbol of peace, a characteristic of Taurus. The name is found in both the Old Testament and the New Testament. The name was readopted by the Puritans after the Reformation and has been in use throughout English-speaking countries since that time.

SUSANNE, SUZANNE French form of Susannah. The name has been in frequent use throughout English-speaking countries since the early-20th century.

SUZETTE French form of Susannah.

TERAH (Latin) 'The earth'.

TERRENA (Latin) 'Of the earth'.

THEIA Name given to a vulcano on the surface of Venus, the ruling planet of Taurus.

THIRZA Form of Tirzah.

TIERRA (Latin) 'Earth'. Name of recent coinage.

TI-MU In Chinese mythology this is the name given to the earth mother, the maker of all creation.

TIRION (Welsh) 'Kind', 'gentle'. Name of recent coinage.

TIRZAH (Hebrew) 'Pleasantness'.

TIVONA (Hebrew) 'Lover of Nature'.

TIVONI (Hebrew) 'Love of Nature'.

TI-YA Alternative name for Ti-mu.

TLAZOLTEOTI (Peruvian Indian) Goddess of love.

TOPAZ Lucky gemstone for Taureans.

TRUGAREDD (Welsh) 'Loving kindness'.

VENITA Forms of Venus. 'The goddess of love'.

VENUS (Greek) 'To love'. Venus is the ruling planet of Taurus. Venus is the goddess of love in Greek mythology.

VERA (Russian) 'Faith', 'truth'. Also (Latin) 'True'. The name was introduced into Britain at the beginning of the 20th century and was particularly popular for the first half of the century.

VERDA (Old French) 'Green', 'spring-like'.

VERELLA A blend of Vera and Ella. Ella is an Old German name meaning 'all'.

VERENA, VERINA Elaborations of Vera.

VERITA Form of Verity.

VERITY (Old French) 'Truth'. Adopted by the Puritans after the Reformation and is still occasionally found today.

VERNA (Latin) 'Spring-like'. Taureans are born in the spring.

VERNE, VERN (French) 'Spring-like'. Shortened forms of Laverne.

VERNICE, VERNIS Forms of Verna.

VERNITA, VERNETA Forms of Verna.

VIRNA, VIRINA Forms of Verna.

VIDA, VINA Shortened forms of Davina, 'beloved' or 'friend'.

VINITA (Latin) 'The goddess of love'. 'Of incomparable loveliness'. Derivative of Venus.

VINNIE, VINNY Shortened forms of Venita.

WILFREDA (Old German) 'The peacemaker'. Feminine form of Wilfred.

WILFRIEDA, WILFREIDA Forms of Wilfreda.

WINIFRED (Welsh) 'Blessed reconciliation'. The name was borne by a Welsh saint of the 7th century.

WINIFRIDA, WINIFREIDA, WINIFRIEDA Forms of Winifred.

WINNIE, WINNY Shortened forms of Winifred.

WINOLA (Old German) 'Gracious friend'.

XENIA (Greek) 'Hospitality'. Rarely found in the English-speaking world.

YELENA (Latin) 'Lily blossom'. The lily is a symbol of peace.

ZULEMA (Arabic) 'Peace'.

Gemini

THE TWINS
21 May - 20 June

RULING PLANET   Mercury – the planet of communication, thought and mind. In mythology Mercury is known as 'the winged messenger of the gods'.

ELEMENT   Air

General characteristics
- Good communicators, speakers.
- Humorous, entertaining, charming.
- Intelligent, intuitive.
- Enjoys variety; versatile.
- Stimulating, inventive.
- Quick, dexterous, youthful.
- Liberal, broad-minded.

Characteristics of young Gemini
- Loves to chatter; friendly.
- Needs space to explore, becomes fractious if cooped up.
- Is bright and alert.
- Loves to learn.
- Often reads at an early age.
- Enjoys activities where he is using his hands and fingers.
- Good sense of humour.
- A good natural mimic.

Geminian lucky connections
Gemstones:	tourmaline and garnet
Colour:	orange
Plants:	orchid and hybrids
Perfume:	lavender
Metal:	quicksilver
Animal:	magpie
Tarot card:	the lovers

GEMINIANS tend to be fast-thinking, fast-moving and fast-talking individuals. They are always on the move, fluttering from one activity to the next with apparent ceaseless energy.

Gemini is ruled by Mercury, the mythological messenger of the gods. Like the fleet-footed Mercury, who was always moving to and fro with many messages, Geminians are always on the go, both in mind and body. In astrology Mercury is the planet of thought and communication, so these mental processes are very important to those born under the sign of Gemini.

You may find that your Gemini baby is unusually alert, even from birth. He may sleep restlessly and wake at the slightest noise. Your Gemini baby may not be a creature of regular sleeping and eating habits. If you wish to establish a more regular pattern for your baby, try rocking him when he fusses or try distracting him with interesting things that he can look at. You could also try talking to him in a spirited fashion as Geminians love language and the sound of your voice will interest him immensely.

Geminians crave variety in their lives and need constant stimulation.

They are inquisitive individuals who like to explore, discovering more about whatever catches their interest, and they enjoy getting their fingers into everything. Try to provide your Gemini baby with as many different types of rattles and playthings as possible, as he will often become bored with a toy very quickly. He is not being difficult on purpose. It is simply that Gemini's love of variety and stimulation is all tied up with their love of learning. In fact Gemini is a sign very much concerned with the intellect.

Their love of learning coupled with their high-energy levels means that Geminians often enjoy doing several things at once. Your child may work at a puzzle, listen to music and chat to someone all at the same time. This need for intellectual stimulation will often mean that Geminians need to discover the relationships between things and how things work. They are often also interested in symbolic systems such as the alphabet and numbers. They enjoy books, puzzles and challenging games, in fact anything that harnesses their thirst for knowledge and understanding. Try to provide your Gemini child with the freedom to explore and provide many opportunities for him to investigate and learn.

Gemini is a sign very much concerned with communication through words and ideas. Gemini children often learn to speak early, as they love to harness the power of language. You may discover that your child chatters away to his toys in quite complicated sentences or retells stories to others in a very enthusiastic fashion. It is important to give attention and respect to your Gemini child's need to express himself verbally. Try composing a poem together, play question and answer games together or try asking him to tell you a story.

Geminians are generally bright and cheerful individuals and have a good sense of humour. Their ability to make you laugh, together with their quick, stimulating minds, will ensure that life with your Gemini child is very rewarding.

Gemini ~ Boys

ADLEY (Hebrew) 'Fair minded'.

ALFRED (Old English) 'Wise counsel'. The name was fairly common in England before the Norman conquest. It was borne in the 9th century by King Alfred the Great. After the Norman conquest the name was little used for centuries until it was revived in the 18th century.

ALIM (Arabic) 'Wise'.

ALURED Form of Alfred.

ALVIS (Old Norse) 'All knowing'. The name occurs in Norse mythology.

ANGEL (Greek) 'Messenger' or 'angel'. Mercury, the ruling planet of Gemini, is known as the messenger of the gods. It is used as both a boys' and girls' name but is seldom found today.

ANGELO Italian form of Angel. The name is occasionally found in English speaking countries, especially in families of Italian descent.

ASHER (Hebrew) 'The laughing one'. The name is found in the Old Testament as one of the sons of Jacob. It has been in infrequent use since the 17th century.

ASHVINS (Indian) 'Twins'.

AVERY 'Wise counsel'. A variant of Alfred.

BALDO (Latin) 'The mutterer'.

BERT 'Bright in mind', 'intelligent'. Shortened from of Hubert.

BOAZ (Hebrew) 'Swiftness'. The name was borne in the Old Testament by the husband of Ruth. It has been used in English speaking countries in the 17th century and is occasionally found today.

BRADY (Gaelic) 'Spirited one'. Mainly found in North America. It was originally an Irish surname.

BRAM Form of Bran.

BRAN (Celtic) 'Raven'. The spirit of eternal youth.

BRICE (Celtic) 'Quick', 'alert'. The name was borne by a 5th-century Bishop of Tours. It remains in occasional use today.

BRYCE (Celtic) 'Quick', 'alert'.

BURR (Norse) 'Youth'.

CAMILLUS (Latin) 'Messenger'. Mercury, the ruling planet of Virgo, is known as the messenger of the gods.

CASPER, CASPAR (Dutch) 'Wise man'. According to legend this name was borne by one of the three wise men who sought the infant Christ.

CASSIDY (Celtic) 'Ingenious'. Mainly found in north America, it is derived from an Irish Gaelic surname. It is used as both a boys' and girls' name.

CASTOR Name given to one of two very bright stars in the constellation of Gemini. Means 'Twin'.

CATO (Latin) 'The wise one'.

CAVELL (French) 'Little lively one'.

CEALLACH (Irish Gaelic) 'Bright-headed'. Pronounced Kell-ach. Traditional Irish Gaelic name.

CLARK, CLARKE (Old English) 'Scholarly', 'learned'. Originally a surname meaning cleric or clerk. Its use as a first name was popularised by the U.S. actor Clark Gable.

CLEARY (Gaelic) 'The scholar'.

CON 'Wisely intelligent'. Shortened form of Conan.

CONAL Form of Conan.

CONAN (Celtic) 'Wisely intelligent' or 'wolf'. The name was introduced into Britain by the Normans. It was in regular use until the 16th century. It is mainly in use as an Irish name in modern times.

CONANT Form of Conan.

CONN (Irish) 'Sense', 'intelligence'.

CONNALL Form of Conan.

CONNEL Form of Conan.

CONROY (Celtic) 'Wise one'.

CONRAD (Old German) 'Wise counsellor'. The name was borne by four medieval German Kings. In English speaking countries the name has been in occasional use since the 15th century.

CONWAY (Celtic) 'One who takes a wise course'.

CORT 'Brave counsellor'. Form of Conrad.

CURT Form of Conrad.

CUTHBERT (Old English) 'Famous and brilliant'. The name was borne by a 7th-century monk St. Cuthbert, Bishop of Lindisfarne in the north of England. The name was in regular use until the 17th century. It was revived during the 19th century but is seldom used today.

DAGDA In Irish Druid mythology Dagda is a father god known as a Good God and Lord of Knowledge. Dagda is the father of Anghus Og, god of love.

DAL Shortened from of Dallas.

DALLAS (Celtic) 'Skilled'. Name of a city in the State of Texas, USA.

DEMPSTER (Old English) 'Wise judge'.

DERMOT (Gaelic) 'Free man'. In Gaelic legend the name was borne by the lover of Grainne. It has been in regular use in Ireland since the 12th century. It is seldom found elsewhere.

DEX, DECK Shortened form of Dexter.

DEXTER (Latin) 'Skilful'. Mainly found in the US. Originally an old English surname but used as a first name since the beginning of the 20th century.

DREW (Celtic) 'The wise one'. Also a shortened form of Andrew.

DRUCE (Celtic) 'Wise man'.

ELDRIDGE (Old English) 'Wise advisor'.

ELVIS (Norse) 'All wise'. The prince of wisdom. The most famous bearer of this name was the US singer Elvis Presley.

EMIL, EMILE (Latin) 'Eager'. The name is derived from a Roman clan name. It is occasionally found in English-speaking countries. The French form Emile became popular in the late 19th century due to the fame of the French writer Emile Zola.

ENLIL Name of a god of air in Mesopotamian mythology.

ERROL (Latin) 'To wander'. Originally a Scottish surname and place name. A famous bearer of the name was the Australian actor Errol Flynn.

ESAU (Hebrew) 'Twins'. The name is found in the Old Testament where Esau sold his birthright to his twin brother Jacob.

FAROLD (Old English) 'Mighty traveller'.

FILBERT, PHILBERT (Old English) 'Very brilliant one'.

FLEET (Old Norse) 'Swift'.

FRANCHOT Form of Francis.

FRANCIS (Latin) 'Free'. One of the best-known bearers of the name was St Francis of Assisi. The name was introduced into England in the early 16th century. It has been in regular use in English speaking countries since the mid-19th century.

FRANK Shortened form of Francis.

FRANZ Form of Francis.

FREEMAN (Old English) 'One born free'.

FREEMONT (Old German) 'Protector of freedom'.

GALEN (Gaelic) 'Little bright one'.

GARNET Lucky gemstone for Gemini. Used as both a boys' and girls' name since the 19th century.

GAVA (Sanskrit) 'Swift'.

GAYLORD (Old French) 'High-spirited'. It is more common as a surname than a first name.

GEARY (Old English) 'The changeable'.

GILES, GILLES, GIL (French) 'Youthful'. (Greek) 'Young goat'. In the 8th century the name was borne by a hermit St. Giles, who was able to heal the lame and crippled. The name was first used in Britain in the 12th century.

GIULIANO (Latin) 'Youthful'. Italian form of Julius.

GWYDDION Name given to the lord of the skies and god of words in Welsh Druid mythology. Both attributes of this god are applicable to Gemini. Gwyddion was the father of Lleu Llaw Gyffes. See Lleu.

HAGAN, HAGGAN, HAGGEN Alternative spellings of Hagen.

HAGEN (Gaelic) 'The young one'.

HALBERT (Old English) 'Brilliant hero'.

HALEY (Gaelic) 'The ingenious one'.

HAMAR , HAMMAR (Norse) Symbol of ingenuity.

HAUORA (Maori) 'Lively'.

HERMES From the name of the Greek messenger of the gods. Known to the Romans as Mercury, which is the ruling planet of Gemini.

HEWETT (Old English) 'Little Hugh'. 'Bright in mind'.

HOBART 'Bright in mind', 'intelligent'. Form of Hubert.

HOGAN (Celtic) 'Youth'.

HOIBEARD Form of Hubert.

HOWELL (Celtic) 'Little', 'alert one'. Anglicised form of the Welsh name Hywel.

HOYT Form of Hubert.

HUB A shortened form of Hubbard.

HUBBARD A form of Hubert.

HUBE Form of Hubert.

HUBERT (Old German) 'Bright in mind, intelligent'. The name was introduced into Britain by the

Normans. It was popular in medieval times and remained in use until the 14th century. It was revived in the 19th century and is still occasionally found today.

HUEY Form of Hubert.

HUGH Form of Hubert. The name was borne by the French aristocracy in the middle ages. It was adopted by the Normans who introduced it into Britain.

HUGHES Form of Hubert.

HUGHIE, HUGHY Form of Hubert.

HUGO (Old German) 'Bright', 'intelligent'. Latin form of Hugh.

HUW Welsh form of Hugh.

HY 'Little alert one'. Shortened form of Hywel.

HYMIE 'Little alert one'. Form of Hywel.

HYWEL 'Little alert one'. Form of Howell. The name was popular in medieval times and is still in occasional use today.

HYWELL 'Little alert one'. Form of Howell.

IDRIS (Welsh) 'Impulsive' or 'fiery'. The name was borne by a character in Welsh mythology. The mountain Cader Idris in Gwynedd is named after him.

IKE Shortened form of Isaac.

IKEY, IKIE Forms of Isaac.

ISAAC (Hebrew) 'The laughing one'. The name is found in the Old Testament. Isaac was the son of Abraham and Sarah. It was popular in English speaking countries at the time of the Reformation. It is seldom found in modern times.

ISAAK Alternative spelling of Isaac.

IZAAC, IZAAK (Hebrew) 'The laughing one'.

JADEN (Hebrew) 'Wise'.

JASPER (Persian) 'Wise man'. Jasper is the anglicised form of the name Caspar. The name was first used in medieval times and is still in occasional use today.

JET (French) 'To throw forward'.

JETHRO (Hebrew) 'Excellent'. The name was borne in the Old Testament by the father of Moses' wife Zipporah. The name was adopted by the Puritans and was in regular use until the late 19th century. It was revived in the 1960's due to the fame of the rock group Jethro Tull.

JODA (Latin) 'Playful'.

JOOLS (Latin) 'Youthful'. Derivative of Julius.

JULE 'Youthful'. French form of Julius.

JULES 'Youthful'. French form of Julius.

JULIAN 'Youthful'. A form of Julius.

JULIUS (Latin) 'Youthful'. From a Roman family name. A famous bearer being Gaius Julius Caeser. The name has been in occasional use in English speaking countries since the 16th century, but in modern times it is more frequently found in the form Julian.

JUNIOR (Latin) 'Young'. Often used in the USA to distinguish between a son and father. In other English-speaking countries the name is sometimes bestowed as a name in its own right.

JUNIUS (Latin) 'Born in June'.

KAN (Japanese) 'Sense', 'intuition'.

KEAN 'Wise', 'learned'. Alternative spelling of Keene.

KEANE 'Wise', 'learned'. Alternative spelling of Keene.

KEENAN 'Wise', 'learned'. Form of Keene.

KEENE (Old English) 'Wise, learned'.

KELLY Anglicized form of Irish Gaelic Ceallach.

KONRAD (Old German) 'Wise counsellor'.

KORT 'Wise counsellor'. Form of Conrad.

KURT 'Wise counsellor'. Form of Conrad.

KYNAN (Celtic) 'Wisely intelligent'.

LANE (Old English) 'To move', 'go'.

LARIS (Latin) 'Cheerful'.

LINDELL (Old English) 'Lithe', 'flexible'.

LLEU First name of Lleu Llaw Gyffes, a god of Celtic Druid mythology who is possibly linked to Mercury. Mercury is the ruling planet of Gemini. Lleu was the son of Gwyddion, lord of the skies and god of words. See Gwyddion.

LOREDO (Latin) 'Learned, wise'.

LUAN (Hawaiian) 'To be at leisure'.

MABON (Welsh) 'Youth'.

MALACHI (Hebrew) 'My messenger'. Mercury, the ruler of Gemini is known as 'the messenger of the gods'. Malachi is the name of the last book of the Old Testament. It was used as a first name after the Reformation but is little used today.

MALACHY Irish form of Malachi. The name was borne by St Malachy, a 12th-century archbishop.

MASSEY 'Twin'. Form of Thomas.

MENDEL (Semitic) 'Wisdom'.

MERCURY Name of the ruling planet of Gemini.

NESTOR (Greek) 'Ancient wisdom'.

OMAR (Hebrew) 'Talkative', 'eloquent'.

PAXTON (Old German) 'Traveller from a distant land'.

PEREGRINE (Latin) 'Wanderer'. In the 2nd century the name was borne by a Greek philosopher. It has been in occasional use in Britain since the 13th century but is seldom found today.

PERRY (Latin) 'Wanderer'. Shortened form of Peregrine.

POLLUX Name given to one of the brightest two stars in the constellation of Gemini.

RAD (Old English) 'Counsellor'.

RADBERT (Old German) 'Brilliant counsellor'.

RAIMOND Form of Raymond.

RAMON Spanish form of Raymond. Found occasionally in English-speaking countries, predominantly the USA.

RANGER (Middle English) 'Wanderer'.

RAY Shortened form of Raymond.

RAYMON Form of Raymond.

RAYMOND (Old German) 'Wise protection'. The name was introduced into Britain by the Normans. It was little used in English-speaking countries until the 19th century. It was very fashionable in the early part of the 20th century and remains in use today.

RAYMUND (Old German) 'Wise protection'.

RAYNOLD, RAYNALD A blend of Raymond and Arnold.

REAMONN Form of Raymond.

REMUS (Roman) Name given to one of the twins in Roman mythology.

ROMULUS (Roman) Name given to one of the twins in Roman mythology.

SAGE (Old English) 'Wise one'.

SCHUYLER (Dutch) 'A scholar', 'a wise man'.

SHANAHAN (Gaelic) 'The wise one'.

SHANNON (Gaelic) 'Wise old one'.

SION 'The swift'.

SKEAT, SKEET 'The swift'. Shortened form of Skeeter.

SKEETER (Old English) 'The swift'.

SKY (Old Norse) A form of Skee, meaning 'a projectile'. Also from Old Norse meaning 'the heavens', 'cloud'. As Gemini is an Air sign this second meaning also has relevance. The name was used mainly in the 1960's when it became fashionable to give names taken from the world of nature.

SOL Shortened form of Solomon.

SOLOMON (Hebrew) 'Wise and peaceful'. King Solomon of the Old

Testament was considered to be a man of great wisdom. In the Middle Ages the name was in regular use in Britain. It was revived by the Puritans but is generally used as a Jewish name today.

SOLAMAN, SOLOMAN, SALOMON Alternative spellings of Solomon.

SOLON (Greek) 'Wise man'.

SPROULE (Old English) 'Energetic', 'active person'.

SPROWLE Alternative spelling of Sproule.

SYLGWYN (Welsh) 'Born at Whitsun'.

TAM 'Twin'. Scottish shortened form of Thomas.

TAMAS (Aramaic) 'A twin'.

TAMBLIN Variation of Thomas.

TAMMANY 'Twin'. Form of Thomas.

TAMMY Form of Thomas.

TANCRED (Old German) 'Think' and 'counsel'. The name was introduced into Britain at the time of the Norman Conquest.

TAO (Chinese) 'Life-force' or 'life-essence'.

TARUNA (Sanskrit) 'Youth'.

TAVIS (Hebrew) 'Twin'. Scottish form of Thomas.

TAVISH 'Twin'. Form of Tavis.

TEVIS 'Twin'. Form of Tavis.

THOM Shortened from of Thomas.

THOMAS (Aramaic) 'A twin'. 'The Twins' are the symbol of Gemini. The name is found in the New Testament, borne by one of the Twelve Apostles. The name has been in regular use throughout English-speaking countries since medieval times. A famous bearer of the name is the 12th-century martyr St Thomas á Becket, Archbishop of Canterbury. The name is still in frequent use today.

TOMKIN (Old English) 'Small Thomas'.

TOMLIN 'Small Thomas'.

TOMOS 'A twin'. Variant spelling of Thomas.

TOM Shortened form of Thomas.

TOMMY Shortened form of Thomas.

QUINN (Gaelic) 'Wise counsellor' or 'leader or chief'. It was originally an Irish surname.

ULICK (Irish) 'Mind', 'spirit' and 'play'.

ULYSSES Classicizing form of Ulick. Hero of Greek mythology. Since the 19th and 20th centuries it has been given as a first name throughout English-speaking countries, especially in the USA. A famous bearer of the name was the eighteenth President of the US, Ulysses S. Grant.

VARIAN (Latin) 'Changeable'.

VERE (Norman) 'Truth'. From the aristocratic family name de Vere. It was introduced into Britain by the Normans.

VITO (Latin) 'Lively', 'vital'.

VIVIEN, VIVIAN (Latin) 'Lively one'. Old French form of a Latin name. The name was borne by a Bishop of Saintes in western France in the 5th century. The spelling 'Vivien' is found in Arthurian legend. The names are used for both boys and girls but the spelling 'Vivian' is more frequently used as a boys' name.

WADE (Old English) 'A traveller'. This name has been in use since medieval times. According to legend it was borne by a sea giant.

WENDEL (Old German) 'A wanderer'. Originally a medieval surname. It has been in occasional use as a first name in English-speaking countries since the 19th century, especially in the USA.

WENDELL (Old German) 'A wanderer'.

ZELOTES (Greek) 'The zealous one'.

ZEVAN (Slavonic) 'Lively'.

ZIVAN (Slavonic) 'Lively'.

ZITO (Greek) 'To seek'.

Gemini ~ Girls

AINGEAL (Irish) 'Angel or heavenly messenger'. Gemini is ruled by Mercury, who is known as the winged messenger of the gods.

AKIRA (Japanese) 'Intelligence'.

ALANI (Hawaiian) 'Orange'. A lucky colour for Gemini.

ALEDA, ALETA, ALITA Variant of Alida.

ALETTE (Latin) A diminutive of 'Wing'.

ALFREDA (Old German) 'Wise counsellor'. Feminine form of Alfred.

ALIDA (Latin) 'Little winged one'. A girl who is as small and lithe as a woodlark.

ALLIE Shortened form of Alfreda.

ALLOULA, ALLULA, ALOULA Alternative spellings of Alula.

ALULA (Latin) 'Winged one'. Gemini is ruled by Mercury, the winged messenger of the gods.

ALURA (Old English) 'Wise counsellor'.

ALVITA (Latin) 'Vivacious'.

ALYSSA (Greek) 'Wise'.

AMIRA (Greek) 'Wise'.

ANGEL, ANGIE ANGELITA Forms of Angela.

ANGELA (Greek) 'Heavenly messenger'. In the 16th century the name was borne by Angela Merici, an Italian saint. The name was introduced into Britain in the 17th century. It was not commonly used until the 19th century and has become increasingly popular in English-speaking countries since the early-20th century.

ANGELICA (Latin) 'Angelic'. Form of Angela. The name was frequently found in Britain in the 18th century and remains in occasional use today.

ANGELINA, ANGELINE Forms of Angela.

ANGELIQUE Form of Angelica.

ANJULIE (Hebrew/Greek) 'Graceful and young'. A combination of Ann and Julie.

ARANI (Maori) 'Orange'. Lucky colour for Gemini.

ARDELIA (Latin) 'Zealous'.

ARITA (Maori) 'Eager'.

ATHENA (Greek) 'Wisdom'.

ATHENE (Greek) 'Wisdom'. In Greek mythology Athene was the name given to the goddess of war and wisdom. The city of Athens is named after her.

BEATHAG 'Wisdom'. A form of Sophia.

BELINDA (Latin) 'Wise beauty'. The name has been in regular use in English-speaking countries since the 18th century.

BENA, BINA (Hebrew) 'The wise one'.

BIBANA (Latin) 'Lively'. Derivative of Vivien.

BLYTHE (Old English) 'Joyous and friendly'. Originally an Old-English surname used occasionally as a first name.

CACHEL (French) 'Hidden wisdom'.

CACHELLA (French) 'Hidden wisdom'.

CACHELLE (French) 'Hidden wisdom'.

CALLENA (Old German) 'Talkative'.

CAMIE Pet from of Camilla.

CAMILLA (Roman) 'Messenger'. Feminine form of Camillus. Gemini is ruled by Mercury, 'the Messenger of the gods'. According to Roman mythology the name was borne by a Roman warrior maiden, queen of the Volscians. It became fashionable in the latter part of the 18th century and remains in use today.

CAMILLE (Roman) Feminine form of Camillus.

CAMINA A blend of Camilla and Nina. Nina is a Russian form of Ann.

CAMINDA A blend of Camilla and Linda. Linda is a Spanish name meaning 'pretty'.

CAMIRA A blend of Camilla and Mira.

CAMITA A blend of Camilla and Rita. Rita is a Spanish form of Margaret.

CAMORA A blend of Camilla and Dora. Dora is fairly modern invention, sometimes taken as a shortened form of Isadora.

CASSIDY, CASSADY (Celtic) 'Ingenious'. Used as both a girls' and boys' name. See Gemini boys' names.

COLLEEN (Irish) 'Young girl'. The name has been in use throughout English-speaking countries since the mid-20th century. Most frequently found in north America and Australia.

CONRADINA 'Wise counsellor'. Feminine form of Conrad.

CONRADINE (Old German) 'Wise counsellor'. Feminine form of Conrad.

DEXTRA (Latin) 'Skilful', 'dextrous'.

DILLYS (Welsh) 'Genuine'. Welsh name of recent coinage.

DILYS (Welsh) 'Genuine'.

DISA (Norse) 'Lively spirit'.

DROMICIA (Greek) 'Fast', 'speedy'.

EFFIE Pet form of Euphemia. It was especially popular in the 19th century.

ELECTRA (Greek) 'Brilliant one'.

ELFREDA (Old German) 'Wise counsellor'. The name was borne by the mother of Ethelred the Unready but was little used until it was revived in the 19th century.

ELFRIDA, ELFRIEDA, AELFREDA Alternative spellings of Elfreda.

ELRA (Old German) 'Elfin wisdom'.

ERLINDA (Hebrew) 'Lively'.

ESPRIT (French) 'Spirit'.

EUPHEMIA (Greek) 'Auspicious speech'. The name was borne by several early saints including a 4th-century virgin martyr. It was first used in Britain in the 12th century and was particularly popular in the 19th century.

FANIA (Latin) 'Free'. Slavic derivative of Frances.

FANNIA Alternative spelling of Fania.

FARAH 'Free'. Derivative of Frances.

FAY (Gaelic) 'The raven'. Symbol of great wisdom. A name of fairly recent coinage, first used in the late-19th century. Its use as a first name may have been influenced by Arthurian legend in that it was borne by Morgan le Fay, the half-sister of King Arthur, known as the Lady of the Lake.

FAYE Alternative spelling of Fay.

FAYETTE Form of Fay.

FILBERTA, FILBERTHA, FILBERTHE (Old German) 'Very brilliant'. Alternative spellings of Philberta.

FLAIR (Latin) 'Instinct for excellence'.

FLETA (Old English) 'Swift'.

FLETTA (Old English) 'Swift'.

FRANCA 'Free'. Spanish form of Frances.

FRANCELLE, FRANCELLA Blends of Frances and Ella. Ella is an old German name meaning 'all'.

FRANCES (Latin) 'Free'. Feminine form of Francis. The name has been in use in English-speaking countries since the 17th century and was particularly popular around the turn of the 20th century.

FRANCESCA 'Free'. Italian form of Frances.

FRANCETTA, FRANCELLA 'Free'. Forms of Frances.

FRANCHESCA, FRANCHESKA Italian form of Frances.

FRANCHON (French) 'Free being'.

FRANCINE, FRANCENE Forms of Frances.

FRANCISCA 'Free'. Form of Francesca.

FRANCOISE 'Free'. French form of Frances.

FRANCY Form of Frances.

FRANCYNE Form of Frances.

FRANKIE Shortened form of Frances.

FRANNIE Shortened form of Frances.

FRANNY Shortened form of Frances.

FRODINE (Old German) 'Wise friend'.

FULCA (Latin) 'Accomplished'.

GAI, GAY, GAE (French) 'Lively' or 'cheerful'. It began to be used as a first name in the early 20th-century but is seldom used today.

GALATIA (Greek) 'Laughing girl'.

GARNET Lucky gemstone of Gemini. The name has been in use as a first name since the 19th century. It has been used as both a girls' and boys' name.

GIULIA (Latin) 'Youthful'. Italian form of Julius.

HEBE (Greek) According to Greek mythology Hebe was the goddess of youth.

HELEN In Greek mythology Helen was the twin of Hermione.

HERMIA Shortened form of Hermione. Greek messenger of the gods.

HERMIONE Feminine form of Hermes. The Greek messenger of the gods, known to the Roman as Mercury. Mercury is the ruling planet of Gemini.

HERMINE Form of Hermione.

HUBERTA (Old German) 'Bright in mind'. Feminine form of Hubert.

HUELA 'Bright in mind'. Feminine form of Hugh.

HUETTE 'Bright in mind'. Feminine form of Hugh.

HUETTA Feminine form of Hugh.

HUGETTE Feminine form of Hugh.

HUGUETTE 'Bright in mind'. Feminine form of Hugh.

ISMAY (Old German) 'Bright'.

ISMENA (Greek) 'Educated'.

JANA (Sanskrit) 'Knows'. First used in English-speaking countries in the 20th century.

JADA (Hebrew) 'Wise'.

JAHNA (Sanskrit) 'Knows'.

JILL 'Youthful'. Shortened form of Jillian, a feminine form of Julian.

JILLIAN, GILLIAN 'Youthful'. Form of Juliana. The name was very popular in medieval times. It was revived in English-speaking countries in the 20th century and remains popular today.

JOCCOAA (Latin) 'Woman of humour'.

JODETTE (Latin) 'Little playful one'.

JOLETTA 'Youthful'. Form of Julia.

JOVITA (Latin) 'Full of joy'.

JUANA Form of June.

JULANDA A blend of Julie and Amanda.

JULANTHA A blend of Julie and Samantha.

JULIA (Greek) 'Youthful', 'young in heart and mind'. Feminine form of Julius. The name arrived in Britain from Italy in the 16th century. It became popular in the 18th century and has remained so since then.

JULIANA 'Youthful'. Feminine form of Julian.

JULIANE A form of Julia.

JULIANNA A blend of Julia and Anne.

JULIANNE French form of Julia.

JULIE 'Youthful'. French form of Julia.

JULIET French form of Julia.

JULIETTA French form of Julia.

JULINA A form of Julia.

JULINDA A blend of Julie and Linda.

JULINE A form of Julie.

JULI Shortened form of Julie.

JULITA, JULITTA A blend of Julie and Rita.

JUNA Derivative of June.

JUNE (Latin) 'Summer's child'. The month in which some Geminis are born. The name has been in use as a first name since the early-20th century.

JUNELLA A blend of June and Ella.

JUNETTE Form of June.

JUNIA 'Summer's child'. Form of June.

JUNIATA Form of June.

KAMILLA (Latin) Feminine form of the Roman name Camillus, meaning 'messenger'.

KARI (Sanskrit) 'Doer'.

KASOTA (Native American) 'Clear sky' (air).

KEENA (Old English) 'Wise', 'learned'. Feminine form of Keene.

KENDRA (English) 'Knowledge'.

KINA 'To move'. Form of Kinetta.

KINETA (Greek) 'Active and elusive'.

KINETTA (Greek) 'Active and elusive'.

KITA (Maori) 'Fast'.

KOMALA (Sanskrit) 'Charming'.

KORI (Maori) 'To play'.

KYNA (Gaelic) 'Great wisdom'.

ISLEAN, ISLIEN (Celtic) 'Sweet voiced'.

ISMENA (Greek) 'Educated'.

LAETITIA (Latin) 'Cheerful', 'joyous'. The name became popular in the 18th century and remains in occasional use today.

LALAGE (Greek) 'Gentle laughter'. The name has been in occasional use since the 19th century.

LALLA (Greek) 'To talk'.

LALLY (Greek) 'To talk'.

LANI (Hawaiian) 'The sky'.

LANIE (Hawaiian) 'The sky'.

LAVENDER (Latin) From the name of the flowering plant. Lavender is a lucky plant for Gemini.

LAVERNE (French) 'Young as spring'.

LEDA (Greek) 'Twins'. In Greek mythology the name was borne by a queen of Sparta who gave birth to two sets of twins, Castor and Pollux and Helen and Hermione.

LIBERTY (Latin) 'Free'.

LINDA Two possible origins: (Old German) 'Serpent' – hence 'wisdom', or (Spanish) 'Pretty'. The name has been in use in English-speaking countries since the late-19th century.

LISA (West African Benin) 'Twins'. The name became popular in English-speaking countries in the latter half of the 20th century.

LITA (Latin) 'Little winged one'. A form of Alida.

LUANA (Hawaiian) 'To be at leisure'.

LYSANDRA (Greek) 'To liberate'.

MABYN (Welsh) 'Youthful'.

MALCA (Old German) 'Active'.

MANON (Sanskrit) 'Imagine'.

MARIPOSA (Spanish) 'Butterfly'.

MAXENTIA (Latin) 'Of great talent'.

MAY (Latin) 'Born in May'. The name was particularly popular in the early-20th century.

MAYU (Japanese) 'True reason'.

MEARA (Gaelic) 'Mirth'.

MERCURY Name of the ruling planet of Gemini.

METIS (Greek) 'Wisdom and skill'.

METYS 'Wisdom and skill'. Alternative spelling of Metis.

MINERVA (Latin) 'Wise and purposeful'. Name of the Roman goddess of wisdom, arts and crafts and war. The name could also be derived from Latin meaning 'mind'.

MOCITA (Sanskrit) 'Liberated'.

NEOLA (Greek) 'The young one'.

NGAIO (Maori) 'Clever'. Pronounced Nye-oh.

ODESSA (Greek) 'A long journey'.

OFELIA, OFILIA, PHELIA Forms of Ophelia.

OPHELIA (Greek) 'Wise lady'. The name appears in Shakespeare's *Hamlet*. It has been in occasional use as a first name since the 19th century.

ORANGE A lucky colour for Gemini.

ORCHID Orchid is a lucky plant for Gemini.

PAIGE (Old English) 'Young child'. The name has been used as a first name since the 20th century. It is found mainly in north America.

PALLAS (Greek) 'Wisdom and knowledge'. Another name for the goddess of wisdom.

PANDORA (Greek) 'Talented', 'gifted one'. In classical mythology Pandora was the name borne by the first woman on earth. According to legend when 'Pandora's Box' was opened it unleashed all the evils of the world with only hope remaining inside.

PANSY (Old French) 'Thought'. The name was first used as a given name in the 19th century.

PETULA (Latin) 'Impatient' or 'to seek'. First used as a given name in the 20th century.

PHILBERTA (Old German) 'Very brilliant'.

PHILBERTHE, PHILBERTHA Alternative spellings of Philberta.

QUITERIA (Latin) 'Vital', 'full of life'.

RABIA (Arabic) 'Fragrant breeze', 'air'.

RADINKA (Old German) 'Playful'.

RAIMUNDA 'Wise protector'. Feminine form of Raymond.

RAMA Shortened form of Ramona.

RAMONA Feminine form of Raymond.

RAMONDA Form of Ramona.

RAYMONDA Form of Ramona.

RAYMONDE (Old German) 'Wise protector'. Feminine form of Raymond.

SABELLA (Latin) 'Wise'.

SADHBH, SADHBHB 'Wisdom'. Forms of Sophie.

SAGINA (Latin) 'Wise one'.

SAGUNA (Latin) 'Wise one'.

SAI (Japanese) 'Intelligence'.

SARADA (Sanskrit) 'Goddess of wisdom'.

SHANNAGH (Gaelic) 'Wise'. Originally an Irish surname.

SHANNAH, SHANNA 'Wise'. Variants of Shannagh.

SKY (Old Norse) 'Projectile' or 'cloud'. Both meanings are relevant to Gemini. Used as both boys' and girls' names. See Gemini boys' names.

SKYE Form of Sky.

SOFIA 'Wisdom'. Alternative spelling of Sophia.

SOLAIRE, SOLAYRE A modern invention combining 'the sun' (Latin) with 'air'.

SONDA A blend of Sonia and Wanda. Wanda is an old German name meaning 'family'.

SONDRA A blend of Sonia and Sandra. Sandra is a short form of Alexandra.

SONESTA A blend of Sonia and Vesta. Vesta is a Latin name given to the Roman goddess of the hearth.

SONIA, SONYA, SONJA 'Wisdom'. Russian and Slavonic forms of Sophia.

SONTARA A blend of Sonia and Tara. The name Tara comes from the name of a hill in Ireland.

SOPHIA (Greek) 'Wisdom'. In Greek mythology Sophia is known as the goddess of wisdom. Several minor saints have borne the name. The name became popular in Britain during the 17th and 18th centuries and remains in use today throughout the English-speaking world.

SOPHIE French form of Sophia.

SOPHY Alternative spelling of Sophie.

SOPHY, SOFIE 'Wisdom'. Forms of Sophia.

SYKIE (Greek) Phonetic form of 'psyche' meaning 'soul', 'mind'.

TAM 'Twin'. Shortened form of Tamsin.

TAMANA A blend of Tamsin and Lana. Lana is a shortened form of Alana.

TAMANDA A blend of Tamsin and Amanda. Amanda is a Latin name meaning 'lovable'.

TAMANDRA, TAMANDRIA Blends of Tamsin and Sandra. Sandra is a short form of Alexandra.

TAMANTHA A blend of Tamsin and Samantha. Samantha is a Hebrew name meaning 'to listen'.

TAMASIN, TAMASINE Forms of Tamsin.

TAMELDA A blend of Tamsin and Imelda. Imelda is an Italian form of German name meaning 'all-embracing battle'.

TAMELLA, TAMELLE Blends of Tamsin and Ella. Ella is an old German name meaning 'all'.

TAMIA A blend of Tam and Mia.

TAMILA A blend of Tam and Mila. Mila is a Hungarian form of Mildred meaning 'mild'.

TAMINA A blend of Tam and Mina. Mina is a form of Carmina.

TAMMY, TAMMIE, TAMME, TAMMI Forms of Tamsin.

TAMSYN, TAMASIN, TAMASINE TAMSIN 'Twin'. Variants of Thomasin. The name was popular in Britain in medieval times and has recently enjoyed a revival.

TAMZYN, TAMZIN, TAMZINE Variants of Tamsin.

TANGERINE A deep orange colour, named from the fruit. Orange is the lucky colour for Gemini.

TANGERENE Alternative spelling of Tangerine.

TANGERYNE Alternative spelling of Tangerine.

TAO (Chinese) 'Life force'.

TASMIN 'Twin'. A form of Tamsin.

TERESA (Greek) 'Summer' or 'the harvester'. The name was used largely in Spain until the 16th century and gradually spread to English-speaking countries. It became more popular in the 19th century and particularly so in the latter half of the 20th century.

TESSA (Greek) 'Summer'.

TESS Shortened form of Tessa.

TERESITA Spanish form of Teresa.

TERESSA A blend of Teresa and Tessa.

TERETTA Diminutive of Teresa.

TEREZA Spanish form of Teresa.

TERRIE, TERRY, TERRI Shortened forms of Teresa.

TERRYL, TERRIL Variants of Terry

TESHA 'Summer'. A form of Tessa.

TESSIE Form of Teresa

THERESA (Greek) 'Summer'.

THERESIA Form of Theresa.

THOMASIN, THOMASINA, THOMASENA 'Twin'. Feminine forms of Thomas.

THOMAZIN, THOMASINE 'Twin'. Feminine forms of Thomas.

TOIREASA Form of Theresa.

TOMASA Form of Thomasina.

TOMASINA Alternative spelling of Thomasina.

TOMMINA 'Twin'. Feminine form of Thomas.

TRACY, TRACEY Forms of Theresa.

TRESA 'Summer'. Form of Teresa.

TRESSA (Cornish) 'Third'. Gemini is the third astrological sign of the zodiac.

ULEMA (Arabic) 'To know'.

ULIMA (Arabic) 'The learned'.

VALIDA 'Very wise'. Form of Velda.

VALMAI (Welsh) 'May-flower'.

VANESSA (Greek) 'Butterfly'. The name was invented in the 18th century by Jonathan Swift for his friend Esther Vanhomrigh. It was a combination of the first syllable of her surname and 'Essa', a pet form of Esther. Vanessa did not become popular as a first name until the 20th century.

VEDA (Sanskrit) 'Knowledge'.

VEDETTE (Sanskrit) 'Wise little one'.

VEDIS 'Knowledge'. Form of Veda.

VELDA (Old German) 'Very wise'.

VELIDA 'Very wise'. Form of Velda.

VELLEDA (Old German) 'Most wise'.

VITESSE (French) 'Swiftness'.

VIV, VIVI Shortened forms of Vivian.

VIVEKA (Latin) 'Little lively one'.

VIVIA VIVIE Forms of Vivian.

VIVIAN 'Alive', 'lively'. The name was used in medieval Britain as a boys' name but it is now more commonly used as a girls' name. A famous bearer of the name was the actress Vivien Leigh, who was christened 'Vivian'.

VIVIANA Form of Vivian.

VIVIEN, VIVIENNE Alternative spellings of Vivian.

VIVIENNA Form of Vivian.

VIVYAN, VYVYAN, VIVIANE, VIVIENE Alternative spellings of Vivian.

WHITNEY (Old English) 'Born at Whitsun' or 'Land near the water'. Some Gemini babies are born at Whitsun. The name is found mainly in North America where it has been popularised by the singer Whitney Houston.

YVELINE (Hebrew) 'Lively one'. Derivative of Eve.

YOUNA (Latin) 'June born'. Derivative of June.

YULAN (Chinese) 'Jade orchid'. The orchid is a lucky plant for Gemini.

ZAKIYA, ZAKYA (Arabic) 'Intelligent'.

ZASU A form of Zaza.

ZAZA (Hebrew) 'Movement'.

ZEFIRA (Italian) 'Breeze'. Gemini is an air sign.

ZELIA (Latin) 'Zealous'.

ZIVA (Greek) 'To seek'.

ZIVANA (Slavic) 'Vivacious'.

Cancer

THE CRAB
21 June - 22 July

RULING PLANET The moon – the cycle of the moon is associated with the changing moods of the Cancerian personality.

ELEMENT Water

General characteristics
- Sensitive, receptive, defensive.
- Kind, compassionate, helpful.
- Loves comfort, domesticity.
- Nuturing, caring, protective.
- Sentimental, nostalgic, dreamy.
- Imaginative, interested in the pyschic etc.; good memory.
- Sensible with money.

Characteristics of the young Cancerian
- Changes mood frequently.
- Loves delicious food and drink.
- Loves colours and pictures.
- Needs love and encouragement.
- Withdraws inwardly from rejection.
- Capable of playing alone for hours.

Cancerian lucky connections

Colours:	yellow-orange and indigo
Gemstones:	pearl, amber and moonstone
Plants:	moonwort, almond and lotus
Perfume:	onycha
Metal:	silver
Animals:	crab, turtle and sphinx
Tarot card:	the chariot

CANCER is the sign of the crab, and like the crab there is a vulnerable softness beneath the outer layer.

Young Cancerians are often rather shy, not wanting to expose their feelings until they are sure of the response they'll receive. If they are hurt in any way they may show a hard outer shell in defence. Because of their sensitivity to emotional hurts and rejections Cancerian children often need lots of parental support.

Because of this sensitivity and need for emotional security, try to make sure that you provide your Cancerian child with many hugs and displays of affection. They will respond to this by showing the very loving and caring side of their nature. For Cancerians love their home and family above all else and if their home life is happy and they have a good relationship with their parents then they will be the most contented of children.

Their love of family life may well manifest itself in your child's play. She will be the perfect little parent to her family of dolls, siblings or even friends. She will love to feed, look after and protect them.

Cancerians are very emotional beings and may suffer from mood swings. You may find that your baby or child gurgles with laughter one minute and is tearful the next. Try to soothe your baby by holding her close, stroking or rocking her. This will provide her with the feeling of security she craves. When trying to soothe an older child try to reassure her if she is sad or fearful. Warmth and affection will give Cancerians the security and reassurance they need to tackle their fears. In this way most Cancerians will overcome their natural shyness and feel secure enough to show the delightful side of their characters. For indeed Cancerians can be truly delightful. They are usually the most thoughtful, helpful, caring and affectionate of individuals.

Cancerians are also very creative and imaginative. Try to provide her with many outlets for her creative side. Drawing and painting for example, or listening to music, singing songs and creating poetry and stories are all activities that your Cancerian child will enjoy.

Water play is always loved by Cancerian children as water is their natural element. At difficult times try to placate your Cancerian baby or child by setting up some water play or give her an extended bath time. This will often soothe away her bad moods.

Cancerians are also often intuitive beings; they might be daydreamers or love to use their imagination. You may often find your Cancerian child telling imaginative stories or singing her own made-up songs to her toys or siblings. She may also invent invisible playmates which is often simply another outlet for her love of make-believe.

Cancerians also often have good memories. Important days in their young lives will stay with them for a long time – often right into adulthood. They can also become very attached to things that remind them of happy times. Little momentos or photos can be important to them. In a similar way old toys often have more significance for her than new. They can give her that feeling of security that she loves so well. She may truly love her old battered teddy bear more than your new offering!

The zodiac sign of Cancer is ruled by the moon. In astrology the moon's cycle of waxing and waning is often likened to the changing moods of the Cancerian personality. But the moon is also associated with oddities and the humour of a Cancerian individual can often be quite crazy and very amusing, reflecting their ability to observe accurately the quirks of human nature.

The moon also influences the emotions and your Cancerian child will need to be handled sensitively. But given the love, warmth and security they need, they will, like the moon, reflect that love and affection back to others in abundance.

Cancer ~ Boys

ABNER (Hebrew) 'Father of light'. Cancer is ruled by the moon which is known to reflect light.

ADRIAN (Latin) 'Man from the sea'. Linked to Neptune. The name in the form 'Hadrian' was borne by a 2nd-century Roman emperor who was responsible for the building of Hadrian's Wall across northern England. The name Adrian was only in occasional use until the mid-20th century when it increased in popularity.

AEGIR Name given to the Scandinavian god of the sea.

AFON (Welsh) 'River'.

AIDAN (Latin) 'Help'.

ALPHONSUS Name given to a large crater on the moon's surface.

ALTON (Old English) 'Old stream source'.

ANTHONY (Greek) 'Flourishing'.

ARTEMAS, ARTEMUS (Greek) The name is connected with Artemis the Greek goddess of the moon. The Moon is the ruling planet for Cancer.

ATWATER (Old English) 'One who lives by the water'.

ATWELL (Old English) 'From the spring'. One who lives by a natural well.

AVON (Welsh) 'River'.

BOURNE, BOURN (Old English) 'A brook'.

BURNE , BURN (Old English) 'A brook'.

BYRNE (Old English) 'A brook'.

CLARENCE (Latin) 'Clear', 'illustrious'.

CLEMENT (Latin). 'Kind, gentle, calm'.

COBURN (Middle English) 'Small stream'.

COLBERT (French) 'Bright', 'famous'. The name was introduced into Britain at the time of the Norman Conquest.

CUTHBERT (Old English) 'Bright', 'famous'. The name was borne by 7th-century and 8th-century English saints. It was revived in the 19th century but is seldom found today.

DAI (Welsh) 'To shine'. Today taken as Welsh form of David but originally from an old Celtic word meaning 'to shine'.

DARWIN (Old English) 'Lover of the sea'.

DELMAR, DELMER (Latin) 'From the sea'.

DELWIN Form of Delmar.

DERON (Old English) 'Water'.

DOUGLAS (Gaelic) 'Dark blue water'. Originally a Scottish surname and place name. As a surname it was borne by one of the most powerful Scottish families. It began to be used as a first name in the 16th century and became particularly popular in English-speaking countries in the first half of the 20th century.

DYLAN (Welsh) 'Man from the sea'. In Welsh mythology the name was borne by a legendary character who became a sea god and was known as 'the god of the waves'. It was used mainly in Wales until the mid-20th century when its use spread to other English-speaking countries.

EDMAR, EDMER (Old English) 'Rich sea'.

ELBOURNE (Old English) 'Elf stream'.

ENKI Name of a god of water and wisdom in Mesopotamian mythology.

EWART (Old French) 'One who serves water'. Originally a Scottish surname. In occasional use as a first name.

FLINT (Old English) 'A stream'.

GARETH (Welsh) 'Gentle'.

GILBERT (Old French) 'Bright'. The name arrived in Britain in the 11th century. It was in regular use in medieval times and is still in occasional use today.

GLADWIN (Old English) 'Bright friend'. Originally a medieval surname.

HAMLET Medieval form of Hamo. The name was in regular use in Britain until the end of the 18th century but is rarely found today.

HAMLYN (Old German) 'Home lover'. A medieval form of Hamo.

HAMMOND Of uncertain origin. It may be a form of Hamo or it may mean 'home protector'.

HAMNET Form of Hamo. The name was borne by the son of William Shakespeare and Anne Hathaway.

HAMO (Old German) 'Home'. The name was introduced into Britain at the time of the Norman Conquest. It was in regular use during the Middle Ages but is little used today.

HERACLES The name of an important mythological character in the creation of the constellation of Cancer. Often known as Hercules.

HOWARD (Old English) 'Guardian of the home'. The name was used by the aristocracy as a family name for hundreds of years. It was adopted as a first name in the 19th century.

HOBART Form of Hubert.

HUBERT (Old French) 'Heart', 'mind', 'bright'. The name was in regular use by the Normans, who introduced it into Britain. It was revived in the 19th century and is still occasionally found in English-speaking countries today.

HUMPHREY (Old German) *Hun*, 'strength', and *frythu*, 'peace'. This name implies a quiet but strong character.

KAI (Japanese) 'Sea'.

KEBY (Cornish) A name of uncertain meaning, possibly 'charioteer'. The chariot is the lucky Tarot card for Cancer.

KELSEY (Old English) 'From the water'. Originally an Old English surname. It is occasionally used as both a girls' and boys' name.

KHENSU Name of an Egyptian moon god. The moon is the ruling planet of Cancer.

LUCAS (Latin) 'Light'. Derivative of Lucius.

LUCIANO (Latin) Italian derivative of Lucius.

LUCIEN (Latin) French derivative of Lucius.

LUCIUS (Latin) 'Light'. The name was in frequent use in ancient Rome. It was borne by three popes. It has been in occasional use in English-speaking countries since the Middle Ages.

LEMARR, LEMAR (Latin) 'Of the sea'.

LYNN, LYN, LIN, LINN (Welsh) 'From the pool or waterfall'.

MALIN 'Drop of the sea'. Masculine form of Mary.

MANNANAN Name given to a sea god in Irish Druid mythology, Mannanan Mac Lir.

MANNAWYDDAN Name of a god of the sea in Welsh Druid mythology.

MARLAND (Old English) 'Dweller in the lakeland'.

MARLIN (Latin) 'The sea'.

MARLON Form of Marlin.

MARLOW Form of Marlin.

MARLY Form of Marlin.

MARNE (Latin) 'Sea'.

MARVIN (Old English) 'Friend of the sea'. Also a Medieval form of Mervyn. Marvin was revived in the 19th century and is found most commonly in the USA.

MERIDETH, MEREDETH Forms of Meredith.

MEREDITH (Celtic) 'Protector of the sea'. The name was only used as a boys' name in Wales until the 20th century. It is now a popular Welsh name used for both boys and girls and is found throughout English-speaking countries.

MERIDITH, MEREDYTH, MERIDYTH Alternative spellings for Meredith.

MERDYDD Form of Meredith.

MERLIN English form of the welsh name Myrddin. Composed of Old Celtic elements meaning 'sea' and 'hill'. In Arthurian legend the name was borne by the famous wizard and advisor to King Arthur.

MORGAN (Welsh) 'Man from the wild sea'. The name has been used in Wales for centuries. Glamorgan, a Welsh county, is named after a 10th-century bearer of the name. The name is occasionally bestowed as a girls' name. Morgan le Fay, the sister of King Arthur, is a famous feminine bearer of the name.

MORIEN (Welsh) 'Sea born'.

MOULTRIE (Gaelic) Origin is uncertain but it possibly means 'sea warrior'.

MUIRIS 'Vigorous sea'. Contracted form of the Gaelic name Muirgheas.

MURCHADH 'Sea battle'. Traditional Gaelic name. Pronounced 'moor-ha'.

MURDO (Scottish) 'Sea'.

MURDOCH Gaelic form of Murdo. The name is most commonly found in Scotland.

MURPHY (Irish) 'Of the sea'.

MURRAY, MORAY (Gaelic) 'Sea'. From the Scottish surname and place name. The name has been in regular use in the English-speaking world since the 19th century.

MURROUGH Anglicized form of Murchadh.

NANNAR Name of a moon god in Mesopotamian mythology.

NEPTUNE In Roman mythology Neptune was the god of the sea.

NEREID In Greek mythology a Nereid is sea nymph.

NEREUS Name given to the Greek god of the sea.

NJORD Scandinavian god of the sea.

NORBERT (Old French) 'North' and 'bright', also 'famous'.

OCEAN (Greek) 'Vast sea'.

OLOKUN (Nigerian Yoruba) 'God of the sea'.

OSIRIS Name of a moon god from Egyptian mythology. Osiris was one of the principle figures in Egyptian mythology. In addition to being the god of the moon Osiris was also a god of fertility and god of the harvest. He was also known as As-ar.

OSBERT (Old English) 'Bright', 'famous'. The name was in frequent use in medieval Britain. It was revived briefly in the 19th century.

ROCKWELL (Old English) 'Rook stream'.

SEABERT, SEBERT (Old English) 'Sea glorious'.

SEABRIGHT (Old English) 'Sea glorious'.

SEABROOKE (Old English) 'Stream by the sea'.

SEWALD (Old English) 'Sea powerful'.

SEWALL Form of Sewell.

SEWARD (Old English) 'Sea guardian'. Originally an Old-English surname used as a first name since the 19th century. Originally a medieval surname it was revived as a first name in the 19th century.

SEWELL (Old English) 'Sea powerful'.

SEYMOUR (Old English) 'Sea'.

SIDWELL (Old English) 'Broad stream'.

SILVER, SYLVER (Old Norse) Name of the precious metal. Silver is the lucky metal for Cancer.

SINCLAIR (Latin) 'Bright', 'shining light'. Originally a Scottish surname from a French place name. It is in frequent use as a Scottish surname. It is occasionally found as a first name since the latter part of the 19th century.

SIWALD (Old English) 'Sea powerful'.

STROTHER (Gaelic) 'Stream'.

STRUAN (Gaelic) 'Stream'.

TALIESIN (Welsh) 'Shining'. 'Shining like the moon'. The name was borne by a legendary Welsh poet of the 6th century. It is occasionally found in modern times.

TEHUTI Alternative name of Thoth.

TELFORD (Latin) 'Shallow stream'.

THOTH (Egyptian) In Egyptian mythology Thoth was a moon god, in addition to being a god of art, science and equilibrium.

TYCHO Name given to crater on the moon's surface.

URIAH (Hebrew) 'God is light'. The name is borne by a character in the Old Testament. It has been in use in Britain since the 17th century and was popular in the 19th century.

URIEL (Hebrew) 'Light'. A form of 'Uriah'.

WESTBOURNE (Old English) 'West stream'.

WESTBROOK (Old English) 'West stream'.

WINSLADE (Old English) 'Friend's stream'.

YEO (Old English) 'River stream'.

ZOHAR (Hebrew) 'Radiant light'.

Cancer ~ Girls

ADRIA (Latin) 'Dark lady from the sea'. Feminine form of Adrian.

ADRIANA, ADRIANE Feminine forms of Adrian.

ADRIENNE, ADRIENNA (Latin) 'Dark lady from the sea'. French feminine forms of Adrian. The name was in frequent use in the mid-20th century.

AILEEN (Greek) 'Light'. Form of Eileen which is a from of Helen. The name is in most frequent use in Scotland.

AISLEEN Derivative of Helen.

ALANA (Celtic) 'Bright, fair child'. Or feminine form of Alan. 'Harmony'.

ALANI (Hawaiian) 'Orange'. Yellow-orange is a lucky colour for Cancer.

ALCINA (Greek) 'Sea Maiden'.

ALCINE (Greek) 'Sea Maiden'.

ALMOND Lucky plant for Cancer.

AMBER (Arabic) Lucky gemstone for Cancerians. The name was in frequent use in the 19th century and was again popular in the mid-20th century both in Britain and the USA.

ARIAN (Welsh) 'Silver white'. Silver is the lucky metal for Cancer.

ARIANWEN (Welsh) 'Silver white'.

ARANI (Maori) 'Orange'. Yellow-orange is a lucky colour for Cancer.

ARANRHOD (Celtic) In Celtic mythology Aranrhod is a moon god in addition to being goddess of the stars.

ARIANWEN (Welsh) 'Silver white'. Silver is the lucky metal for Cancer.

ARTEMIS (Greek) In Greek mythology Artemis was the goddess of the moon.

ARTEMISIA (Greek) 'Of Artemis'. The name was borne in the 4th century by the Queen of Caria, who was responsible for the construction of The Mausoleum of Halicarnassus, one of the Wonders of the Ancient World. The name has been used from time to time in Britain for the last two hundred years.

BEVERLEY, BEVERLY (Old English) 'Beaver stream'. Originally a surname derived from a Yorkshire place name. It was used as a boys' name in the late-19th century but is now more frequently found as a girls' name.

CALTHA (Latin) 'Yellow flower'. Yellow-orange is a lucky colour for Cancer.

CANDRA, CANDRE (Sanskrit) 'Moon'.

CANDY Shortened form of Candra.

CARMENTIA (Roman) The name of the Roman goddess of water, childbirth and prophesy.

CELANDINE (Greek) 'Yellow water flower'. Yellow-orange is a lucky colour for Cancer.

CELANDON Form of Celandine.

CELENE, CELINE 'Moon goddess'. Alternative spelling of Selina.

CELIE Shortened form of Celene.

CELINDA Form of Celene.

CERIDWEN (Welsh) 'Poetry, 'white'. The name was borne by the Welsh goddess of poetic inspiration. It is seldom found outside Wales.

CHANDRA, CHANDRE (Sanskrit) 'The moon'. The moon is the ruling planet of Cancer.

CHARIS (Greek) Form of Charity.

CHARISSA A modern name and an elaboration of Charis.

CHARITA Form of Charity.

CHARITY (Latin) 'Benevolent and loving'. Taken originally from the three Christian virtues. The name was in regular use by the Puritans but is seldom used today.

CHARRY Form of Charity.

CHERRY Form of Charity.

CHIA (Columbian Indian) 'The goddess of the moon'.

CHIARA (Italian) 'Clear'. 'As light as the moon'.

CLAIRE (Latin) 'Bright', 'shining'. Bright as the moon. This is the French spelling of the name. It has been widespread in English-speaking countries since the mid-20th century.

CLARA (Latin) 'Bright', 'shining'. The name has been in use in English-speaking countries since medieval times. It became particularly popular in the 19th century and remains in occasional use today.

CLARE (Latin) 'Bright', 'shining'. This has been the usual spelling of the name since medieval times.

CLARICE (Latin) Derivative of Clara. French or Italian form of Clara. The name has been in use in English-speaking countries since the 13th century.

CLARINDA Elaboration of Clara. The name was first used in 16th-century literary works.

CLARISSA Form of Clarice.

CLARITY (Latin) 'Clearness'.

CLEONE (Greek) 'Light', 'clear'.

CORAL, CORALE (Latin) 'From the sea'. The name became popular in the 19th century.

CORALINE, CORALIE French forms of Coral. They have been in use in English-speaking countries for over a hundred years.

CORDELIA (Welsh) 'Jewel of the sea'. The name was borne by the daughter of King Lear.

CORDELIE, CORDIE Forms of Cordelia.

CYAN (Greek) 'Dark blue'. Indigo is a lucky colour for Cancer.

CYNTHIA (Greek) Alternative name for Diana, goddess of the moon. It has appeared in literature for many centuries and has been used as a first name in English-speaking countries since the 17th century. Frequently used in the USA in the mid-20th century.

CYNTHIE, CYNTH, CYN Forms of Cynthia.

CYRENE (Greek) 'A water nymph'.

DANA Alternative form of Danu.

DANU In Irish Druid mythology the name is borne by a river goddess. She is also known as a mother goddess of the land. The name means 'sacred gift'.

DEANNA Variant of Diana.

DELIA (Greek) Another name for the moon goddess. The name is found in literature from the 17th century and remains in use today.

DELMA (Spanish) 'Of the sea'.

DELMARE Form of Delma.

DERORA (Hebrew) 'Flowing stream'.

DIANA (Roman) 'Goddess of the moon'. The name has been in use in Britain since the 16th century. It was frequently used in literature but did not become widely used as a first name until the late-19th century.

DIANE French form of Diana. The name has been in use in English-speaking countries since the early-20th century and for a while became more widespread than Diana.

DIANNA Variant of Diana.

DINAH Variant of Diana.

DINA Variant of Diana.

DODI Form of Doris.

DORIA Forms of Doris.

DORICE, DORISE, DORRIS Forms of Doris.

DORIS (Greek) 'From the sea'. Name given to the daughter of Oceanus. The name became popular in the late-19th century and early-20th century.

DORITA Form of Doris.

EDLYN (Old English) 'Happy brook'.

EILEEN (Irish) 'Light'. Form of Helen. The name became widespread in English-speaking countries in the early-20th century and remains in use today.

EIRIAN (Welsh) 'Silver'. Silver is a lucky metal for Cancer.

EIRWEN (Welsh) 'Snow', 'white', 'fair'.

ELAINE 'Light'. Old French form of Helen. The name was borne in Arthurian legend by the mother of Sir Lancelot's son, Sir Galahad. It has become fashionable in Britain since the mid-20th century.

ELANE, ELAIN Forms of Elaine.

ELEANOR (French) 'Light'. A medieval form of Helen. The name has been used in Britain since the 12th century and remains in use today.

ELEANORE, ELEANORA, ELINOR, ELINORE, ELINORA Forms of Eleanor.

ELINOR, ELENORA, ELEONORE, ELNORE Forms of Eleanor.

ELENA 'Light'. Italian and Spanish form of Helen.

ELLA A pet form of Ellen.

ELLEN 'Light'. Variant of Helen. This form of the name was more common in medieval times than Helen. It became particularly popular in the USA in the 20th century.

ELLENE A form of Helen.

ELLYN A form of Helen.

ERWINA (Old English) 'Friend from the sea'.

FILOMENA (Latin) 'Daughter of light'.

FLAVIA (Latin) 'Yellow-haired'. Yellow-orange is a lucky colour for Cancer. The name has occasionally been found in English-speaking countries but has never been frequently used.

GELASIA (Greek) 'Laughing water'.

GELASIE Form of Gelasia.

GILBERTA, GILBERTINE (Old German) 'Bright'. Feminine form of Gilbert.

GRETA German or Swedish from of Margaret. The name was little used in English-speaking countries until the late 1920s.

GRETCHEN German pet form of Margaret.

GRETEL German pet form of Margaret.

GWENDOLINE, GWENDOLYN, GWENDOLEN, GUENDOLEN (Welsh) 'White circle' which is interpreted as possibly meaning 'the moon'. In Arthurian legend the name was borne by the wife of Merlin. The name has been in fairly regular use in English-speaking countries since the latter half of the 19th century.

GWENLLIAN Form of Gwendoline.

HATHER (Egyptian) A moon goddess in Egyptian mythology. Hather was also a water goddess and goddess of love.

HELEN (Greek) 'Light' or 'the bright one'. In Greek mythology the name was borne by the beautiful Helen of Troy who was known as 'the face that launched a thousand ships'. It came into widespread use in the 16th century and increased in popularity since the mid-20th century.

HELENA (Greek) 'Light'. Form of Helen.

HENG-O Name given to a moon goddess in Chinese mythology.

HINA (Tahiti) Name given to the Tahitian moon goddess.

HYACINTH (Greek) A flower name meaning blue gem or sapphire. Indigo is a lucky colour for Cancer. The name is borne in Greek mythology by a beautiful youth who was accidentally killed by Apollo and from whose blood sprang a hyacinth flower. The name was used as a boys' name for centuries. Its use as a girls' name is a fairly recent phenomenon.

HYACINTHA, HYACINTHIA Forms of Hyacinth.

ILEANE A form of Helen.

ILONA, ILLONA, ILLONE Forms of Helen.

ILONA Hungarian form of Helen.

IMBRIUM Name of a 'sea' on the surface of the moon. Means 'sea of showers'.

INDIGO Lucky colour for Cancer.

INDIRA (Sanskrit) 'Moon'.

ISLEEN 'Light'. Form of Eileen and therefore Helen.

IRVETTE (English) 'Sea friend'.

IRVETTA Form of Irvette.

JEMIMA (Hebrew) 'Bright as day' or 'dove'. The name was borne in the bible by one of the daughters of Job. It became particularly fashionable in the early part of the 19th century and remains in use today.

JEMMA Pet form of Jemima.

JUNE Taken from the name of the month in which many Cancerians are born.

JACINTHA, JACINTHIA Forms of Hyacinth.

KAIYA (Japanese) 'Sea'. Feminine form of Kai.

LAKAIYA Kaiya with a 'La' prefix.

LANA (Celtic) 'Bright', 'fair child'. Form of Alana.

LANNA (Celtic) 'Bright', 'fair child'. Form of Alana.

LAOISE (Irish Gaelic) 'Radiance'. Pronounced 'lee-sha'. Derivative of Lug, name of the goddess of light.

LEIHINA (Hawaiian) 'Wreath of the moon'.

LENA, LINA 'Light'. Forms of Eleanor.

LEONORA, LEONORE, LENORA 'Light'. Forms of Eleanor. The name has been in use from time to time in English-speaking countries since the 19th century.

LEORA, LORA Forms of Leonora.

LEUCOTHEA The name of a sea goddess in Greek mythology.

LEVANA (Hebrew) 'Moon'.

LEWANNA (Hebrew) 'As clear as the moon'.

LOTUS (Greek) From the name of the flower. The lotus is a lucky plant for Cancer.

LUANNA Form of Lewanna.

LUCETTE (Latin) 'Little light'.

LUCIA (Latin) 'Light'. Feminine form of Lucius. The name Lucia was borne by a 4th-century saint and was widespread in medieval Britain. It is seldom found today.

LUCILLA Pet form of Lucia.

LUCILLE French form of Lucilla.

LUCINDA Derivative of Lucia.

LUCY Old French form of Lucia. The name was in widespread use in English-speaking countries in medieval times. It was particularly popular in the 18th century and again in the latter part of the 20th century.

LUCYNA (Latin) 'Light'.

LUNETTA (Latin) 'Little moon'.

LYNN, LYN (Celtic) 'A waterfall'. In widespread use in English -peaking countries since the mid-20th century.

LYNNE Alternative spelling of Lynne.

MADGE Pet form of Margeret.

MAE Form of May. This form of the spelling became particularly popular in the USA in the 20th century due to the fame of actress Mae West.

MAIR 'Drop of the sea.' Welsh form of Mary.

MAIRE Irish Gaelic form of Mary.

MAIRENN (Irish) 'Fair sea.'

MAIRI Scottish Gaelic form of Mary.

MAISIE Scottish pet form of Margaret.

MALIA Hawaiian form of Mary.

MAMIE Short form of Mary.

MARA Form of Mary.

MARAMA (Maori) 'Moon'. The moon is the ruling planet of Cancer.

MAREA Alternative spelling of Maria.

MARGARET (Greek) 'Pearl'. The pearl is a lucky gemstone for Cancer. The name was borne by a legendary saint of the 3rd century. It was introduced into Britain in the 11th century and became very popular in medieval times. It has remained in frequent use since that time.

MARE (Latin) 'Sea'.

MAREETHA, MARITHA. Blends of Mary and Aretha. Aretha is a Greek name meaning 'virtue'.

MARELLA, MARELLE A blend of Mare and Ella. Ella is an Old-German name meaning 'all'.

MARGARETA, MARGARETTA, Hungarian for Margaret.

MARGARITA Form of Margaret.

MARGE Pet form of Majorie.

MARGERY, MARGERIE Forms of Margaret.

MARGETHE, MARGARETHA, MAIGRGHREAD Forms of Margaret.

MARGETTE, MARGETTA, MARGALO, MERGET Forms of Margaret.

MARGIE Pet form of Marjorie.

MARGO, MARGOT French form of Margaret.

MARGOLAINE A blend of Margo and Elaine.

MARGUERITA Form of Margaret.

MARGUERITE French form of Margaret. Used as a flower name in English-speaking countries since the turn of the 20th century.

MARI Welsh form of Mary.

MARIA Latin form of Mary.

MARIABELLA Combination of Maria and Bella. Interpreted as 'beautiful Mary', therefore 'beautiful drop of the sea'. The name has been in occasional use in English-speaking countries since the 17th century.

MARIAH Elaborated spelling of Maria.

MARIAN, MARIANNE Combination of Mary and Ann. Ann is a Hebrew name meaning 'graceful'.

MARIE French form of Maria.

MARIELLA Italian pet form of Maria.

MARIETTA Italian pet form of Maria.

MARILEE A combination of Mary and Lee. Lee is an Old-English name meaning 'meadow' or 'wood'.

MARILENE Variant of Marilyn.

MARILYN Elaboration of Mary with the addition of Lyn.

MARILYNN, MARYLYN, MARILENE Alternative spellings of Marilyn.

MARIMNE 'Drop of the sea'. Form of Miriam.

MARINA (Latin) 'Of the sea'. The name was introduced into Britain in medieval times and was revived in the 20th century

MARION French form of Marie.

MARIS (Latin) 'The sea'.

MARISA, MARISSA Elaboration of Maria.

MARISE Form of Marisa.

MARISELLA, MARISELA 'The sea'. Spanish form of Maris.

MARISKA Russian form of Maria.

MARITA Blend of Mary and Rita.

MARITZA Hungarian form of Mary.

MARIWIN A blend of Mary and Winifred.

MARJORIE, MERJERY Forms of Margaret.

MARNA Swedish form of Marina.

MARNINA (Hebrew) 'To rejoice'.

MARNI, MARNIE, MARNEY (Hebrew) 'To rejoice'.

MARNIA 'The sea'. A form of Marina.

MAROLA (Latin) 'Sea'.

MARY An anglicized form of the French Marie, or the Latin Maria. It is a form of Miriam, from the Latin 'drop of the sea' or 'star of the sea'.

MAURA (Celtic) Form of Mary.

MAY Pet form of Mary. Often used as an independent name. It became popular in the 20th century and is still occasionally found today.

MAYA Latin variation of May. Also an alternative spelling of the Roman goddess Maia, influenced by the English name May.

MEAGAN, MEAGHAN Forms of Megan.

MEGAN 'Pearl'. Welsh form of Margaret. The pearl is a lucky gemstone for Cancer.

MEGGIE, MEGGY Pet forms of Margaret or Megan.

MEGHAN Alternative spelling of Megan. Used more frequently in the USA.

MEINWEN (Welsh) 'White, fair, blessed'.

MEREL Form of Muriel.

MERIEL Form of Muriel.

MERIS Form of Merrie.

MERISSA, MERRISSA Blends of Meryl and Clarissa. Clarissa is a form of Clare, a Latin name meaning 'clear, bright'.

MERLYN, MERLINE Feminine forms of Merlin.

MERRY, MERRIE, MERRYN (Old English) 'Joyful, pleasant'.

MERRIEL, MERRIELLE Forms of Merrie.

MERRILL, MERRIL, MERIL Forms of Meryl.

MERYL A recent form of Muriel. It has been popularized by the US actress Meryl Streep.

META Form of Margaret.

MIA Danish and Swedish form of Maria.

MIMI Italian form of Maria. The name has been in use as an independent name since the 19th century.

MIMOSA (Latin) 'Imitative, sensitive'.

MIO (Japanese) 'Waterway'.

MIRIAM 'Drop of the sea'. Old Testament form of Maryam. The name was borne in the Old Testament by the elder sister of Moses. The name was popular in the 17th century and remains in regular use throughout English-speaking countries.

MITA A form of Mitzi.

MITZI 'Drop of the sea.' German form of Maria.

MOANA (Maori) 'Sea'.

MOIRA Anglicized form of Irish Gaelic Maire, a form of Mary.

MOON (Old French) 'The moon'. The moon is the ruling plant of Cancer.

MOONWORT A lucky plant for Cancer.

MORVOREN, MORVA (Cornish) 'Maid of the sea, mermaid'.

MOLLY Pet from of Mary.

MORGAN (Welsh) 'Man from the wild sea'. The name has been used in Wales for centuries as a boys' name. Glamorgan, a Welsh county, is named after a 10th-century bearer of the name. The name is occasionally bestowed as a girls' name. Morgan le Fay, the sister of King Arthur, is a famous feminine bearer of the name.

MORGANA Feminine form of Morgan.

MOYA Derived from Moyra.

MOYRA Alternative spelling of Moira.

MUIRE Form of Muriel.

MUIREALL (Scottish Gaelic) 'White sea.' Pronounced mwir-an.

MUIREANN, MUIRINN (Irish Gaelic) 'White sea'.

MURIEL , MERIEL, MURIAL (Irish) 'Sea-bright'. The name has been used in its many forms throughout Britain since medieval times. It was revived throughout English-speaking countries in the 19th century.

MYSIE Form of Maisie.

NALANI (Hawaiian) 'Calmness of the heavens'.

NANDA (Sanskrit) 'Giver of joy'.

NAOMI (Hebrew) 'Pleasantness, delight'. The name was borne in the Old Testament by the wise mother-in-law of Ruth. The name came into general use in the 17th century and became increasingly popular in the latter half of the 20th century.

NARA (English) 'Nearest and dearest'.

NECTARIS Name of a 'sea' on the surface of the moon. Means 'sea of nectar'.

NERICE (Greek) 'From the sea'.

NERIMA (Greek) 'From the sea'.

NERINA Form of Nerissa.

NERINE (Greek) 'From the sea'. It is also the name given to a sea nymph in Greek mythology.

NERISSA (Greek) 'From the sea' or 'sea-nymph'. The name was borne by a minor character in Shakespeare's *The Merchant of Venice*. The name is found occasionally in English-speaking countries.

NERITA (Greek) 'From the sea'.

NERICE (Greek) 'From the sea'.

NIA Welsh form of Niamh.

NIAMH (Irish Gaelic) 'Brightness or beauty'. Pronounced 'Nee-uv'. In Irish mythology, this is the name given to the daughter of the sea god.

NUBIUM Name of a 'sea' on the surface of the moon. It means 'sea of clouds'.

NELL 'Light'. Pet form of Ellen.

NEOMA (Greek) 'From the sea'.

NEVA (Spanish) 'As white as the moon'.

NEVADA Form of Neva.

NIA Welsh form of Niamh.

NYAME (West African Ashanti) 'The goddess of the moon'.

NYREE (Maori) 'Wave'.

ONDINE (Latin) 'From the sea waves'. Form of Undine.

ONYCHA Lucky perfume for Cancer.

OOLA (Celtic) 'Sea jewel'. Form of Ulla.

OVINA (Latin) 'Gentle as a lamb'.

PEARL (Latin) 'Precious jewel'. The pearl is a lucky stone for Cancer. It has been in use as a first name since the mid-19th century. The name was borne by the 20th-century US novelist Pearl Buck.

PEARLE, PERLE , PERL Alternative spellings of Pearl.

PEARLIE, PERLIE Forms of Pearl.

PEARLINE A blend of Pearl and Pauline. Pauline is a French feminine form of Paul, meaning 'small'.

PEGGY, PEG Pet forms of Margaret. During the early part of the 20th century the name was often used as a name in its own right.

PERLINE Form of Pearl.

PERLINA Form of Pearl.

PELAGIE (Greek) 'Mermaid'.

PHOEBE (Latin) 'Bright'. Partly identified with Artemis, goddess of the moon. The name occurs in the New Testament. It came into general use in English-speaking countries in the 17th century, becoming widespread in the latter half of the 19th century. It remains in use today.

PHILOMENA (Greek) 'Lover of the moon', 'loved'. The name came into use during the 19th century, popularised by the alleged discovery of the remains of St Philomena.

PHOTINA (Greek) 'Light'.

RAN Name given to the Scandinavian goddess of the sea.

REANNA Modern alteration of the Welsh name Rhiannon.

REANNE Variant of Reanna.

RHIANNON (Welsh) Name from Celtic mythology. A minor deity associated with the moon. The name did not come into use as a first name until the 20th century.

RITA Short form of Margarita, the Spanish form of Margaret. In English-speaking countries the name has been in regular use as a name in its own right since the early 20th century.

ROSEMARY (Latin) 'Sea dew'. Did not come into use as a first name until the 19th century. It became particularly popular in the mid-20th century.

ROSEMARIE French form of Rosemary.

SAFFRON (Arabic) From the name of a type of crocus or the orange spice obtained from it. Yellow-orange is a lucky colour for Cancer.

SALENA, SALINA Forms of Selina.

SAPPHIRA (Greek) 'Eyes of sapphire colour'. Dark blue (indigo) is a lucky colour for Cancer. The name occurs in the New Testament.

SEDNA (North American Eskimo) 'Goddess of the sea'.

SELA 'Moon Goddess'. Shortened from of Selina.

SELIA, SELIE Shortened forms of Selina.

SELINA, SELENA (Greek) Name of the moon goddess in Greek mythology. The name has been in use in English-speaking countries since the 17th century. It became particularly popular in the late-20th century.

SELINDA Blend of Selena and Linda.

SELINE, SALENE (Greek) Forms of Selina.

SENA (Greek) Form of Selina.

SERENITATIS Name of a 'sea' on the surface of the moon. The name means 'sea of serenity'.

SHIZU (Japanese) 'Quiet, 'clear'.

SILVER Lucky metal for Cancerians.

SORCHA (Irish and Scottish Gaelic). 'Brightness'. Pronounced 'sorr-kha'.

TALLULA Alternative spelling of Tallulah.

TALLULAH (Native American) 'Laughing water'. 'One who bubbles like a spring'.

TALLU, TALLA, TALLIE Shortened form of Tallulah.

TANGERINE, TANGERENE, TANGERYNE (Old English) A deep orange colour.

TATE, TAIT, TEYTE (Old English) 'Cheerful'.

THAISA (Greek) 'The sea'.

THALASSA (Greek) 'From the sea'.

THIRZA (Hebrew) 'Pleasantness'.

TIRZA, TIRZAH Forms of Thirza.

TISHA (Latin) Pet form of Letitia 'Joy'.

TRANQUILLITATIS Name of a 'sea' on the surface of the moon. It means 'the sea of tranquillity'.

ULLA, ULA (Celtic) 'Jewel of the sea'.

UNDINE, UNDINA (Latin) From the sea waves. In mythology, a female water spirit.

URANIA (Greek) 'Heavenly', 'divine'.

URIELLE (Hebrew) 'The Lord's Light'.

XAN (Greek) 'Yellow'.

XANTHE (Greek) 'Yellow', 'bright'.

YEMANJÁ (Afro Brazilian) 'Goddess of the sea'.

YOKO (Japanese) 'Ocean child'.

ZAKA (Hebrew) 'Bright', 'clear'.

ZEHARA (Hebrew) 'Light'.

ZOHARA (Hebrew) 'Light'.

Leo

ॠ

THE LION

23 July – 22 August

RULING PLANET   The Sun. In astrology the sun is the source of life and creativity.

ELEMENT   Fire

General characteristics

- Fun-loving, playful, entertaining.
- Creative.
- Romantic, affectionate, amorous.
- Honest, loyal, honourable.
- Enjoys the limelight, drama.
- Needs to be adored.
- Hospitable, appreciative.
- Sporty, takes risks.
- Child-like.

Characteristics of young Leo

- Warm and friendly.
- A sunny disposition.
- Energetic.

- Loves to be the centre of attention.
- Adventurous and can be reckless.
- Loves physical play and sports.
- Is generous to others.
- Loves parties.

Leonine lucky connections

Gemstones:	catseye and chrysolite
Colours:	yellow and orange
Plants:	sunflower and laurel
Perfume:	olibanum
Metal:	gold
Animal:	lion
Tarot card:	fortitude

LEO is ruled by the sun, and like the sun Leonines are warm and sunny individuals who are always full of energy. Just as the sun is the centre of our universe, so Leonines expect most things in life to orbit around them!

Leonines love the limelight, always wanting to be the king or queen of their own particular castle. They are courageous and proud, almost regal in the way they command themselves.

Even as a baby your little Leonine will love to be the centre of the household. You may find that your baby will settle into a regular routine fairly readily, which is just as well as he will probably demand what he wants when he wants, in no uncertain terms!

Most of your baby's demands will often be for attention. Leonines love to be centre stage and your baby will bask in the adoration of playful and chatty adults. The existence of an appreciative audience will often entice him to give a repeat performance of his latest achievements, be it grabbing his toes, rolling over or saying "Dada".

Leo's need for attention and the desire to command others can sometimes make them appear rather bossy. Most Leo children, however, do not maintain their power over others by bullying, but through generosity and affection. Their fun-loving and sunny nature, coupled by their warmth and loyalty ensures that they can easily endear themselves to others. So much so that most other children or adults will forgive the odd display of arrogance! They are capable of loving their family and friends with great magnitude, forming deep bonds with their close family and becoming loyal and trustworthy friends.

You may find that in an effort to appear important to other children your Leo child may display a tendency to boast or show off. You could try to curb this tendency by explaining to your child that such behaviour is undignified. You may find that this has the desired effect as Leonines always wish to keep their dignity.

Leos, along with other fire signs, have an intense need to express themselves. They are often very creative and tend not to do things by halves. If they want to paint a picture, they will want it to be a big picture! Try to provide the opportunities to do this even if it means painting outdoors.

Leos also love to dress up so try to provide some play clothes and props. With their flair for drama and organisational ability you may find your Leo child organising his playmates into an impromptu production!

Leos love physical play and sports so try to provide opportunities for your child to engage in such activities. You may find that having run off some of that burning energy your Leo child is just a little calmer to live with!

Above all, Leonines need love and honest appreciation. Plenty of hugs and praise for achievements will keep his generous, fun-loving nature alive. Keeping your little Leo happy in this way will ensure that you have a joyful, entertaining and kind-hearted child who will gladly give you plenty of love, warmth and loyalty in return.

Leo ~ Boys

AIDAN, AIDEN (Irish Gaelic) 'Fiery one'. The name was borne by several early Irish saints including a famous 7th-century monk. The name enjoyed a revival in the early-19th century and remains in regular use today.

ALBERT (Old German) 'Noble one'. The name was introduced into Britain by the Normans. It became popular throughout English-speaking countries following the marriage of Queen Victoria to Prince Albert in 1840.

ALBERTO (Old German) Form of Alberto.

ALONSO, ALONZO Forms of Alphonso.

ALPHONSE, ALPHONSUS Forms of Alphonso.

ALPHONSO, ALFONSO (Old German) 'Noble' and 'ready'. The name has been in use in Spain since the 7th century.

ALROY (Latin) 'Royal'.

AMERIGO Form of Emery.

ANDOR Form of Andrew.

ANDRÉ French form of Andrew.

ANDREAS (Greek) 'Courageous man'. The original form of Andrew found in the New Testament. It is becoming increasingly popular in English-speaking countries.

ANDREW English form of Andreas. St Andrew, an apostle of Jesus Christ and patron saint of Scotland, was one of the earliest and most famous bearers of the name. The name has been popular in Scotland for hundreds of years and was in regular use in Britain in the Middle Ages. Its use spread to the USA where it was borne by two presidents, Andrew Jackson and Andrew Carnegie. The name became particularly popular in the latter half of the 20th century after the birth of Queen Elizabeth II's son Prince Andrew.

ANEIRIN A Welsh name of uncertain origin. It may be derived from a Latin name meaning 'man of honour' or from Welsh, meaning 'gold'. Either meaning is appropiate for Leo.

ANEURIN Variant spelling of Aneirin.

AODH (Gaelic) Pronounced 'ee'. Name of the Celtic sun god. The name means 'Fire'. The name was popular in early times. From the Middle Ages it was often found in the form of Hugh, and in more recent times as Eugene. The Gaelic form is now coming back into use.

APOLLO (Greek) Name of the Greek sun god.

ARCHIBALD (Norman French) 'Genuine and brave'. The name was introduced into Britain by the Normans. It is most commonly found in Scotland.

ARIEL (Hebrew) 'Lion of God'. The name is found in the Bible as a place name. In modern Israel the name is used as a boys' name but in the USA it is more commonly found as a girls' name.

ASA (Zoroastrian) 'The sun'. It is also a Hebrew name meaning 'healer'.

ATEN (Egyptian) 'The sun'.

ATUM (Egyptian) 'The sun'.

AUBERON (From an Old French name from German origin) 'Noble' and 'bear-like'. Auberon was the name of the king of the fairies in medieval romance.

AUBREY (Old German) 'Elf ruler'. In German mythology this was the name of the king of the elves. The name was introduced into Britain at the time of the Norman Conquest and was fairly common in medieval times. It was revived in the 19th century. In the USA it is used mainly as a girls' name.

AUGUST (Latin) 'Majestic'. German form of Augustus. It is occasionally found in English-speaking countries.

AUGUSTIN, AUGUSTINE (Latin) 'Venerable'. The name was borne by two saints in the 1st and 6th century. In medieval times it was found in the form 'Austin'. The original form of the name was revived in the 19th century and remains in occasional use today.

AUGUSTUS (Roman/Latin) 'Great', 'magnificent'. The name was borne by several Roman emperors. It was also given to several German princes. It was introduced into Britain by the Hanoverians in the early-18th century and remained popular until the turn of the 20th century.

AURELIAN (Latin) 'Gold'. The name was borne by a 3rd-century Roman emperor.

AUSTEN Form of Augustus.

AUSTIN Medieval form of Augustus.

AYLMER (Old English) 'Noble', 'famous'.

BAS, BASIE, BAZ Shortened forms of Basil.

BASIL (Greek) 'Royal'. In the 4th century the name was borne by St Basil the Great, bishop of Caesarea, who was regarded as one of the Fathers of the Eastern Church. The name was introduced into Western Europe by the Crusaders but the name was little used in Britain until the 19th century.

BRENDAN (Old Celtic) 'Prince' or 'fiery one'. The name was borne by two 6th-century Irish saints one of whom, Brendan the Voyager, was said to be the first European to set foot on North American soil.

BRIAN, BRYAN (Irish) 'High, noble'. The name was borne by Brian Boru who became high king of all Ireland in 1002. Originally found only in Ireland the name is now used throughout English-speaking countries.

CARL (Old German) Derivative of Charles.

CARLOS (Old German) Spanish derivative of Charles.

CENRIC (Middle English) 'Royal'. The original form of Kendrick. The name Cenric died out in the 17th century.

CHARLES (Old German) 'Strong, virile man'. The name became popular in the 9th century due to Charles the Great who became the first ruler of the Holy Roman Empire. The name has been borne by several European monarchs. The name was introduced into Britain at the time of the Norman Conquest although it was rarely found until the 17th century when it became popularized by the reigns of King Charles I and II. In the mid-19th century it had become one of the most popular boys' names in English-speaking countries.

CHUCK (Old German) Derivative of Charles.

CHU-JUNG Name given to the spirit of fire in Chinese mythology.

COLBRAN (Old German) 'Man of fire'.

CURT Shortened form of Curtis.

CURTIS (Old French) 'Courteous'. The name has been in regular use since the 19th century.

CYNRIC (Welsh) 'Of Royal birth'.

CYRIL (Greek) 'Lord'. The name was borne by several saints. It has been found in Britain since the 17th century and became popular in the early part of the 20th century.

CYRUS (Persian) 'The sun god'. In the 6th century BC the name was borne by King Cyrus the Great who founded the Persian empire. The name was adopted by the Puritans but is more well known in the USA than in Britain.

DENEBOLA Name given to the brightest star in the constellation of Leo.

DEVLIN (Celtic) 'Heroic, brave'.

DONAL (Irish) 'World ruler'. Irish form of Donald.

DONALD (Scottish) 'World ruler'. The name was borne by several early Scottish kings and has been in use in Scotland for centuries. It gradually spread to other English-speaking countries and was particularly popular in the first half of the 20th century.

DUNCAN (Scottish) 'Noble' or 'chief'. The name was borne by a 7th-century Scottish saint and a 10th-century Irish saint. It has been frequently found in Scotland for centuries and is occasionally found in other English-speaking countries.

EARL (Old English) 'Nobleman' or 'prince'. From a surname originally borne by members of an earl's family or from the title itself. It has been in use as a first name since the 17th century, being most commonly found in the USA.

EDAN (Celtic) 'Flame'. Scottish and Irish form of Aidan. The name was borne by St Edan, an Irish disciple of St David, the patron saint of Wales.

EDEL (Old German) 'The noble one'.

EDELMAR (Old English) 'Noble and famous'.

EDGAR (Old English) 'Prosperity', 'riches'. In the 10th century the name was borne by a king of England, Edgar the Peaceful, who was a great grandson of Alfred the Great. It has been in occasional use since the Norman Conquest and increased in popularity in the early 19th century.

EDMUND (Old English) 'Rich protector'. The name was borne by St Edmunds, a 9th-century martyr who was also King of East Anglia. The Suffolk town of Bury St Edmunds is

named in his honour. The name was also borne by two English Kings in the 10th and 11th century and by another saint, Edmund Rich, who was a 13th-century Archbishop of Canterbury.

EDRIC (Old English) 'Fortunate ruler'.

EDWALD (Old English) 'Prosperous ruler'.

EDWARD (Old English) 'Prosperity, riches'. 'Guardian'. The name has been in regular use since the early Middle Ages. Its association with the British royal families began in the 9th century when it was borne by King Edward the Elder, son of Alfred the Great. Perhaps the most influential bearer of the name was Edward the Confessor who reigned in the 11th century.

EGAN (Gaelic) 'Formidable, fiery, strong'.

ELBERT (Old German) 'Noble and industrious'.

ELI, ELY (Hebrew) 'The highest'.

ELLARD (Old English) 'Noble', 'brave'.

ELMER (Old English) 'Noble, famous'. Originally a surname its use as a first name in the US began in the 19th century, in honour of the brothers Ebenezer and Jonathan Elmer who were leading activists in the American Revolution.

ELRIK (Old German) 'Regal'.

ELROY (Latin) 'Royal'. 'The King'. Form of Leroy.

EMERY (Old German) 'Industrious ruler'. The name was introduced into Britain by the Normans.

EMMERY, EMORY Forms of Emery.

EMERSON, EMMERICH Forms of Emery.

EMYR (Welsh) 'Ruler', 'king'. The name was borne by a 6th-century Breton saint who settled in Cornwall.

ERIC (Old Norse) 'All powerful ruler', 'kingly'. It was introduced into Britain from Scandinavia before the Norman Conquest, but was seldom used until the latter half of the 19th century. Its popularity increased during the early part of the 20th century when it spread to the USA.

ERICH, ERICK Forms of Eric.

ERIK Scandinavian form of Eric.

ERLE, EARLE, ERL Forms of Earl.

ERLING (Old English) 'Son of a nobleman'.

ERROL Form of Earl. The name was made popular in the first half of the 20th century by the fame of the Australian actor Errol Flynn.

EUGENE (Old French) 'Well-born, noble'. Borne by four popes and various early saints, it was made popular in Europe by Prince Eugene of Savoy. In the late-19th century Eugene became popular in the USA.

EURWYN (Welsh) 'Golden haired'. Gold is a lucky metal for Leo.

FAGAN, FAGIN (Gaelic) 'Little fiery one'.

FALCON The symbol given to Ra, the Egyptian sun-god in mythology.

FERGAL (Irish) 'Valour'. The name was borne by an 8th-century king of Ireland.

FERDINAND (Old German) 'Courageous peacemaker' or 'adventurous'. The name was used traditionally in Spanish royal families from an early date. It spread to Britain in the 16th century.

FERNANDO Form of Ferdinand.

FARON, FARRAN, FARREN Forms of Ferdinand.

FIACHRA (Irish Gaelic) 'King'. In Irish legend, the name was borne by one of the children of Lir, who were turned into swans by their stepmother. The name was also borne by an Irish saint and missionary.

FINTAN (Irish) 'White fire'.

GALLARD Form of Gaylord.

GALOR, GAYLOR Forms of Gaylord.

GAYLORD (French) 'The happy noble man'. More commonly used as a surname than as a first name.

GEN Shortened form of Eugene.

GENE Shortened form of Eugene. Found particularly in North America.

GRADY (Gaelic) 'Illustrious and noble'.

GRANT (French) 'The great one'. Originally a surname, used as a clan name in Scotland. The name was adopted as a first name in the 19th century in the USA, presumably in honour of President Ulysses S. Grant, and spread to other English-speaking countries.

GWILYM 'Protector'. Welsh form of William.

HAL Pet form of Henry, sometimes used as an independent name.

HANK Dutch pet form of Henry, often used as a name in its own right.

HARDY (Middle English) 'Brave'. Originally a surname, it has been in use as a first name since the 19th century.

HARRY 'Home ruler'. Pet form of Henry. Often used as a name in its own right.

HELIOS (Greek) 'The sun'. The name of a sun god in Greek mythology.

HELIUS (Greek) 'The sun'. Alternative name of Helios.

HENRY (Old French) 'Home ruler'. The name was introduced into Britain by the Normans and was borne by eight kings of England. The name remained in frequent use throughout English-speaking countries until the 20th century when its popularity began to decline.

HERACLES (Greek) The name of an important character in the creation of the constellation of Leo.

HERCULES Alternative name for Heracles.

HERU Name of a sun-god in Egyptian mythology. Heru is also protrayed as a lion in mythology, so furthering the connections with Leo.

HEW, HUW Welsh spelling of Hugh, derived from a Celtic word for 'fire' or 'inspiration'. Both meanings are appropriate for Leo.

HORUS Alternative name for Heru in Egyptian mythology.

HYPERION (Greek) 'The sun'.

IDRIS (Welsh) 'Fiery lord'. In Welsh mythology there is a character named Idris. The mountain Cader Idris in Gwynedd, is named after him.

IGNATIUS (Latin) 'Fire'. The name was borne by St Ignatius of Antioch, a 2nd-century martyr, and also by St Ignatius of Loyola, the founder of the Jesuits (1491-1556).

IGNACE 'Fire'. A form of Ignatius.

IGNACIO A form of Ignatius.

IGNATE A form of Ignatius.

INIGO 'Fire'. A Spanish form of Ignatius.

IOLO (Welsh) 'Handsome lord'. Pet form of Iorwerth.

IORWERTH (Welsh) 'Handsome lord'.

KAI (Persian) 'King'.

KALON (Greek) 'Noble'.

KANTI (Sanskrit) 'Sun's rays'. The name is used as both a boys' and girls' name.

KEIRAN, KAIRAN (Greek) 'Rays of the sun'.

KENDRICK (Old English) 'Royal'. Originally an English surname which was derived from the name Cenric.

KENNEDY (Old English) 'Royal'. In modern times it is sometimes given as a first name in honour of the assassinated American president John F. Kennedy.

KENRICK (Old English) 'Royal'. The name was used mainly as a surname until the 19th century when it began to be used as a first name.

KENNETH (Scottish) 'Born of the fire god' and 'handsome'. The name was borne by King Kenneth I MacAlpin, who reigned over Scotland in the 9th century. The name has been used in Scotland for centuries. It only began to spread to other parts of Britain in the late-19th century. By the mid-20th century it was in frequent use throughout English-speaking countries.

KEYE (Gaelic) 'Son of the fiery one'.

KING From the vocabulary word for a male monarch. Originally used as a surname or nickname for members of a royal household.

KINGSLEY, KINGSLIE (Old English) 'King's wood or meadow'. It has been used as a first name since the 19th century. A famous bearer of the name is British novelist Kingsley Amis.

LARS Shortened form of Laurence.

LAURENCE, LAWRENCE (Latin) 'From Laurentum', a town in Latium. Laurentum was an ancient Italian town which was named after its laurel groves. The laurel is a lucky plant for Leo. The name was popular in medieval Britain and has been in regular use since then. The name was popularised in the 20th century by Lawrence of Arabia and by the British actor Laurence Olivier.

LEANDER (Greek) 'The lion man'. The name was borne by a character in Greek mythology who was the lover of Hero, to whom he swam every night. The name was also borne by St Leander who became the archbishop of Seville in the 6th century.

LENNARD Variant spelling of Leonard.

LEO (Latin) 'Lion'. The name was borne by St Leo the Great, a pope of the 5th century. It was also born by several other popes and saints. The name has been in regular use in English-speaking countries since medieval times and is still in use today.

LEON Form of Leo.

LEONARD (Old French) 'Brave, strong lion'. The name was introduced into Britain by the Normans and has been in occasional use since the Middle Ages. In the 19th century it was revived in English-speaking countries and became very popular.

LEOPOLD (Old German) 'Bold man'. The name became popular in Britain in the 19th century after the uncle of Queen Victoria and Prince Albert, the Belgian King Leopold I. Queen Victoria also gave the name to her youngest son.

LEROY (French) 'The king'. From an Old French surname or nickname. As a first name it has been in regular use since the late-19th century, being especially popular in the USA.

LIAM (Old German) 'Resolute protector'. Irish form of William.

LION, LYON (Middle English) 'Lion'. Used as a nickname in medieval Britain.

LIONEL (Old French) 'Young lion'. Medieval pet form of Leon or Lyon. The name has been in use as an independent name since the Middle Ages.

LLEWELYN (Welsh) 'Lion-like'. In the 13th century the name was borne by two Welsh princes. The name is a traditional Welsh name which has been in use in that country for centries but is seldom found elsewhere.

LONNIE (Old German) 'Noble' and 'ready'. Form of Alonso.

LORCÁN (Irish) 'Fierce'. The name was borne in the 12th century by St Lorcán O'Tuathail, the archbishop of Dublin.

LOREN Varient of Laurence. From the plant name Laurel, a lucky plant for Leos.

LORENZO Spanish or Italian form of Laurence.

LORIN, LORRIN Variant spellings of Loren.

LORNE 'Laurel tree'. Masculine form of Laura. Laurel is a lucky plant for Leo.

LYULF, LYULPH (Old English) 'Flame' and 'wolf'. The name is seldom used today.

MAGNUS (Latin) 'Great'. The name was borne by several Scandinavian kings. It began to be used in Scotland and Ireland in the Middle Ages.

MANUS Form of Magnus.

MAX Short form of Maximilian.

MAXIMILIAN (Latin) 'Greatest'. The name was borne by a 3rd-century martyr St Maximilian. The name is seldom found in this form in English-speaking countries.

MAXWELL An extension of Max.

MAYNARD (Norman) 'Strength, brave'. The name was introduced into Britain by the Normans. In modern times it is more frequently found as a surname.

MEILYR (Welsh) 'Chief ruler'. A traditional Welsh name.

MEREDITH (Welsh) 'Great chief'. The name was little used outside Wales until the 20th century. It is now used throughout English-speaking countries, both as a masculine and feminine name.

NAPOLEAN Of uncertain origin but possibly from Neapolis, the Italian city of Naples. Influenced by leone 'lion'.

NOLAN (Latin) 'Noble and famous'. In modern times the name is occasionally used as a first name.

NYE 'Man of honour' or 'gold'. Shortened from of Aneurin.

OBERON Form of Auberon.

ORLIN, ORLON (Latin) 'Golden'. Gold is the lucky metal for Leo.

ORVILLE, ORVIL, ORVAL (French) 'Golden town'. From a French place name. The name was borne by Orville Wright, the US aviator who designed and built the first powered aircraft capable of controlled flight.

ORWIN (Old German) 'Golden friend'.

PADDY Shortened form of Patrick.

PADRAIG Irish Gaelic form of Patrick.

PATRICK (Latin) 'Noble'. It is the name of St Patrick, the patron saint of Ireland. It was little used as a first name however until the 17th century.

PENROD (Old German) 'Famous leader'.

QUINCY, QUINCEY (Latin) 'Fifth'. Leo is the fifth sign of the zodiac. The name was borne by the US president John Quincy Adams in the 19th century.

QUINTIN (Latin) 'Fifth'. Leo is the fifth sign of the zodiac. It spread to Britain at the time of the Norman Conquest.

RA The name of the sun god in Egyptian and other mythologies.

RAA (Maori) 'The sun'.

RAGHNALL (Irish Gaelic) 'Decisive ruler'.

RANALD (Scottish) 'Decisive ruler'. Anglicized form of Raghnall.

RANDALL 'Decisive ruler'. Medieval form of Raghnall.

REAGAN, REAGEN, REGEN Variant spellings of Regan.

REGAN (Gaelic) 'Royalty', 'a king'. From an Irish surname. Also used as a girls' name.

REGINALD (Old German) 'Powerful leader'. The name came into use in the 15th century and became more popular in the 19th and 20th century.

RENAUD (Old German) French form of Reginald.

REX (Latin) 'King'.

RICARD Form of Richard.

RICCARDO (Old German) Italian form of Richard.

RICHARD (Old German) 'Powerful and wealthy ruler'. The name was introduced into Britain at the time of the Norman Conquest. It was very popular in medieval times. Famous bearers of the name include Richard I, known as Richard the Lionheart, and St Richard of Wyche a 13th-century bishop of Chichester. In the 20th century it was one of the most popular masculine names in English-speaking countries.

RICHMOND (Old English) 'Powerful protector'.

RICK, RICKIE, RICKY 'Famous, wealthy ruler'. Pet forms of Roderick. Sometimes used as names in their own right.

ROD, RODDY 'Famous wealthy ruler'. Shortened forms of Roderick.

RODERICK (Old German) 'Famous, wealthy ruler'. The name was introduced into Britain by Scandinavian settlers and later by the Normans. Roderick is found throughout English-speaking countries but has never been common.

RODRICK, RODRIC, RODERIC Forms of Roderick.

RONALD (Old German) 'Mighty and wealthy ruler'. Scottish form of the Old Norse equivalent of Reginald. Since the Middle Ages the name has been in regular use in Northern England and Scotland. It subsequently spread to other English-speaking countries in the late-19th century and remains in frequent use today.

ROMARIC (Old German) 'Glorious nobleman'.

RORY, RORIE (Celtic) 'Red or fiery king'. The name was borne by a 12th-century Irish king Rory O'Connor. Rory has been frequently in use in Scotalnd and Ireland for centuries, but is seldom found elsewhere.

ROY (Gaelic) 'Red'. However it is sometimes taken as a reanalysis of the Old French roy, meaning 'king'.

ROYAL (English) 'Royal'. From the English word meaning 'royal'. It is occasionally found as a first name especially in the US.

ROYLE Associated with the vocabulary word 'royal'. Originally a surname taken from a place name in Lancashire.

RULE (Latin) 'The ruler'.

RYAN (Gaelic) 'Little king'. Anglicized form of Ríoghan, a traditional Gaelic name. It was originally an Irish surname, but since the mid-20th century it has been occasionally used as a first name in Britain and the USA. A famous bearer of the name is the American actor Ryan O'Neal. In North America it is also used as a girls' name.

SAMSON, SAMPSON (Hebrew) 'Sun child'. In the Old Testament Samson, leader of the Israelites, made use of his great strength to defeat the Philistines. The name was used in Britain in the Middle Ages and the 17th century but is rarely found today.

SAVITRI (Indian) 'The sun'.

SIMBA (Swahili) 'Lion'.

SHAKURU (North American Pawnee) 'The sun'.

SHAMASH (Mesopotamian) 'The sun'.

SOL (Latin) 'The sun'.

STEFAN (Greek) Form of Stephen.

STEFANO (Greek)) Italian form of Stephen.

STEPHEN, STEVEN (Greek) 'The Crowned One'. The name was borne by St Stephen, the first Christian martyr. It was used in Britain in the 11th century and remains popular today.

STEVE, STEVIE Pet forms of Stephen.

SUNREY 'Ray of sun'.

SURYA (Indian) 'The sun'.

SVEN (Greek) Scandinavian form of Stephen.

TIERNAN (Irish Gaelic) 'Descendant of Tighearnan', meaning 'descendant of a lord'. The name was in regular use in medieval Ireland.

TIERNEY (Irish Gaelic) 'Descendant of Tighearnach', meaning 'descendant of a lord'. Tighearnach was the name of a 6th-century saint. Tierney is used both as a boys' and girls' name, although in North America it is well-established as a girls' name.

ULRIC (Old German) 'Rich and noble ruler'. The name was borne by several saints including a 10th-century German bishop St Ulric of Augsburg. It was in use in Britain until the 13th century. It was reintroduced from Germany several centuries later.

URIKA (Old German) 'Rich and famous ruler'. Form of Roderick.

UTU (Mesopotamian) Name of a sun god in Mesopotamian mythology.

VALENTINE (Latin) 'Vigorous'. The name came into general use in Britain during the Middle Ages but has never been regularly used.

VALERE (Old German) 'Fierce ruler'.

VASIL (Greek) Form of Basil.

VLADIMIR (Slavic) 'Glorious Monarch'.

WALDO (Old German) 'Mighty', 'the ruler'. A famous bearer of the name was Ralph Waldo Emerson the 19th-century American poet and essayist.

WILEY Form of William.

WILHELM Form of William.

WILKIE, WILKES Forms of William.

WILL, WILLIE, WILLY Shortened forms of William.

WILLARD Form of Wiliam.

WILLET Form of William.

WILLIAM (Old German) 'Resolute defender'. The name was introduced into Britain by William the Conqueror in the 11th century. It has also been borne by three other British kings and several saints. After the Norman Conquest the name rapidly became one of the most popular boys' names in English-speaking countries, a position it retained until the early-20th century. In modern times a famous bearer of the name is Prince William, elder son of the Prince and the late Princess of Wales.

WILLIAMSON Form of William.

WILLIS From a surname with the meaning 'son of Will'. Introduced as a first name in the 19th century.

WILMER (Old German) 'Will' and 'fame'. The name died out as a first name in the Middle Ages, but was still found as a surname. It is seldom found in modern times.

WILMOT Medieval form of William.

WILSON Form of William.

WIRT Form of Wirth.

WIRTH (Old German) 'The master'.

XERXES (Persian) 'The king'.

YI (Chinese) 'The sun'.

YORATH (Welsh) 'Lord' and 'worth'. Form of Iorwerth.

Leo ~ Girls

ADAR (Hebrew) 'Fire'.

ADELA 'Noble'. Variant of Adele. The name was introduced into Britain by the Normans and was borne by the youngest daughter of William the Conqueror.

ADELAIDE (German) 'Noble'. The name was borne in the 10th century by St Adelaide, the wife of the Holy Roman Emperor Otto the Great. The name became popular in Britain in the early-19th century due to the fame of of Queen Adelaide, the consort of King William IV. The capital of South Australia is named in her honour.

ADELE (French) 'Noble'. The name was borne by a 7th-century saint. The name fell out of use in the Middle Ages but was revived in the 19th century.

ADELINA Latinized form of Adeline.

ADELINE French form of Adele.

ADELINE (Old German) 'Noble'. The name existed in the Doomsday book in 1086 and was in regular use throughout the medieval times. It regained popularity in the 19th century.

AIDEEN (Gaelic) 'Fire'. Feminine form of Aidan.

AILEEN Form of Eileen.

AINE (Gaelic) 'Fire'. Feminine form of Aidan.

AISLEEN Form of Helen.

AITHNE (Irish) 'Little fire'. The name has been popular in Ireland for centuries.

ALANI (Hawaiian) 'Orange'. Orange is a lucky colour for Leo.

ALARICE (Old German) 'Ruler of all'.

ALECIA Form of Alice.

ALEXANDRA (Greek) 'Defender of men'. Feminine form of Alexander. The name has been in use in Britain since the 13th century. It became popular in the 20th century due to the marriage of Princess Alexandra of Denmark to King Edward VII.

ALEXIS (Greek) 'To defend'.

ALEXIA Variant of Alexis.

ALICE Variant of Adelaide. The name Alice has been in regular use throughout Britain since the 12th century. The name increased in popularity in the 19th century with the publication of Lewis Carroll's *Alice's Adventures in Wonderland*.

ALICIA Form of Alice.

ALINA (Old German) 'Noble'. Pet form of Adeline, occasionally found as a name in its own right.

ALINDA (German) 'Noble and tender'. A name of recent times, considered to be a blend of Alina and Linda.

ALINE (Old German) 'Noble'. Pet form of Adeline.

ALISHA Form of Alicia.

ALISIA Form of Alice.

ALISSA, ALISA Forms of Alicia.

ALYS Variant spelling of Alice.

ALYSSA, ALISSA Variant spelling of Alisia.

AMENA (Celtic) 'Honest', 'one of incorruptible truth'.

AMINA, AMINE Forms of Amena.

ANDREA 'Warrior'. Feminine form of Andrew. The name has been in use since the 17th century.

ANEIRA (Welsh) 'Honour' or 'gold'. Feminine form of Aneurin.

ALPHONSINE Feminine form of Alphonso.

APOLLONIA (Greek) 'The sun god'. Feminine of Apollo. The name was borne by a 3rd-century saint.

APPOLINA APPOLINE Forms of Apollonia.

ARANI (Maori) 'Orange'. Orange is a lucky colour for Leo.

ARIAL (Welsh) 'Vigour'.

ARIELLE (Hebrew) 'Royal'.

ARIEL (Hebrew) 'God's lioness'. The name is found in the Blible as a place name. In modern Israel the name is used as a boys' name but in the USA it is more commonly found as a girls' name.

ARIELL (Hebrew) 'God's lioness'.

ARIELLA Variation of Ariell.

AUDREY (Old English) 'Noble', 'strength'. An altered form of Etheldreda which was the name of a 6th-century saint who was popular in the Middle Ages. The name was revived in the first half of the 20th century when it came particularly popular, partly due to the fame of the actress Audrey Hepburn.

AUDRINA Derivitive of Audrey.

AUGUST The month in which Leos are born.

AUGUSTA (Latin) 'Majestic'. Feminine of Augustus.

AUREA (Latin) 'Golden'.

AURELIA (Latin) 'Golden'. The name was borne by several early saints. It has been in occasional use in Britain since the 17th century.

AUREOLA, AUREOLE Forms of Auriel.

AURIOL Form of Aurelia.

AURIEL Name of uncertain origin. It may be from Latin, meaning 'gold', or it may be a form of Oriel meaning 'fire' and 'strife'. Both origins are appropriate for Leo. The name has been in use in Britain since the 19th century.

BASILIA (Greek) 'Regal'. Feminine form of Basil.

BASILIE Feminine form of Basil.

BASILLA 'Regal'. Feminine form of Basil.

BAST Name of a goddess in Egyptian mythology who possessed the attributes of a cat or lioness. She has further connections with fire and the sun, both of which are linked to Leo.

BEDELIA Form of Bridget.

BERTHA (Latin form of German name) 'Bright, famous'. The name fell out of use in the Middle Ages but was revived in English-speaking countries in the 19th century.

BIDDIE, BIDDY Pet forms of Bridget.

BIRGITTA Scandinavian form of Bridget.

BRENNA Form of Brianna.

BRIANNA (Irish) 'High, noble'. Feminine form of Brian.

BRIDE Form of Bridget. Although rarely used in modern times it was once a popular form of the name in England and Scotland.

BRIDIE, BRIDEY, BRYDIE Forms of Bride.

BRIDGET, BRIGIT (Irish/Celtic) 'The high one' or 'strength'. It was a name

borne by a Celtic goddess. It has been in use in Britain, particularly in Ireland, since the 17th century.

BREITA, BRIETA Forms of Bridget.

BRIE Shortened form of Brietta, a form of Bridget.

BRIETTA Form of Bridget.

BRIGETTE Form of Bridget.

BRIGHID Form of Bridget.

BRIGID Form of Bridget. The name was borne by an Irish abbess who died in the early-6th century and became one of the patron saints of Ireland. In Britain she was known as St Bridget or St Bride.

BRIGIDA Form of Bridget.

BRIGITTA Form of Bridget.

BRIGITTE French form of Bridget.

BRITA Shortened form of Birgitta.

CALTHA (Latin) 'Yellow flower'. Yellow is a lucky colour for Leo.

CARLA (Old German) Feminine form of Carl, a form of Charles.

CARLETTA 'Strong', 'virile'. Form of Charles.

CELANDINE (Greek) 'Yellow water flower'. Yellow is a lucky colour for Leo.

CELANDON Form of Celandine.

CELOSIA (Greek) 'A flame'.

CHRYSOLITE Lucky gemstone for Leo.

CLEOPATRA (Greek) 'Glory'. The name was borne by many female members of the Egyptian royal family, the most famous being the lover of Mark Antony. The name has been in occasional use in English-speaking countries.

CLIO (Greek) 'Glory'. In Greek mythology the name was borne by one of the muses and one of the nymphs.

CRESSIDA, CRESSYDA (Greek) 'Gold'. In medieval legend Cressida was the name borne by a faithless Trojan princess. The name became particularly popular in the 20th century.

DAPH, DAFF Shortened froms of Daphne.

DAPHNE (Greek) 'Laurel'. Laurel is a lucky plant for Leo. In Greek mythology the nymph Daphne avoided the attentions of Apollo by turning into a laurel bush. The name has been in use in English-speaking countries since the early-20th century.

DEVONA (Old German) 'Brave and dependable maid'.

EARLA (Old English) 'Noblewoman', 'princess'. Feminine form of Earl. The name is of recent coinage and is found mainly in the US.

EARLINA Feminine form of Earl.

EARLINE, EARLENE, EARLEEN Feminine forms of Earl.

EDA, EDIE Pet forms of Edith.

EDANA (Gaelic) 'Little fiery one'. One of a warm and loving nature. Feminine form of Edan.

EDITH (Old English) 'Prosperity, riches'. The name was born by a 10th-century nun St Edith, or St Eadgyth, an illegitimate daughter of Edgar the Peaceful. The name has been in regular use in English-speaking countries since the Middle Ages and became particularly popular around the turn of the 20th century.

EILEEN Form of Helen. The name was popular in Britain in the late-19th century and later spread to other English-speaking countries.

ELAINE Originally an Old French form of Helen but now taken as a name in its own right. The name occurs in Arthurian legend, borne by the mother of Sir Lancelot's son, Galahad. The name Elaine was revived in the 19th century and was particularly popular in the late-20th century.

ELATA (Latin) 'Lofty', 'noble', 'a woman of high birth and beauty'.

ELDORA (Spanish) 'Gilded or golden'. Gold is the lucky metal for Leo.

ELEANOR, ELINOR Possibly French forms of Helen. The name was introduced into Britain in the 12th century by Eleanor of Aquitaine, wife of King Henry II.

ELEANORA, ELINORA, ELENORA Forms of Eleanor.

ELEANORE, ELINORE, ELINOR, ELNORE Forms of Eleanor.

ELENA Spanish or Italian form of Helen.

ELLEN Form of Helen. This form of Helen was the most popular form from medieval times until the Renaissance. It was also very popular in the USA during the 20th century.

ELLENE, ELLYN Forms of Helen.

ELOISE, ELOISA (Old German) 'Noble' and 'ready'. Possibly forms of Aloysia, a feminine form of Louis.

ELYSSA 'Noble'. Form of Alicia.

EMINA (Latin) 'Highly placed maiden'. 'Daughter of a noble house'.

ENA Shortened form of Eugenia.

ERICA, ERIKA (Latin) 'Ruler'. The name has been in regular use in English-speaking countries since the latter part of the 19th century.

ERMA 'Noble', 'majestic'. Form of Irma.

ERME 'Noble', 'majestic'. Form of Irma.

ERMINIA (Latin) 'Royal'.

ETHEL (Old English) 'Noble maiden'. Originally a shortened form of feminine names beginning with Ethel, such as Etheldreda or Ethelinda. The name began to be used as a name in its own right in the late-19th century.

ETHELDREDA (Old English) 'Noble strength'. The name was borne in the 7th century by St Etheldreda, founder of a monastery at Ely, and the wife of a Northumbrian king. The name has largely been superseded by Ethel but is still found occasionally.

ETHELDA, ETHELINDA, ETHELINE Elaborated forms of Ethel.

ETHNE (Irish) 'Little fire'. The name and its various forms have been popular Irish names for centuries.

ETHYLYN, ETHYL Forms of Ethel.

EUCLEA (Greek) 'Glory'.

EUGENIA (Greek) 'Well-born', 'noble'. Feminine form of Eugene. The name was borne in early times by a Roman martyr. The name has been in occasional use since medieval times.

EUGENIE (Greek) 'Noble', 'well-born'. French feminine form of Eugene. The name has been in use in English-speaking countries since the 19th century.

EVELEEN Form of Eileen.

FERNANDA (Old German) 'Adventurous' or 'courageous peacemaker'. One who is daring and courageous. Feminine form of Ferdinand.

FERDINANDA, FERNANDINA Forms of Fernanda.

FLAVIA (Latin) 'Yellow haired'. Yellow is a lucky colour for Leo. The name has occasionally been found in the English-speaking countries but has never been in frequent use.

FULVIA (Latin) 'Golden girl'. The most famous bearer of the name was the wife of Mark Antony in ancient Roman times. The name was revived in the 18th century.

GENIE, GENE, GINA, GENA Shortened forms of Eugenia.

GERTRUDE (German) 'Strength'. The name has been in occasional use since the Middle Ages but did not become popular until the late-19th century.

GLORIA (Latin) 'Glory'. 'An illustrious person'. The name came into use in 1898 when George Bernard Shaw used it for one of his characters in the play *You Never Can Tell*. The name became very popular in the 20th century.

GLOIRE, GLORI, GLORY Forms of Gloria.

GLORIANA, GLORIANNA Forms of Gloria.

GLORIANE, GLORIANNE Forms of Gloria.

GOLD Gold is the lucky metal for Leo.

GOLDA (Old English) 'Gold'.

GOLDIE (Old English) 'Gold'.

HAIDEE Form of Heidi.

HARRIET 'Home ruler'. Anglicized form of French Henriette, a feminine form of Henry. The name was popular in the 18th and 19th centuries and remains in use today.

HARRIETTE Variant of Harriet.

HARRIOT Form of Harriet.

HEIDI 'Noble', 'kind'. Swiss pet form of Adelaide.

HELEN (Greek) 'Sun', 'sunbeam', 'light', 'the bright one'. In Greek mythology, the beautiful Helen (of Troy) was known as 'the face that launched a thousand ships'. In medieval Britain the name was popular due to the fame of St Helen. It was also popular in the latter half of the 20th century.

HELENA Latin form of Helen. The name was born by St Helena (or Helen) who was the mother of the Roman emperor Constantine the Great. St Helena allegedly found the cross of Jesus Christ in the early-4th century.

HELIANTHA (Greek) 'Sunflower'. Lucky flower for Leos.

HENRIETTA 'Home ruler'. Latin form of the French Henriette.

HESTIA Name of a goddess of fire in Greek mythology.

HONEY Pet form of Honora. Also from the Old English vocabulary word. Often used as a term of endearment.

HONOR, HONOUR (Latin) 'Honour'. The name was first popularized by the Puritans in the 17th century. It was revived in the 20th century, a famous bearer of the name being the British actress Honor Blackman.

HONORA (Latin) 'Honour'.

HONORIA Form of Honora.

IDELIA (Old German) 'Noble'.

IGNATIA (Latin) 'Woman of fiery temperament'. Feminine form of Ignatius.

ILLONA, ILLONE Forms of Helen.

ILONA Hungarian form of Helen.

IORA (Latin) 'Gold'. Gold is the lucky metal for Leo.

IRMA (Old German) 'Noble, majestic'. The name has been in occasional use since the late-19th century.

IRMINA, IRMINE Variations of Irma.

IRME Form of Irma.

ISLEEN Form of Eileen, from Helen. 'Light', 'sunbeam'.

JOCEA, JOSSE Medieval forms of Joyce.

JOCELYN, JOSCELIN, JOSCELINE Related to the name Joyce. The name was introduced into Britain by the

Normans. It was originally a boys' name and particularly popular in the Middle Ages. It was revived in the early-20th century as a girls' name.

JOYCE (Norman) 'Lord'. The name was borne by a 7th-century Breton saint. In medieval Britain the name was given as both a boys' and girls' name in a variety of forms. It was revived in the late-19th century and became popular throughout English-speaking countries.

JULY Month in which some Leos are born.

KANTI (Sanskrit) 'Sun's rays'. Used as both a boys' and girls' name.

KEFIRA (Hebrew) 'Young lioness'.

KEIRA (Greek) 'Rays of the sun'. Feminine form of Keiran.

KEIRANNE A blend of Keira and Anne.

KINBOROUGH (Old English) 'Royal fortress'. The name was regularly used in England until the 18th century, but is rarely found today.

KOA (Hebrew) 'Princess'.

LAIS (Greek) 'Adored'.

LARAINE (French) 'The queen'. Found mainly in the USA. A form of Lorraine.

LAREINE, LAREINA Alternative spellings of Laraine.

LAURA Feminine form of Laurus, meaning 'laurel'. Lucky plant for Leo. The laurel is the symbol for victory or triumph. The name became well-used in English-speaking countries in the mid-19th century.

LAURANA A blend of Laura and Anna. Anna is a Hebrew name meaning 'grace'

LAURANDA A blend of Laura and Amanda. Amanda is a Latin name meaning 'loveable'.

LAURANTHA A blend of Laura and Samantha. Samantha is a Hebrew name meaning 'to listen'.

LAUREL (Middle English) Taken from the name of the evergreen shrub. Laurel is a lucky plant for Leo. The name was particularly popular in the USA and Canada in the mid-20th century.

LAURELIA A form of Laura.

LAURELLE, LAURELLA Elaborated forms of Laurel.

LAURELLEN, LAURELEN Blends of Laura and Ellen.

LAUREN Varient of Laura. Laurel - lucky plant for Leos.

LAURENA, LAUREEN, LAURENE French forms of Laura.

LAURETTA, LAURETTE Diminutive of Laura.

LAURIANE, LAURIANNE French forms of Laura.

LAURINA Form of Laura.

LAURIE Pet form of Laura and Laurel.

LAURINDA Variant of Laura.

LAWRIE Pet form of Laura.

LEALA (Middle English) 'Loyal'.

LENA 'Sun, sunbeam','the bright one'. Abstracted form of Helena. It is also a Latin name meaning 'enchanting one'.

LEOLINA (Welsh) 'Little lion'.

LEONA 'The lion'. Feminine form of Leon.

LEONARDA Feminine form of Leon.

LEONE 'The lion'. French feminine form of Leon.

LEONIA 'The lion'. Feminine form of Leon.

LEONIE 'The lion'. French feminine form of Leon. The name is found throughout English-speaking countries.

LEONIS A bright star in the constellation of Leo.

LEONORA, LEONORE, LENORA
'Light'. Forms of Eleanor. The name has been in use from time to time in English-speaking countries since the 19th centuries.

LEONTINE, LEONTYNE (Greek) 'Lion-like'.

LEORA, LORA Form of Leonora.

LERA Variant of French 'le roi' meaning 'the king'.

LEXINE (Scottish) Elaboration of Lexy.

LEXY 'Defender of men'. Pet form of Alexandra.

LINA Form of Lena.

LIONA 'Lion'. Altered form of Leona.

LISA (West African Benin, Togo) 'The sun'. Also considered to be a pet form of Elizabeth.

LOLLY Pet form of Laura.

LORA 'Laurel'. German form of Laura. Lucky plant for Leos.

LORAL Alternative spelling of Laurel.

LOREEN, LORENE Form of Laura.

LORELL, LORELLE Alternative spelling of Laurel.

LOREN Variant spelling of Lauren.

LORENA Elaboration of Loren.

LORETTA Variant of Lauretta.

LORETTE Variant of Laurette.

LOREY Pet form of Lorell.

LORI Variant of Laurie. From the plant name Laurel. Lucky plant for Leos.

LORINDA Form of Laura.

LYSSA 'Noble'. Short form of Alyssa. From the name Adelaide.

MATELDA, MAITILDE Variations of Mathilda.

MATHILDA (Old German) 'Brave little maid. One as courageous as a lion'. The name was introduced into Britain by Queen Matilda, the wife of William the Conqueror. It was revived in the 18th century and remains in use throughout English-speaking countries today.

MATILDA, MATILDE, MATHILDE Variations of Mathilda .

MAUD, MAUDE Shortened versions of Mathilda.

MAXINE 'Greatest'. Derivative of Max. The name has been in regular use in English-speaking countries since the early part of the 20th century.

MEGARA (Greek) Wife of Heracles, an important mythological character in the creation of the constellation of Leo.

MEREDITH (Welsh) 'Great chief'. The name was little used outside Wales until the 20th century. It is now used throughout English-speaking countries, both as a masculine and feminine name.

MERRY Shortened form of Meredith.

MITHRA (Iranian) 'The sun'.

MONA (Irish) 'Noble'. The name was little used outside Ireland until the late-19th century when it began to spread to other English-speaking countries.

MÓR (Scottish and Irish Gaelic) 'Great'. In medieval Ireland this was the most popular girls' name. It is still found in Ireland and Scotland today.

MORAG (Gaelic) 'Great' or 'sun'. The name is most frequently found in Scotland where it is very popular. It is also found throughout other English-speaking countries.

MOREEN (Irish) 'Great'. Pet form of Mór.

NERYS (Welsh) 'Lord'. A name of recent coinage. A famous bearer of the name is the British television actress Nerys Hughes.

NOLA 'Famous', 'noble'. Feminine form of Nolan.

NORA, NORAH Shortened form of Honora. Often used as a name in its own right. The name was introduced into Ireland at the time of the Normans and is still in use today.

NOREEN Form of Honora.

NORREY, NORRIE, NORRY Pet forms of Honora.

OLIBANUM Lucky perfume for Leo.

OPHIRA (Hebrew) 'Gold'. Gold is the lucky metal for Leo.

ORA (Latin) 'Gold one'.

ORABEL (Latin/French) 'Golden beauty'. Gold is the lucky metal for Leo.

ORABELLA, ORABELLE (Latin/French) 'Golden beauty'.

ORALIE, ORALEE Of uncertain origin, possibly a form of Aurelia, 'golden'.

ORIANA (Latin) 'Golden one' or 'sunrise'. The name occurs in several literary works including Tennyson's ballard Oriana. However it is rarely found as a first name in modern times.

ORIEL (Old German) 'Fire' and 'strife'.

ORIETTA (Latin) 'Little golden girl'.

ORLA (Irish) 'Golden princess' or 'golden lady'. In medieval Ireland this was a popular girls' name which is now being revived.

ORLANA, ORLANE Forms of Orlena.

ÓRLAITH (Irish/Gaelic) 'Gold princess'. The original form of Orla.

ORLENA (Latin) 'Golden brilliance'.

ORLINA (Latin) 'Golden'.

PAT, PATSY Shortened forms of Patricia.

PATRICIA (Latin) 'Noble'. The name was rarely used until the late-19th century and became particularly popular in the mid-20th century.

PATTIE, PATTY Shortened forms of Patricia.

PYRENA, PYRENIA (Greek) 'Fiery one'.

QUEENA Form of Queenie.

QUEENIE, QUEENY (English) 'Queen'. It is either used as a name in its own right or as a pet form of Regina.

RAINA, RAINE Of uncertain origin, but thought to be from a French word meaning 'queen'. It may also be a feminine form of Rayner (Old German) meaning 'mighty army'.

RANA (Sanskrit) 'Of royal birth'.

REGAN (Latin) 'Queen'. Form of Regina. The name occurs as one of the daughters in Shakespeare's *King Lear*.

REGINA (Latin) 'Queen-like'. The name was in use as a first name in the Middle Ages. The name was revived in the 19th century and is still in use in modern times.

REGINE (Latin) Form of Regina.

REINA, REINE (French) 'Queen'.

REINITA (Spanish) 'Little queen'.

RICA 'Ruler of all'. Shortened form of Ulrica.

RICADONNA (Italian) 'Lady who rules'.

RICARDA (Old German) 'Powerful and wealthy ruler'. Italian feminine form of Richard.

RODERICA (Old German) 'Rich and famous ruler'. Feminine of Roderic.

RONALDA (Old Norse) 'Mighty and powerful ruler'. Feminine of Ronald.

ROYALE (French) 'Regal being'.

RULA (Latin) 'Sovereign leader'.

TILDA 'Brave little maid'. Shortened version of Mathilda.

TILLY Shortened version of Mathilda.

SADIE (Hebrew) Pet form of Sarah. Sadie has been in use as a name in its own right since the 19th century.

SAFFRON (Arabic) From the name of a type of crocus or the orange spice obtained from it. Orange is a lucky colour for Leos.

SALENA, SALINA Forms of Sally.

SALLY Form of Sarah.

SANDRA (Greek) 'Defender of men'. A form of Alexandra. During the 20th century the name became fashionable as a name in its own right.

SARAH (Hebrew) 'Princess'. In the Old Testament Sarah was the wife of Abraham and mother of Isaac. It has been in use in Britain since medieval times and in the early 1980s it became one of the most popular girls' names in the English-speaking world.

SARAI Form of Sarah.

SARANNA A blend of Sarah and Anna. The name has been in use since the 18th century.

SARETTE (Hebrew) 'Princess'. Form of Sarah.

SARINA Form of Sarah.

SARITA Form of Sarah.

SARITA (Hebrew) Form of Sarah.

SAVITRI (Indian) 'The sun'.

SERAPHINA (Hebrew) 'Fiery' or 'winged'. The name was borne by two saints in the 13th and 15th centuries.

SHAKURU (North American Pawnee) 'The sun'.

SHAMASH (Mesopotamian) 'The sun'.

SHARA Derivative of Sharon.

SHARON, SHARRON (Hebrew) 'A princess of exotic beauty'. Also taken from the Plain of Sharon in the Holy Land. The name was taken up as a first name in the 17th century. It spread to England from the USA in the early 20th century.

SHERRY, SHARRY SHARI, SHARRI Forms of Sharon.

SHIMONA (Hebrew) 'Little princess'.

SOLA (Latin) 'The sun'.

SOLAIRE, SOLAYRE (Latin) A modern invention combining 'the sun' with 'air'.

SOLANA A blend of Sola and Lana. Lana is a form of Alana, meaning 'noble' or 'harmony'.

SOLANDA A blend of Sola and Amanda. Amanda is a Latin name meaning 'loveable'.

SOLANDRA A blend of Sola and Sandra. Sandra is a shortened form of Alexandra, 'defender of men'.

SOLANE A blend of Sola and Jane. Jane is a Hebrew name meaning 'Jehovah is gracious'.

SOLANN, SOLANNE A blend of Sola and Anne. Anne is a Hebrew name meaning 'grace'.

SOLANTHA A blend of Sola and Samantha. Samantha is an Hebrew name meaning 'to listen'.

SOLARA A blend of Sola and Lara. Lara is a Latin name meaning 'cheerful'.

SOLATA A blend of Sola and Lata. Lata is a name of uncertain origin.

SOLEA A blend of Sola and Lea. Lea is a Hebrew name meaning 'languid'.

SOLEILA A blend of Sola and Leila. Also from French meaning 'sun'.

SOLELLA, SOLEIL (French) 'Sun'.

SOLENA, SOLINA Blends of Sola and Lena. Lena is a Latin name meaning 'enchanting one'. It is also a pet form of Helena.

SOLINDA, SOLYNDA Blends of Sola and Linda. Linda is a Spanish name meaning 'pretty'.

SOLIZA A blend of Sola and Liza. Liza is a pet form of Elizabeth, a Hebrew name meaning 'God is satisfaction'.

SOLOLA A blend of Sola and Lola. Lola is a pet form of Delores, a Spanish name meaning 'lady of sorrows'.

SOLORNA A blend of Sola and Lorna. Lorna is a name invented by the British novelist R.D. Blackmore for the heroine in Lorna Doone.

SOLYN, SOLYNNE Blends of Sola and Lyn. Lyn is a pet form of Linda, a Spanish name meaning 'pretty'.

STEPHANIE, STEFANIE (Greek) French feminine forms of Stephen, 'the crowned one'. The name has been in regular use in English-speaking countries since the early part of the 20th century.

SUNFLOWER The sunflower is a lucky plant for Leo.

SURYA (Indian) 'The sun'.

TANGERINE, TANGERENE, TANGERYNE A deep orange colour. Orange is a lucky colour for Leo. The name is derived from the fruit from Tangier.

TIERNEY (Irish Gaelic) 'Descendant of Tighearnach', meaning 'descendant of a lord'. Tighearnach was the name of a 6th-century saint. Tierney is used both as a boys' and girls' name, although in North America it is well-established as a girls' name.

TRICIA, TRISHA (Latin) 'Noble'. Shortened forms of Patricia, often used as names in their own right.

TRUDIE, TRUDI, TRUDY Shortened form of Gertrude, often used as an independent name.

ULRICA (Old English or Old German) 'Ruler of all'. Feminine form of Ulric.

ULRIKA Alternative spelling of Ulrica.

VALDA (Old German) 'Ruler'. The name is in occasional use in English-speaking countries.

VAL, VALLIE Shortened form of Valentina.

VALENCIA Form of Valentina. 'Strong and courageous'.

VALENTINA (Latin) 'Strong and courageous'. Feminine form of Valentine.

VALENTIA Form of Valentina.

VALIDA Form of Valentina.

VALESKA (Slavic) 'Glorious ruler'.

VELDA Form of Valda.

VESTA Name given to the Roman god of fire.

WALESKA Form of Valeska.

WILHELMINA (Old German) 'Resolute defender'. A feminine form of William. The name has been in use in English-speaking world since the 18th century.

WILLA Pet form of Wilhelmina.

WILLIAMINA Feminine form of William. Not usually found outside Scotland.

WILMA Form of Wilhelmina. Found mainly in Scotland, the USA and Canada.

XAN (Greek) 'Yellow'. Yellow is a lucky colour for Leo.

XANTHE (Greek) 'Yellow'. The name is found in classical mythology.

YELLOW A lucky colour for Leo.

ZAHEERA, ZAHAVA (Hebrew) 'Golden'.

ZANDRA (Greek) 'Defender of men'. Shortened form of Alexandra.

ZARA (Hebrew) 'Princess'. Origin uncertain but possibly a form of Sarah. The name is found in several literary works although it was little used as a first name until the late-20th century. The name was given by Princess Anne to her daughter in 1981.

ZSA ZSA (Hebrew) 'Princess'.

Virgo

♍

THE VIRGIN
23 August – 22 September

RULING PLANET	Mercury. In astrology Mercury is the planet associated with communication and the mind.
ELEMENT	Earth

General characteristics
- Aims for perfection.
- Self-critical.
- Honest, responsible, dedicated.
- Health, healing.
- Modest, gentle, helpful.
- Emotionally warm, sensual.
- Efficient, hard-working, reliable.

Characteristics of young Virgoans
- Can be shy.
- Is quick and alert.
- Learns facts quickly.
- Reliable and honest.
- Usually tidy but can be messy.
- Enjoys helping adults.
- Often learns to talk and read at an early age.
- May be a fussy eater.

Virgoan lucky connections
Gemstones:	opal, agate, peridot
Colours:	brown, cream, yellow-green
Plants:	herbs, narcissus, vervain
Perfume:	narcissus
Metal:	mercury
Animals:	mink, porcupine, bat
Tarot card:	the hermit

VIRGOS possess a natural reserve which can often make them appear shy of strangers. They like to assess you with slow deliberation before they eventually categorise you. They can, therefore, be difficult to get to know. But once they warm to you they can be talkative individuals with an active, enquiring mind. Indeed young Virgos will often question things in great detail. They will want to know the who, when, where and why of situations and facts in enormous depth. Detail is a hallmark of Virgos. They scrutinise and study everything and are eager to absorb and use any fascinating scraps of information.

Even baby Virgos will quietly and carefully observe their surroundings. Only when they are really sure about their immediate world, and the people who inhabit it, will they be prepared to explore it. They also enjoy being spoken to and enjoy listening to conversations even if they are too young to participate. As with many things Virgo babies will watch you carefully as you speak, often imitating the sounds and movements you make with your mouth.

Virgo babies enjoy having toys that they can manipulate, toys they can pull, bang or knock with. Virgos are the doers of this world and they like to see tangible results for their labours. As they grow older they will enjoy toys that are intricate, for example puzzles, jigsaws and sorting boxes. Anything that demands exacting manipulation and provides a sense of achievement – for example a fully completed jigsaw – will satisfy a Virgo toddler.

This sense of achievement is vital to Virgos as they can often be self-critical and lacking in confidence. This can often be caused by the fact that they demand perfection of themselves. Activities that give them a sense of achievement and satisfaction will help to boost their self-esteem.

Older Virgo children will enjoy helping with chores for they are conscientious little beings who thrive on helping others. They are capable of hard work and their scrupulous attention to detail can make them really useful little helpers. It is this attention to detail and their conscientious streak that makes Virgos so neat and organised. They usually like things 'just so', with everything in its own little place. However they can also be very messy. Their bedroom may look like a disaster area; although it can be the very picture of chaos it is usually organised chaos. Your little Virgo will know where everything is in her messy bedroom; what every little scrap of paper or picture means and where it belongs. Tidying up is best done with her consent and participation, to avoid unnecessary upsets.

Even though your Virgo child can be self-critical it is important not to criticise her yourself. Such criticism can hurt her deeply and will do nothing to boost her sometimes shaky confidence and self-esteem. Try to encourage and praise her whenever possible. If she displays bad behaviour try to explain why such behaviour is not good for anyone, rather than criticise her as a person. She will respond to this much more positively.

Give her warmth and understanding, a cuddle when she needs it and an outlet for her practical and creative abilities. Such an approach will help your Virgo child to gain confidence in herself and to find peace and contentment.

Virgo ~ Boys

ADAM (Hebrew) 'Of the red earth'. Adam of the Old Testament, the father of the human race, was said to be created from the red earth. The name was particularly popular in the 13th century, the mid-19th century and again in the 1960s.

ADAMNAN 'Little Adam'. The name was borne by St Adamnan, an Irish 7th-century saint.

ADDIS Form of Adam.

ADDISON (Old English) 'Earth'. Son of Adam.

AIDAN (Latin) 'To help'.

AIKEN (Old English) 'Earth'. Little Adam.

AIKIN, AICKIN Forms of Aiken.

AMAETHON In Welsh druid mythology Amaethon is known as the god of agriculture. The story of Virgo has links with the harvest and fertility of the land. In mythology Amaethon is the brother of Arianrhod.

ANGEL (Greek) 'Messenger' or 'angel'. Mercury, the ruler of Virgo, is named after the Greek god Hermes, the messenger of the gods.

ANGELO Form of Angel.

ARVAL (Latin) 'Cultivated land'.

ASA (Hebrew) 'Healer'. In the Old Testament the name is borne by a king of Judah. The name was adopted by the Puritans in the 17th century and remains in occasional use today.

AS-AR Alternative name of the god Osiris from Egyptian mythology. See Osiris.

BOYD (Scottish Gaelic) 'Yellow'. Yellow-green is a lucky colour for Virgo. The name has been used in Scotland for centuries. It has been used both as a first name and surname.

BRAN In Welsh Druid mythology, the name is borne by a guardian of the land. He was also known as a god of war, who defended British lands.

BRON (Old English) 'Brown'. Brown is the lucky colour for Virgo.

BRONSON (Old English) 'Son of Brown'.

BROWN Lucky colour for Virgos.

BRUNO (Old German) Dark or brown complexion. The name was used among the Germanic ruling families during the Middle Ages. It was borne by three German saints in the 10th and 11th centuries. The name has been used occasionally in English-speaking countries since medieval times.

BURNETT, BURNET (Old French) 'Brownish'.

CALORIS Name given to huge crater on Mercury which was caused by a rock crashing into the planet.

CAMILLUS (Latin) 'Messenger'. Mercury, the ruling planet of Virgo, is known as the messenger of the Gods.

CERNUNNOS In Celtic mythology the name is borne by a fertility god. The story of Virgo is linked to fertility and the harvest.

CHIK English gypsy name, meaning 'earth'.

CLAY From the Old English, claeq,'clay', a fine-grained earth.

CONLEY (Irish) 'Pure, chaste'.

CONSTANT (Latin) 'Steadfast'. Medieval form of the name Constantine. The name Constant was used by the Puritans and revived in the 19th century.

CONSTANTINE (Latin) 'Steadfast'. The name was borne by the Roman emperor Constantine the Great, the first Christian emperor. It was also borne by three medieval Scottish kings. Although the name has been in occasional use in Britain since the Dark Ages it is seldom found in English-speaking countries.

CORIANDER (Greek) From the herb name. Herbs are lucky plants for Virgos.

COSIMO Form of Cosmo.

COSME Form of Cosmo.

COSMO (Greek) 'Order' and 'universe'. Hence 'the perfect order of the universe'. The name was borne by a 4th-century martyr. It was introduced into Britain in the 18th century by the Scottish Dukes of Gordon and has been in occasional use in the English-speaking countries since that time.

COSTIN 'Steadfast'. A form of Constantine.

CREAM Lucky colour for Virgos.

DARIUS (Greek) 'Possesses good'. The name was borne by several Persian kings.

DARRAGH (Gaelic) 'Fertile'. The name was borne by an Irish fertility god.

DEMETER In Greek mythology Demeter was the goddess of the harvest and all living plants. She was one of the central characters in the story of the creation of Virgo.

DON, DONNY Shortened forms of Donovan.

DONNAN (Irish) 'Brown'.

DONOVAN (Irish) 'Dark brown'. Brown is a lucky colour for Virgo. Originally an Irish surname its use as a first name began in the early-20th century.

DOVEY (Hebrew) 'To whisper', suggesting a quiet character.

EARTHAN (Old English) 'Of the Earth'.

EFREM Form of Ephraim.

ELLESWORTH (Old English) 'A farmer', 'lover of the earth'.

ENOCH (Hebrew) 'Educated, dedicated'. This name was favoured by the 17th-century Puritans.

EPH Shortened form of Ephraim.

EPHRAIM (Hebrew) 'Fruitful'. The name is borne in the Old Testament by one of the sons of Joseph. It was adopted by the Puritans in the 17th century and is still found today.

ERROL (Latin) 'To wander'. Mercury, the ruling planet of Virgo, is often known as the 'wandering star' because it moves so quickly about the sky.

EUNAN (Irish and Scottish) 'Earth'. Gaelic version of Adam.

EUSTACE (Greek) 'Stable', 'tranquil' or 'fruitful'. The name was introduced into Britain at the time of the Norman Conquest. It was fairly popular in the late Middle Ages and is occasionally found today.

FELIM (Irish Gaelic) 'Eternally virtuous'. The name was borne by several early Irish saints and kings.

GAIAN (Greek) 'Child of the Earth'.

GALLEN (Greek) 'Healer'.

GEORG Alternative spelling of George.

GEORGE (Greek) 'Earth, the farmer'. The name was borne by St George, the patron saint of England. The legend of St George and the Dragon is thought to be a medieval Italian invention. The name became popular in Britain after the accession of King George I in 1714. Its popularity in the USA grew with the initiation of George Washington as the first president of the USA (1732-99). The name remains popular today.

GEORGES Form of George.

GEORGIE, GEORDIE Pet forms of George.

GORDIE, GORDY Pet forms of George.

GEORGY, GEORG Pet forms of George.

GOWER (Celtic) 'The pure one'.

HAL Form of Hale.

HALE (Old English) 'Safe, sound, health and whole'.

HECTOR (Greek) 'Holding fast, anchor.' Suggests a responsible and hard-working character.

HERMES From the name of the Greek messenger of the gods. Known to the Romans as Mercury. Mercury is the ruling planet of Virgo.

HERMIT The lucky tarot card for Virgos.

HUMPHREY (Old German) *Hun*, 'strength', and *frythu*, 'peace'. This name implies a quiet but strong character.

ISADORE Form of Isidore.

ISIDORE (Greek) 'The gift of Isis'. A Greek name even though Isis was an Egyptian goddess. The name was borne by St Isidore of Seville, a 7th-century bishop and scholar who attempted to convert Spanish Jews to Christianity. The name was used as a Jewish name in Spain and later spread to Britain and the USA.

JASON (Greek) 'Healer'. In the 17th century the name was popular with the Puritans. It increased in popularity in the USA and Britain in the mid-20th century.

JORGE variation of George. 'Earth, farmer'.

JORIN Variation of George.

JORIS Variation of George.

JUGEN Variation of George.

KORIANDER (Greek) From the name of the herb. Herbs are lucky plants for Virgos.

LEIGHTON, LAYTON (Old English) 'Herb garden'. Herbs are lucky plants for Virgo. The name was originally a surname and place name, but has been in use as a first name since the 19th century.

LLEU First name of Lleu Llaw Gyffes, a god of Celtic Druid mythology who is possibly linked to Mercury. Mercury is the ruling planet of Virgo.

MALACHI (Hebrew) 'My messenger'. Mercury, the ruling planet of Virgos, is known as the 'messenger of the gods'.

MALACHY Alternative spelling of Malachi.

MERCURY The ruling planet of Virgo. Mercury is also the lucky metal for Virgos.

MINK Lucky animal for Virgos.

MOYA (Ngoni) 'Good health'.

MYRON (Greek) Sweet-smelling oil, myrrh. Myrrh is a lucky herb for Virgos.

NARCISSUS (Greek) Narcissus is a lucky plant for Virgo. The name is borne by a character in Greek mythology who fell in love with his own reflection and was transformed into the Narcissus flower. Occasionally given as a first name in English-speaking countries.

ORLANDO Italian form of Roland. 'Famous land'.

OSIRIS Name of the fertility or corn god (god of the harvest) from Egyptian mythology. Osiris was one of the principle figures in Egyptian mythology. The myth of Osiris bears a close resemblance to the myth of the Greek goddess Deineter and Persephone. The story of Virgo is based on the story of these two goddesses of Greek mythology. In addition to being the god of corn Osiris was also a moon-god. He was also known as As-ar.

RAFAEL Alternative spelling of Raphael.

RAPHAEL (Hebrew) 'God has healed'. The name was borne by one of the archangels mentioned in the Apocrypha. Occasionally still found today. A famous bearer of the name was the Italian painter Raphael.

ROLAND, ROWLAND, ROLYND (Old German) 'Famous land'. The name was introduced into Britain at the time of the Norman Conquest. Rowland was the usual spelling of the name until the 19th century when the French form Roland became more popular.

ROLEY, ROLLIN Forms of Roland

ROLLAND, ROLLO Forms of Roland.

SEXTUS (Latin) 'Sixth'. Virgo is the sixth sign of the zodiac.

SOMBRERO Name given to a galaxy which lies in the constellation of Virgo. It is one of the largest galaxies ever known.

SPICA Name given to the brightest star in the constellation of Virgo.

STACEY, STACY (Greek) 'Fruitful'. From Eustace.

TARRAGON (Greek) From the name of the herb. Herbs are lucky plants for Virgos.

THU God of the earth in Chinese mythology.

VAL Shortened form of Valentine.

VALENTINE (Latin) 'Strong' or 'healthy'. St Valentine's Day is believed to be a pagan custom and has no connection with the Christian saints who bear the name. The name came to general use in Britain during the Middle Ages but never achieved widespread popularity. The name is occasionally given as a girls' name.

VERVAIN Lucky plant for Virgos.

VULCAN God of thunder, one of the rulers of Virgo. The mythical Vulcan was said to have had a confident and brilliant mind.

VIRGIL (Latin) 'Maidenly, like a virgin'. The Roman poet Virgil (or Vergil) wrote the Aeneid, the story of Aeneus' journey after the fall of Troy.

WARE (Old English) 'Prudent one'. An astute person.

YORICK Danish form of George. 'Earth'.

YURI (Greek) 'Earth, a farmer'. Russian derivative of George.

ZACCHAEUS A name of uncertain origin. It may be from Aramaic, meaning 'pure', or it may be a form of Zachariah, meaning 'the Lord has remembered'.

Virgo ~ Girls

ABRA (Hebrew) 'Earth Mother'.

ACACIA 'Innocent'.

ADAMINA (Hebrew) 'Earth'. A feminine form of Adam.

ADRANA (Greek) 'Maiden from Ardrea'.

AG, AGGIE, AGGY Forms of Agatha.

AGATA Form of Agatha.

AGATHA (Greek) 'Good'. One of fine virtue. The name was borne by a 3rd-century Sicilian martyr. In modern times a famous bearer of the name was Agatha Christie, the British detective story writer.

AGATHE Form of Agatha.

AGATHY Form of Agatha.

AGAVE (Greek) 'Illustrious and noble'.

AGGIE Form of Agnes.

AGNA Form of Agnes.

AGNELLA Form of Agnes.

AGNES (Greek) 'Pure', 'chaste'. 'The untouchable virgin'. The name was borne by a young Roman virgin martyr who became a popular saint in the Middle Ages. The name was revived in the 19th century and remains in use today.

AGNETA Form of Agnes.

AINDREA Alternative spelling of Andrea.

AINGEAL (Irish) 'Angel' or 'messenger of the gods'. Mercury, the ruler of Virgo, is often described as the 'winged messenger of the Gods'.

AISHA (Arabic) 'Woman'.

AISSA (Arabic) 'Woman'.

ALBINIA 'White woman'. Form of Elvira. The name was introduced into Britain from Italy in the 17th century.

ALETTE (Latin) A diminutive of 'wing'. Mercury, the ruler of Virgo, was known as the 'winged messenger of the gods'.

ALIDA (Latin) 'Little winged one'. Mercury, the ruler of Virgo, was known as the 'winged messenger of the gods'.

ANCILLA (Latin) 'Handmaiden'.

ANIS, ANNIS Forms of Agnes.

ALMA (Hebrew) 'Woman'.

ALTHEA (Greek) 'The healer'. The name is taken from the Greek name of a marsh mallow plant, Althaia, which is valued for its healing powers. In Greek mythology Althea was the name of the mother of Meleager who was famous for his heroism in *The Iliad*.

ALTHETA Form of Althea.

ALTHEE Form of Althea.

ALULA (Latin) 'Winged one'. Mercury, the ruler of Virgo, is often described as the 'winged messenger of the Gods'.

ALZENA (Arabic) 'The woman'. 'The embodiment of all feminine charm and virtue'.

ANATOLA (Greek) 'Woman of the East'. Particularly relevant to a Virgo born in the East.

ANDREA (Latin) 'Womanly', 'The epitome of all feminine beauty and charm'. The name dates back to the 17th century.

ANDREANA Form of Andrea.

ANDRE, ANDREE Form of Andrea.

ANDRIA Alternative spelling of Andrea.

ANDRIANA Elaborated form of Andrea.

ANGEL (Greek) 'Messenger' or 'angel'. Mercury, the ruler of Virgo is known as the 'winged messenger of the gods'.

ANGELA (Greek) 'Messenger' or 'angel'. Mercury, the ruler of Virgo, is named after the Greek god Hermes, the winged messenger of the gods.

ANGELINA, ANGELINE Elaborated forms of Angela.

ANGIE Pet form of Angela.

ANNICE Form of Agnes.

ANNONA Alternative spelling of Anona.

ANONA (Latin) 'Yearly crops'. The Roman goddess of the crops. Virgo is linked to goddess of the harvest and crops.

ANQET Name of the Egyptian goddess of the fertile waters. Also known as Isis. Virgo is associated with harvest and fertility.

AO (Maori) 'Planet earth'.

ARETA (Greek) 'Virtue'.

ARETHA (Greek) 'Virtue'.

ASTRAEA In classical mythology the name given to the goddess of innocence and purity, who is identified with Virgo.

BELL Alternative spelling of Belle.

BELLA Form of Belle.

BELLE (French) 'Beautiful woman'.

BELVA Form of Belle.

BELVIA Form of Belle.

BENIGNA (Latin) 'Gentle, kind and gracious'. 'A great lady'.

BRIGHID Name of a goddess of healing, poetry and smith-craft in Irish Druid mythology.

BRUNA (Old German) 'Dark or brown complexion'. Brown is a lucky colour for Virgo.

BRUNETTA Feminine form of Bruno.

CACIE (Greek) 'Innocent'. Form of Acacia.

CAILIN (Irish) 'Young girl'. A from of Colleen.

CAITANYA Blend of Caitlin and Tanya. Tanya is a pet form of Tatiana.

CAITLIN Irish for of Kathleen.

CAITRIONA 'Pure'. Form of Catriona, from Catherine.

CAITRIN 'Pure'. Form of Catherine.

CAL, CALLY, CALLIE Shortened forms of Calantha.

CALANTHA (Greek) 'Beautiful blossom'. A woman of childlike beauty and innocence.

CALANTHE Form of Calantha.

CALELLA (Celtic) 'Handmaiden'.

CALTHA (Latin) 'Yellow flower'. Yellow-green is a lucky colour for Virgo.

CAMILLA (Roman) 'Messenger'. Feminine form of Camillus.

CANDACE, CANDICE (Latin) 'Pure', 'glittering', 'brilliant white'. 'One who is most pure and virtuous'. The name was borne by several Ethiopian queens, one of whom is mentioned in the New Testament. Since the 17th century the name has been in occasional use throughout English-speaking countries. It was particularly fashionable in the USA and Canada in the mid-20th century. A famous bearer of the name is the US actress Candice Bergen.

CANDIDA (Latin) 'White' – associated with purity.

CANDIE, CANDY Shortened forms of Candice.

CARMA Form of Carmel.

CARMEL (Hebrew) 'God's fruitful vineyard' or 'garden'. Virgo is associated with the harvest and living crops. Carmel is the name of a mountain in the Holy Land. It is largely given to children from Roman Catholic families.

CARMELA Italian form of Carmel.

CARMELITA Italian form of Carmel.

CARMELLA Form of Carmel.

CARMELINA, CARMELINE Forms of Carmel.

CARMEN Spanish form of Carmel. The name became popularized in English-speaking countries by Bizet's opera *Carmen*.

CARMIE Form of Carmel.

CASTA (Latin) 'Of pure upbringing'.

CASTE (Latin) 'Of pure upbringing'.

CASEY Diminutive of Catherine.

CASTA, CASTE (Latin) 'Of pure upbringing'.

CATALINA Form of Catherine.

CATERINA Form of Catherine.

CATHARINE, CATHARINA Forms of Catherine.

CATHERINE (Greek) 'Pure'. The name has been borne by several saints including St Catherine of Alexandria, a 4th-century martyr, after whom the Catherine Wheel was named. The name and its various forms became popular in Britain and many English-speaking countries. It remains in regular use today.

CATHLEEN Variant of Catherine, from the Irish Gaelic form Caitlin.

CATHY, CATHIE Diminutive of Catherine, sometimes used as independent names.

CATRIN Welsh variant of Catherine.

CATRIONA Scottish Gaelic variant of Catherine. It was rarely used outside Scotland until the mid-20th century.

CERELIA, CERELLIA (Latin) 'Fruitful woman'.

CERIDWEN (Welsh) One of the names given to the goddess of the earth, Gaia. The name is little used outside Wales.

CLAIRINE (Latin) 'Bright maiden'.

COLEEN, COLENE, COLLINE, COLINE Alternative spellings of Colleen.

COLLEEN (Irish) 'Young girl'. The name is seldom used as a first name in Ireland but, since the mid-20th century, it has been in frequent use in other English-speaking countries, especially north American and Australia.

CONSTANCE (Latin) 'Steadfast'. The name has been in regular use in Britain since the time of the Normans, with whom it was popular. It was frequently found throughout the English-speaking countries in the early part of the 20th century but is seldom used today.

CONSTANTINA (Latin) 'Steadfast'. Feminine form of Constantine.

CORA (Greek) 'Maiden'. The name Cora first appeared in the early-19th century in the novel *The Last of the Mohicans* by James Fenimore Cooper. Its use gradually spread to other English-speaking countries and it remains in use today.

CORABETH Blend of Cora and Elizabeth.

CORABELLA 'Beautiful maiden'. Combination of Cora and Bella.

CORABELLE 'Beautiful maiden'. Combination of Cora and Belle.

CORALIE Variant of Cora.

CORANDA A blend of Cora 'maiden', and Amanda 'loveable'.

CORANTHA A blend of Cora 'maiden', and Samantha 'listener'.

CORELLA Form of Cora.

CORETT, CORETTE Forms of Cora.

CORETTA Form of Cora.

CORIANTHA (Greek) From the herb name. Herbs are lucky plants for Virgos.

CORIN, CORINNE , CORRINNE 'Maiden'. Forms of Cora.

CORINA, CORINNA , CORRINA Forms of Cora.

CORISSA (Greek) 'Most modest maiden'.

CORRENA Form of Cora.

CORRIE, CORIE Forms of Cora.

CORIN Form of Cora.

CORINTHE A blend of Cora 'Maiden' and Ianthe, Greek for 'violet flower'.

CORISSA (Latin/Greek) 'Most modest maiden'. Variant of Cora.

CORISSE (Latin/Greek) 'Most modest maiden'.

CORITA Variant of Cora.

CORNELIA (Latin) 'Womanly virtue'. The name was borne in the 2nd century B.C. by the mother of two Roman revolutionaries. The name is found from time to time in English-speaking countries.

CORONA (Spanish) 'Crowned maiden'.

CORONIE (Spanish) 'Crowned maiden'.

CORREEN, CORRENE Forms of Cora.

CORRENA Form of Cora.

DAFFODIL (Greek) From the flower name. The daffodil is the common name for Narcissus, a lucky plant for Virgo.

DAMITA (Latin) A form of Dama, meaning 'lady'.

DANA Alternative name of Danu. The name is found mainly in North America. It is sometimes also found as a boys' name.

DANU Name of a mother goddess of the land, also a fertility and river goddess, in Irish Druid mythology. The name means 'sacred gift'.

DARA (Hebrew) 'Charity, compassion and wisdom'.

DARIA (Greek) Feminine form of Darius. The name was borne by a 3rd-century saint.

DARINA (Irish Gaelic) 'Fertile'. A feminine form of Darragh.

DEBBIE, DEBBY Shortened forms of Deborah.

DEBORA, DEBRA Form of Deborah.

DEBORAH (Hebrew) 'The bee'. An industrious woman who looks for what is sweet in life. The name is found in the Old Testament. It has been found in English-speaking countries since the 17th century and was particularly popular in the mid-20th century.

DELICIA (Latin) 'Delightful maiden'. It has only recently been used as a first name.

DELFINE Alternative spelling of Delphine.

DELPHINE (Greek) 'Calmness and serenity'. The name became popular in the early-19th century in France but has never been particularly common in the English-speaking world.

DEMETER (Greek) Goddess of fertility. Demeter is an important character in the story of Virgo in Greek mythology.

DEMETRIA (Greek) 'Fertility'. Alternative name of the goddess of fertility.

DONA, DONAH Alternative spellings of Donna.

DONELLA A blend of Donna and Ella. Ella is an old German name meaning 'all'.

DONNA (Italian) 'Lady'. Since the early-20th century the name has been in regular use in English-speaking countries. It is particularly popular in the USA and Canada in the mid-20th century.

DORA, DORI, DORY Shortened forms of Isadora.

DUANA (Gaelic) 'Little dark maiden'.

DUENA, DUENNA (Spanish) 'Chaperon'. The name given to a woman responsible for the morals and manners of young girls in their charge.

DUNA Form of Duana.

DWANA Form of Duana.

DURETTA (Spanish) 'Little steadfast one'.

EARTHA (Old English) 'From the earth'.

EDLYN (Old English) 'Noble maiden'. It can also mean happy brook.

EIR (Norse) 'Peace and mercy'. In Norse mythology Eir is the goddess of healing.

ELLA (Old English) 'Beautiful fairy maiden'. Beauty bestowed by fairies as a birth gift. The name was introduced into Britain by the Normans. It was revived in the 19th century. It is sometimes regarded as a short form of names beginning or ending with 'Ella'. It is often now used as a name in its own right.

ELVERA Alternative spelling of Elvira.

ELVIRA (Spanish/Latin) 'True', 'white woman'. The name was not commonly found in English-speaking countries until the 19th century. The name occurs in Mozart's 18th-century opera *Don Giovanni*.

ELVIRE Form of Elvira.

ERDA (Old German) 'Child of the earth'.

EIR (Norse) 'Peace and mercy'. The goddess of healing.

EMINA (Latin) 'Noble maiden'.

EMMA (Old German) 'Great and worldly healer'. The name was introduced into Britain by the Normans. It was popular in medieval England in part due to the fact that the name was borne by the mother of Edward the Confessor. The name was revived in the 18th century and remains in popular use today.

ENID (Celtic) 'Purity of the soul'. The name was borne in Arthurian legend by the wife of Geraint. It was revived in the latter half of the 19th century.

EUSTACIA (Latin) 'Tranquil maiden', 'fruitful'. Feminine form of Eustace.

EUSTACIE Form of Eustacia

FENNEL (Latin) From the herb name. Herbs are lucky plants for Virgos.

FREYA Name of the Norse goddess of love and fertility. It also means 'lady'. It has been in occasional use in English-speaking countries since the early-20th century.

GAEA (Greek) 'The Earth'. Goddess of the earth.

GAIA Alternative spelling of Gaea.

GAIANE (Greek) 'Child of Earth'.

GALIANA (Old German) 'Lofty maiden'.

GALIENA (Old German) 'Lofty maiden'.

GE (Greek) In Greek mythology Ge was the name of the earth goddess who gave birth to the heavens.

GEORGANA Feminine from of George.

GEORGENE, GEORGINE Feminine forms of George.

GEORGETTE (Greek) 'Earth, farmer'. Feminine form of George.

GEORGIA 'Earth, farmer'. Latin feminine form of George. Particularly popular in the USA. The American state of Georgia was named after the British King George II.

GEORGIANA Feminine form of George. It was fairly popular in the 18th and 19th centuries but is rarely used in modern times.

GEORGY, GEORGIE Pet forms of George.

GEORGIE Pet form of Georgia or Georgina.

GEORGINA Feminine form of George.

GEVIRA (Hebrew) 'Lady, queen'.

GIANE (Greek) 'Child of the earth'.

GINGER 'Pure, untouched'. Shortened form of Virginia.

GINNY, GINNIE Shortened form of Virginia.

GIROGIA Form of Georgina.

GLENNA (Celtic) 'Maiden from the valley'. Feminine form of Glen.

HAIDEE (Greek) 'Caressed' or 'modest'. The name was borne by a character in *Don Juan*, the 19th-century poem by Byron.

HERB Herbs are lucky plants for Virgo.

HERMINA (Latin) 'Belonging to the Earth'. Derivative of Hermoine.

HERMIONE (Latin) 'Of the earth'. The name is also a form of Hermes, the messenger god, known to the Romans as Mercury. Mercury is a ruling planet of Virgo.

HERTA 'Earth mother'. Form of Hertha.

HERTHA (Old German) 'Earth mother'.

HYGEIA Name borne by the Greek goddess of health.

IDONEA Of uncertain origin. Possibly Old Norse, meaning 'work' or Latin, meaning 'suitable'. It has been in occasional use in Britain since the 13th century.

IDYLLA (Greek) 'Perfection'.

IMOGEN (Latin) 'Innocent maiden'. The name was borne by the heroine in Shakespeare's play *Cymbeline*. The source used for this play spells the name as Innogen. Imogen was thus the result of a printing error. The name Imogen is still in use today.

INES, INEZ 'Pure','chaste'. Forms of Agnes.

INEX (Greek) 'Pure'. Portugese derivative of Agnes.

INNOGEN (Latin) 'Innocent', or (Celtic) 'Girl' or 'maiden'. Both meanings are appropriate for Virgo.

ISADORA (Greek) 'The gift of Isis'. See the story of Isis overleaf. The name is a feminine form of Isadore.

ISIS A goddess of harvest and food from Egyptian mythology. Isis is the wife of Osiris, the god of corn. In Egyptian mythology she comes in many guises. She is known as Usert, goddess of the fruitful earth, and also as Anqet, goddess of the fertile waters. In addition she is known as Sati, the force which brings forth the powers of spring and the Nile flood, and as Knut, the light-giver of spring.
The story of Virgo is based on the story of Demeter, the goddess of harvest in Greek mythology. There are parallels between this story and the story of Isis.

ISSIE, ISSY, IZZY Shortened forms of Isadora.

JESSALYN (Hebrew) 'Wealthy woman'.

JINNY 'Pure, untouched'. Shortened form of Virginia.

JONQUIL (Spanish) From the flower name. Jonquil is a type of Narcissus. The narcissus is a lucky plant for Virgo. The name has been in use since the mid-20th century.

KAITLYN Irish form of Kathleen.

KALANTHA, KALANTHE 'Beautiful blossom', 'a woman of childlike beauty and innocence'. Alternative spelling of Calantha.

KALINA (Greek) 'Pure'.

KALYA (Sanskrit) 'One who is healthy'.

KALYANA (Sanskrit) 'One who is virtuous'.

KANYA (Sanskrit) 'Virgin Goddess'.

KARAN Form of Karen.

KAREEN 'Pure'. From Catherine.

KAREN 'Pure'. A Danish form of Katarina, from Catherine. In the early-20th century the name was introduced into the USA by Danish immigrants. It has only been used in Britain since the mid-20th century but has become very popular.

KARIN A Swedish variant of Karen.

KARINA Swedish form of Katherine.

KASIA (Greek) 'Pure'.

KASSIE 'Pure'. Alternative spelling of Cassie, from Catherine.

KATARINA Swedish form of Katherine. Occasionally used in English-speaking countries.

KATE 'Pure'. Diminutive of Catherine. The name has been in constant use since medieval times. It was used by Shakespeare in *The Taming of the Shrew*. It enjoyed a surge of popularity in the late-19th century and again in more recent times.

KATERINA, KATERINE, KATERYN Forms of Catherine.

KATHERINA, KATHARINA Forms of Katherine.

KATHERINE, KATHARINE (Greek) 'Pure'. From Catherine.

KATHLEEN Variant of Catherine, from the Irish Gaelic Caitlin.

KATHRYN Variant of Catherine which has been in regular use since the mid-20th century.

KATHY Diminutive of Catherine. Sometimes used as an independent name.

KATIE, KATY 'Pure'. Diminutives of Catherine.

KATINKA (Greek) 'Pure'. Russian derivative of Katherine.

KATRINA, KATRINE 'Pure'. Variations of Catriona, a Scottish form of Catherine.

KAY Diminutive of Katherine, of any name beginning with the letter 'K'.

KHUT An alternative name for Isis, the goddess of the harvest in Egyptian mythology. See Isis.

KIONA (American Indian) 'Brown hills'. Brown is a lucky colour for Virgo.

KISHA (Russian) 'Pure'.

KIT Diminutive of Catherine or Kathleen.

KITTY Diminutive of Catherine or Kathleen. It is the oldest known pet form of these names.

KOLINA (Greek) 'Pure'.

KOO (Maori) 'Girl'.

KORA (Greek) 'Maiden'.

KORE (Greek) 'Beautiful maiden'.

KOREN (Greek) 'Beautiful maiden'.

KORENZA (Italian) Form of Koren.

LALANA (Sanskrit) 'Woman'.

LARISSA (Greek) 'Cheerful maiden'.

LAVEDA (Latin) 'Purified one'.

LAVENDER From the name of the flowering shrub which is classed as a herb. Herbs are lucky plants for Virgos.

LAVETTA, LAVETTE Forms of Laveda.

LIL Shortened form of Lilian or Lily.

LILIAN, LILLIAN (Latin) 'Lily'. The lily is a symbol of purity. In Britain the name has been in use since the 16th century, increasing in popularity at the turn of the 20th century.

LILIAS, LILLIAS Scottish forms of Lilian.

LILLA, LILLAH Form of Lily.

LILY, LILLIE Forms of Lilian. From the name of the flower. The Lily is the symbol of purity. The name has been in use since the 19th century.

LOLETA, LOLITA (Spanish) 'Maiden of sorrow'.

MACHA Name given to a wild fertility goddess of Irish Druid mythology. Macha was also known as a protector of the land.

MADONNA From the Italian title of the Virgin Mary, meaning 'my lady'. The name has been applied to many renaissance paintings representing the mother of Christ. Its use as a first name has begun in fairly recent times, often among Americans of Italian descent. The famous recent bearer of the name is Madonna Ciccone.

MAHINA A form of Mahira.

MAHIRA (Hebrew) 'Industrious'.

MAHRA Form of Mahira.

MAIDA (Middle English) 'Maiden'.

MAIDEL Form of Maida.

MAIDIE , MADY (Middle English) 'Maiden'. Originally used as an affectionate nickname occasionally now used as a first name.

MAIYA (Sanskrit) An aspect of the goddess Gaia, the goddess of the earth.

MARTA Form of Martha.

MARTHA (Aramaic) 'Lady' or 'lady of the house'. Martha of the New Testament was preoccupied with housework, which has given rise to the association of the name with domestic work and practical common sense. The name was used as a first name in Britain since the 16th century.

MARTHE Variation of Martha.

MARTY, MARTI, MARTIE Shortened versions of Martha.

MARVA (Hebrew) The herb sage. Herbs are lucky plants for Virgos.

MATTIE, MATTY Variations of Martha.

MAYDA, MAYDE (Old English) 'Maiden'.

MAYDENA Form of Maida 'Maiden'.

MEL Shortened form of Melanie.

MELANIA Form of Melanie.

MELANIE, MELLONEY (Greek) Alternative name given for Demeter in Greek mythology. Demeter was the goddess of the cornfields and is linked to the story of Virgo. Melanie means 'black' or 'dark'.

MELINA 'God's fruitful vineyard'. Derivative of Carmel.

MENTHA (Latin) 'Mint'. Herbs are lucky plants for Virgos.

MERCURY Name of the ruling planet of Virgo. Also the name of the messenger of the gods in Roman mythology.

MINK Lucky animal for Virgos.

MISA Form of Missie.

MISSIE American usage meaning 'young girl'.

MODESTY (Latin) 'Chasteness', 'modesty'.

MORENA (Spanish) 'Brown'. Brown is a lucky colour for Virgo.

MORENWYN (Cornish) 'Fair maiden'.

MORWEN Form of Morwenna.

MORWENNA (Welsh) 'Maiden'. The name was borne by a 5th-century Celtic saint, in whose honour the Cornish village Morwenstow was named. The name is found mainly in Wales and Cornwall.

MYFANWY (Welsh) 'Little woman'. The name has increased in popularity in recent times.

MYRRH (Greek) The flowering herb Sweet Cicely. Herbs are lucky plants for Virgos.

MYRA, MIRA (Greek) Sweet smelling oil, myrrh.

MYRZA A form of Myrrh.

NAOMH (Irish Gaelic) 'Holy' or 'saint'. Pronounced 'neev'. It has only been used as a first name in fairly recent times.

NARCISSUS Lucky plant and perfume for Virgos.

NEMISSA (Native American) 'Star maiden' in native American mythology.

NESSA 'Pure', 'chaste'. Form of Agnes.

NESSI, NESSIE Forms of Agnes.

NEST, NESTA Form of Agnes.

NEYSA Form of Agnes.

NONA Shortened form of Anona, the Roman goddess of the crops.

NONNIE Shortened form of Anona.

NORDICA (Old German) 'Northern maiden'.

ONAWA (American Indian) 'Maiden who is wide awake'.

OPAL (Sanskrit) From the name of the precious stone. Opal is a lucky gemstone for Virgo.

ORLA (Irish) 'Golden lady'.

PAMONA (Latin) 'Fruitful and fertile'.

PARTHENIA (Greek) 'Virgin'. The virgin, or maiden, is the symbol of Virgo. The name is occasionally found in English-speaking countries.

PAT, PATTI, PATTIE, PATTY Shortened forms of Patricia.

PATRICE Form of Patricia.

PATRICIA (Latin) 'Well-born maiden'. The name was borne in the 7th century by one of the patron saints of Naples. It did not become popular in English speaking countries until the late-19th century.

PATRIZIA Form of Patricia.

PATSY Form of Patricia.

PAVITA (Sanskrit) 'Made pure'.

PEONY (Latin) 'Healer'.

PERIDOT Lucky gemstone for Virgo.

PERSEPHONE (Greek) Goddess of the Underworld. Persephone is an important character in the story of Virgo in Greek mythology.

PIA (Latin) 'Pious'.

POMONA (Latin) 'Fruitful', 'fertile'.

PRUDENCE (English) Prudence. The name was first used in the 13th century and is still used occasionally in English-speaking countries.

QUINBY (Scandinavian) 'Womanly'.

RABI (Arabic) 'The harvest'.

RAPHAELA, RAFAELA Feminine forms of Raphael.

RHIAN (Welsh) 'Maiden'.

RHIANNON (Welsh) 'Maiden'. The name Rhiannon is borne by a Welsh goddess of the land in Druid mythology. The name is also associated with the moon in Celtic mythology. It has only been given as a first name since the 20th century.

RHIANWEN (Welsh) 'Maiden'.

ROLANDA, ROLANDE (Old German) 'Famous land'. Feminine forms of Roland.

ROLANTHA A blend of Rolanda and Samantha. Samantha means 'listener'.

ROLARA A blend of Rolanda and Lara. Lara means 'cheerful'.

ROLENE A blend of Rolanda and Ilene. Ilene means 'light'.

ROMAIRE A blend of Rolanda and Maire. Maire is a form of Mary – 'sea' or 'wished for child'.

ROSEMARY (Latin) From the name of the flowering herb. It means 'dew of the sea'.

ROSEMARIE, ROSEMAIRIE, ROSIE Variations on Rosemary.

RUE (Old German) A herb name. Herbs are lucky plants for Virgos.

SALVIA (Latin) Sage herb. Herbs are lucky plants for Virgos.

SATI (Sanskrit) 'Virtuous wife'. It is also an alternative name for Isis, the Egyptian goddess of the harvest. See Isis.

SENGA 'Pure', 'chaste'. Form of Agnes.

SHEDEA (North American Indian) Wild herb. Herbs are a lucky plant for Virgo.

SHUSHANA, SHUSHANNA Forms of Susannah. Has been in occasional use in the English-speaking world since the 17th century.

SOMBRERO Name given to a galaxy which lies in the constellation of Virgo. It is one of the largest galaxies ever known.

SOPHRONIA (Greek) 'Prudent'. The name is occasionally found in the English-speaking world.

SOREL, SORREL, SORELLE (Old French) From the name of the herb sorrel. Herbs are lucky plants for Virgos.

SPICA Name given to the brightest star in the constellation of Virgo.

STACEY, STACY, STACIE Forms of Eustacia.

SUE Shortened form of Susan.

SUKEY Form of Susan. The form of the name was in use in the 18th century.

SUSAN Form of Susannah. The name has been in regular use since the 18th century and was particularly popular in the mid-20th century.

SUSANNAH, SUSANNA, SUZANNA (Hebrew) 'Lily'. The lily is a symbol of purity, and so linked to the symbol of Virgo, the virgin. The name Susannah is found in both the Old Testament and New Testament. It was in use at the time of the Reformation and has been in regular use in English-speaking countries since then.

SUSIE, SUZEY Forms of Susan or Susannah.

SUZETTE French form of Susannah.

TALITHA (Aramaic) 'The maiden'. The name occurs in the New Testament. It has been in use as a first name since the mid-19th century.

TARUM (Sanskrit) 'Maiden'.

TERAH (Latin) 'The earth'.

TERESA (Greek) 'The harvester'. The name was used largely in Spain until the 16th century and gradually spread to English-speaking countries. It became more popular in the 19th century and particularly so in the latter half of the 20th century.

TERESSA, TERESITA Forms of Teresa.

TERRENA (Latin) 'Earth'.

TERRI, TERRIE, TERRY Forms of Teresa.

TESS Form of Teresa.

TESSA, TESSIE, TESSY Form of Teresa.

THERESA Form of Teresa.

THERESE, TERESE Forms of Teresa.

THERESIA Form of Theresa.

TIERRA (Spanish) 'Land', 'earth'.

TI-MU In Chinese mythology this is the name given to the earth mother, the maker of all creation.

TI-YA Alternative name for Ti-mu.

TOIREASA Form of Teresa.

TRACEY, TRACEY Forms of Teresa.

TRINETTE (Greek) 'Pure little girl'.

USERT Goddess of the fruitful earth in Egyptian mythology. Also known as Isis, the goddess of the harvest in Egyptian mythology. See Isis.

VALONIA (Latin) 'Maiden from the vales'.

WYNNE (Welsh) 'Fair maiden'.

VALEDA (Old German) 'Wholesome'.

VALONIA (Latin) 'Maiden from the vales'.

VAL Shortened form of Valentine.

VALENTINE (Latin) 'Strong' or 'healthy'. Given as both a girls' and boys' name. See Virgo boys' names.

VALERIA (Latin) 'To be strong or healthy'.

VALERIE French form of Valeria. Since the late-19th century this is the form of the name usually found in English-speaking countries. The name was particularly popular in the mid-20th century.

VERVAIN Lucky plant for Virgos.

VEVINA (Gaelic) 'Sweet woman'.

VIRGINIE Form of Virginia.

VIRGI, VIRGIE, VIRGY Shortened forms of Virginia.

VIRGINIA (Latin) 'Virgin, pure and untouched'. The American state of Virginia was named in honour of Elizabeth I, 'the Virgin Queen'. It was also the name bestowed on the first child to be born of English parentage in the New World, on Roanoke Island in 1587.

WYNNE (Welsh) 'Fair maiden'. From a Welsh surname.

WYNE, WIN Alternative spellings of Wynne.

XANTHE (Greek) 'Yellow'. Yellow-green is a lucky colour for Virgo. The name was borne by several minor characters in classical mythology.

YARROW (Old English) From the name of the flowering herb.

YELLOW Yellow-green is a lucky colour for Virgos.

YNES, YNEZ 'Pure', 'chaste'. Forms of Agnes.

ZABRINA (Old English) 'Well-born maiden'.

ZANA Name of uncertain origin. It may be Persian, meaning 'woman', or it may be a form of Suzanna. Either origins are relevant to Virgo.

ZEA (Latin) The herb rosemary. Herbs are lucky plants for Virgos. It also means 'ripened grain' which is also linked to Virgo. The story of how the constellation of Virgo was formed revolves around the goddess of the harvest.

ZEBRINA From the name of the flowering herb. Herbs are lucky plants for Virgos.

ZELE, ZELIE Form of Zelia.

ZELIA (Greek) 'Zealous one'. One with a true devotion to duty.

ZELINA Form of Zelia.

ZENA (Persian) 'Woman'.

ZENAIDE Variant of Zena or Zenaida.

ZENAIDA 'Zeus gave life'. From Zenobia. Zeus was an important god in the story of Virgo in Greek mythology.

ZENDA Form of Zenobia.

ZENIA Form of Zenobia.

ZENINA Form of Zenobia.

ZENNA Shortened form of Zenobia.

ZENNIE Shortened form of Zenobia.

ZENOBIA (Greek) 'Zeus gave life'.

ZENORBIE Form of Zenobia.

ZETTA (Old English) 'Sixth'. Virgo is the sixth sign of the zodiac.

ZHENYA Origin uncertain. Possibly a form of Zena 'Woman'.

Libra

THE SCALES
23 September – 22 October

RULING PLANET   Venus. In astrology Venus is the planet of love, beauty and personal values.

ELEMENT   Air

General characteristics

- Harmony, balance, diplomacy.
- Gentle, loving, peaceful.
- Good manners, personal appearance.
- Good taste, refinement.
- Tactful, good communicator.
- Good listeners, interested in others.
- Enjoys music and an attractive environment.

Characteristics of the young Libran

- Is often a beautiful baby.
- Charming and friendly.
- Enjoys the company of others.
- Is kind and affectionate.
- Can be reasonable and fair in dealing with others.
- Is often clean and tidy.

Libran lucky connections

Gemstone:	emerald
Colours:	green, pink, purple
Plants:	rose, myrtle, aloe
Perfume:	galbanum
Metal:	copper
Animal:	elephant
Tarot card:	justice

LIBRA is the sign of the scales and it is a characteristic of this sign that they like everything to be in balance. They love harmony and they will do everything in their power to make life as pleasant and tranquil as possible. Rarely will you need to chastise your young Libran, for their aim in life is to please. They will constantly wish to gain your approval and will readily agree to your wishes. Not that they will always do what you want them to do. In aiming to please they may agree to tidy their room, but you may find that an hour later, they've tidied very little, and they're still trying to decide which toy gets put in its box and which one stays on the shelf.

Indecision is a Libran hallmark. Seeing a number of options before them Librans may spend hours, if not days, trying to decide which one to pick. Asking your Libran child what they want for dinner may be fraught with problems for he may still be making up his mind two hours later. Perhaps its better to limit his choice, or maybe, not even to ask at all...

Librans are charming, friendly individuals. Even as babies their ready smile and beguiling laughter will make them a hit with everyone. They relish company and enjoy the attention and fuss that is made of them. This love of company can often be a problem when you need to go out, or even to leave the room for your Libran baby will not be slow to voice his disapproval. Bedtime too may be a problem, when he is left alone without company. Try playing soft, relaxing music. He will sense your presence nearby and his natural enjoyment of gentle sound will help him to relax.

Music is just one peaceful pastime that Librans enjoy. They are pleasure-loving creatures and can happily spend quiet hours playing, reading or simply daydreaming. Sometimes peace and tranquillity is all they need and they enjoy times of solitude. At other times they will revert to the social creatures they truly are.

Librans are frequently attractive individuals. As babies they will often possess a calm beauty with their wide-eyed smile and cheerful demeanour. Even as young children they will often be clean and tidy and as they grow older, they will make a real effort with their appearance.

Librans appreciate the finer things in life such as small luxuries and the beauty of their surroundings. Older children may really enjoy being allowed to make choices, as to the decoration of their bedroom for example. Their choices will often achieve good results as Librans frequently possess a good eye for colour.

The sociable side of your Libran child's nature will make him a good playmate and you will rarely have to deal with any squabbles. Your little diplomat will readily sort out any discord all by himself. He will intensely dislike arguments of any sort and will do his best to remedy any problems. He will usually succeed. Charming, pleasant, keen to regain calm in his world, you will discover that he is a born peacemaker. Not that that necessarily makes him a pushover. In many cases regaining harmony will not be a case of relenting, but often a case of pleasantly, gently coaxing the other party, be that yourself or his friends, into believing that his way really is the best way after all.

Libra ~ Boys

ABSALOM (Hebrew) 'The father is peace' or 'father of peace'. In the Old Testament it was the name borne by the son of King David.

ADEEL (Arabic) 'Just, honest'.

ADIL (Arabic) 'Just, honest'.

ALAIN French form of Alan.

ALAN (Celtic) 'Cheerful harmony'. The name entered Britain at the time of the Norman invasion. It was popular in medieval times and remains in regular use.

ALAND, AILEAN, AILIN Forms of Alan.

ALLAN, ALLEN, ALLYN Forms of Alan.

ALDEN Form of Aldwin.

ALDIS, ALDOUS, ALDUS Form of Aldo.

ALDWIN, ALDWYN (Old English) 'Old friend'. The name was popular in the Middle Ages and is still occasionally found today.

ALIM (Arabic) 'Wise, learned'.

ALOE From the name of the plant. Aloe is a lucky plant for Libra.

ALUN Welsh form of Alan.

ALWYN, ALWIN Forms of Alvin.

AMYAS, AMIAS (Old French) 'Loved'. The name was in use as early as the 12th century.

ANGHUS OG Name of the god of love in Irish Druid mythology. The name is also spelt as Aonghus Og.

ANGUS Anglicized form of Anghus or Aonghus, god of love in Irish mythology.

ANGWYN (Welsh) 'Handsome'.

AXEL (Old English) 'Father of peace'.

BELLAMY (Greek) 'Fair friend'.

BONAMY (French) 'Good friend'. The name originates from a Guernsey surname. It is occasionally found as a first name in English-speaking countries.

BUDDY, BUD From an informal term of address used in the US, meaning 'friend'. More usually used as a nickname than as a first name.

CALLUM, CALUM Forms of Malcolm.

CARADOC (Welsh) 'Love'. The name borne by a British king in the 1st century. The name is still in occasional use in Wales but infrequently found elsewhere.

CARADOCK Form of Caradoc.

CASEY Shortened form of Casimir.

CASIMIR (Polish) 'Proclamation of peace'. Occasionally used in Britain and the USA.

CERI (Welsh) 'Loved one'.

COLM, COLUM Shortened forms of Columbus.

COLMAN (Irish) 'Dove'.

COLUMBUS (Latin) 'Dove', the symbol of peace. The name was borne by St Columbus, a 6th-century Irish abbot and missionary who converted Scotland and Northern England to Christianity.

COLVER Form of Culver.

COPPER Copper is a lucky metal for Libra.

CORWIN, CORWEN (French) 'Friend of the heart'.

CRADDOCK (Welsh) 'Amiable'.

CULVER (Old English) 'Gentle as the dove', 'peaceful'. The symbol of peace.

CUPID (Roman) Name of the Roman god of love.

DAFDD Welsh form of David.

DAI Shortened form of David.

DANTE (Latin) 'Enduring'. Form of Durand.

DAREL, DARELL, DARRELL (French) 'Loved one' or 'darling'. The name has been in use as a first name since 1860 and was particularly popular in the mid-20th century.

DARRYL, DARYL (Old English) 'Loved one' or 'darling'.

DARRY Shortened version of Darryl.

DAVE, DAVY Shortened forms of David.

DAVID (Hebrew) 'Beloved' or 'friend'. It was borne by a 6th-century bishop St David, the patron saint of Wales. It is one of the most popular masculine names in English-speaking countries.

DEMPSTER (Old English) 'The judge'.

DEWI Welsh form of David.

DURAN (Latin) 'Enduring'. Form of Durand.

DURRANT (Latin) 'Enduring'.

EDWIN, EDWYN (Old English) 'Rich friend'. The name was borne by King Edwin of Northumbria after whom, it is believed, the city of Edinburgh was named. The name was little used after the 12th century until its revival in the 19th century. It remained in regular use until the mid-20th century.

EHREN (Old German) 'Honourable one'.

EIRAN (Irish) 'Peace'.

ELLIS (Old Welsh) 'Kind', 'benevolent'.

ENLIL Name borne by a god of air in Mesopotamian mythology. Libra is an air sign.

ERASME Form of Erasmus.

ERASMUS (Greek) 'To Love'. The name has been in occasional use since the 17th century but is rarely found today. St Erasmus was the patron saint of sailors.

ERASTUS (Greek) 'The beloved'.

EROS (Greek) Name of the Greek god of love.

ESME (Old French) 'Loved' or 'esteemed'. The name was popular in Scotland in the 16th century and its use spread to England where it was used as both a boys' and girls' name.

EUSTACE (Old French) 'Well, good'. The name was borne by St Eustace, a Roman soldier martyred in the 2nd century. The name was introduced into Britain by the Normans. It was in regular use during the Middle Ages and remains in use today.

EZRA (Hebrew) 'The one who helps'. Borne by a prophet of the Old Testament. It was adopted by the Puritans and used in Britain and the USA until the end of the 19th century.

FARQUHAR (Gaelic) 'Friendly man' or 'very dear one'. The name was borne by an early King of Scotland. The name is still used occasionally in Scotland but is little used elsewhere.

FERDINAND (Old German) 'Courageous peacemaker'. The name has been used in Spanish royal families from an early date. The name spread to Britain in the 16th century where it has been in occasional use ever since.

FREDERICK (Old German) 'Peaceful ruler'.

FREY (Old English) 'The lord of peace and prosperity'. From the name of the Norse god.

GALBANUM Name of the lucky perfume for Libra.

GARETH (Welsh) 'Gentle'.

GEOFFREY, JEFFREY (Old German) 'Gift of peace'. The name spread from France into Britain in the 11th century. The name became little used after the 16th century but was revived in the late 19th century.

GLADWIN (Old English) 'Kind friend'.

GODFREY (Old German) 'God's peace'. The name was introduced into Britain at the time of the Norman Conquest. The name was fairly well used in the Middle Ages and is in occasional use today.

GOODWIN (Old English) 'Good friend'. Originally a surname, transferred use to that of a first name.

GLADWYN (Old English) 'Glad friend'. Originally a surname, transferred use to that of a first name.

GWYDDION In Welsh mythology the name is borne by the lord of the skies. Libra is an air sign. In mythology Gwyddion is the father of Lleu Llaw Gyffes.

HARMAN, HARMOND (Greek) 'Peace, harmony'.

HEDDWYN (Welsh) 'Peace' and 'white'.

HUGH (Old French) 'Heart, mind, spirit'. The name was used by the aristocracy in medieval France, in Britain until the end of the 18th century but is rarely found today.

HUMPHREY (Old English) Means both 'strength' and 'peace'. The name existed in Britain before the Norman Conquest but was influenced by the Normans to form the name as we know it today. Humphrey is still in occasional use today, a famous bearer of the name being the US actor Humphrey Bogart.

ING In Norse mythology Ing is the name given to the god of peace.

ION (Greek) 'Purple-coloured jewel'. Purple is a lucky colour for Libra.

JARED (Hebrew) 'Rose'. The rose is a lucky plant for Libra. The name is found in the Old Testament and was adopted by the Puritans in the 17th century. It was revived in the latter half of the 20th century.

JARON (Bohemian) 'Firm peace'.

JARRED, JARROD Alternative spellings of Jared.

JEDIDIAH (Hebrew) 'Beloved or friend (of the Lord)'. The name was used by the Puritans in the 17th century but is rarely found today.

JONAH (Hebrew) 'Dove', the symbol of peace. The name was borne by a prophet of the Old Testament. The name was readopted by the Puritans after the Reformation and is still occasionally in use today.

JONAS Form of Jonah. The name was fairly common in medieval Britain.

JUSTIN, JUSTYN (Latin) 'Just'. The name was borne by several early saints including a 2nd-century Christian apologist St Justin Martyr. Justin was rarely found outside Ireland until the latter half of the 20th century, when it became particularly popular in other English-speaking countries.

KAMA (Sanskrit) 'Love'. Name of the Hindu god of love, equivalent to Cupid in Greek mythology.

KANE (Welsh) 'Beautiful'. The name is in occasional use as a first name in English-speaking countries, Australia in particular.

LEWIN (Old English) 'Beloved friend'.

MALCOLM (Gaelic) 'Servant or disciple of Columba'. Columba means 'dove' the symbol of peace. Malcolm was the name borne by four Scottish kings. It was used in Scotland from the end of the Middle Ages until the early-20th century when it spread to other English-speaking countries.

MANFRED (Old German) 'Peaceful man'. The name was introduced into Britain by the Normans.

MINGO (Gaelic) 'Amiable'.

MUNGA (Scottish) 'Dearest friend'. Gaelic form of Mungo.

MUNGO (Scottish) 'Dearest friend' or 'beloved'. The name is mainly found in Scotland.

NEVIN (Old English) 'Middle'.

OLIVER (Latin) 'The olive tree' hence 'the symbol of peace'. The name was fairly well-used in Britain during and after the Middle Ages. The name became less popular in the late 17th century but was revived in the 19th century and remains in use today.

ORWIN (Old German) 'Golden friend'.

OSCAR (Old Irish) 'Friend'. The name was rarely found in Britain from the time of the Norman conquest until the 18th century. The name was borne by two Swedish kings in the 19th century. In more recent times the name has been associated with Oscar Wilde, the Irish poet and dramatist, and with the annual awards for achievement in the film industry made by the American Academy of Motion Picture Arts and Science.

PAICE (Old French) 'Peace'.

PHILEMON (Greek) 'Affectionate' or 'kiss'. The name is the title of one of the books of the New Testament. The name was adopted by the Puritans but is little used today.

PHILO (Greek) 'Friendly love'.

RAS Shortened form of Erasmus or Erastus.

RASMUS (Greek) Form of Erasmus. 'Beloved'.

RASTUS (Greek) 'To love'. The name occurs in the New Testament as a shortened form of the Latin name Erastus.

SAITH (Welsh) 'Seven'. Libra is the seventh sign of the zodiac.

SELWYN Name of uncertain origin. It may be from Old English meaning 'prosperous friend' or it may be a combination of two Welsh words meaning 'ardour' and 'fair'.

SEPTIMUS (Latin) 'Seventh'. Libra is the seventh sign of the zodiac.

SHANNON (Hebrew) 'Peaceful'.

SHEEHAN (Gaelic) 'The peaceful one'.

SIEGFRIED (Old German) 'Peaceful victory'. The name has been in occasional use in the English-speaking world since the late-19th century.

SOLOMAN (Hebrew) 'Peace'. King Solomon of the Old Testament was considered someone of great wisdom. In the Middle Ages the name was in regular use in Britain. It was revived by the Puritans but is generally used as a Jewish name today.

STILLMAN, STILMAN (Old English) 'Quiet and gentle man'.

TAFFY 'Beloved' or 'friend'. Pet form of David.

TAI (Chinese) 'Peace'.

TEX Generally used as a nickname for someone from Texas, the name is sometimes given as a first name in the USA. 'Texas' is derived from an Indian name meaning 'Friends'.

TIBON (Hebrew) 'Lover of Nature'.

TIVIAN Derived from Tibon.

TIVON Derived from Tibon.

VENN (Gaelic) 'Fair'.

VERDANT (Latin) 'Green, spring-like'. Green is a lucky colour for Libra.

WILFRED, WILFRID, WILFRYD (Old English) 'Hope for peace'. The name was borne by St Wilfrid, a 7th-century Bishop of York. The name was revived in the 19th century and was in regular use until the mid-20th century.

WINFRED (Old English) 'Peaceful friend'. The name is rarely found in modern times.

YARILO (Slavonic) 'God of love'.

Libra ~ Girls

ACCORD (Old French) 'Harmony'.

AIMEE (French) 'Beloved friend'.

AINE (Irish) Pronounced 'ah-na'. Name given to the ancient Irish god of love. The name means 'delight' or 'pleasure'.

ALAIN, ALAYNE, ALYNE (Celtic) 'Harmony'. Feminine forms of Alan.

ALANA, ALANNA, ALAYNA, ALANNAH (Celtic) 'Harmony'. Feminine forms of Alan.

ALANDA Recent feminine form of Alan.

ALIKA (Nigerian) 'Outstanding beauty'.

ALLENE, ALLYN Feminine forms of Alan.

ALVA Form of Alvina.

ALVINA (Old English) 'Beloved friend'. Also the name given to a 'continent' on the surface of Venus, the ruling planet of Libra.

AMABEL (Latin) 'Loveable' or 'my beautiful one'. The name was in regular use in medieval times and was revived in the 19th century.

AMANDA (Latin) 'Lovable'. The name has possibly been in existence since the Middle Ages, although some schools of thought believe that it was invented in the 17th century. The name became increasingly popular in the mid-20th century.

AMATA Form of Amy.

AMECIA (Latin) 'Love'.

AMELINDA (Latin) 'Beloved and pretty'.

AMERA A blend of Amy and Vera. 'Love and faith'.

AMIA (Latin) 'Love'. Form of Amy.

AMICA (Latin) 'Friend'.

AMICE Of uncertain origin. Possibly a form of Amy or a French form of Amica.

AMICIA Form of Amice.

AMINTA (Latin) 'Loving'.

AMORETTA (Latin) 'Loved one'.

AMY (Old French) Form of Aimee. 'Loved'. The name has been in use since the 13th century. It enjoyed a revival in the 19th century but did not become popular in the USA until the late-20th century.

ANDRIS (Welsh) 'Very fair'.

ANGHARAD (Welsh) 'Much loved'. The name was in use in medieval Welsh folk tales.

ANGWEN (Welsh) 'Beautiful'.

ANNABEL, ANNABELLE (Latin) 'Lovable'. A form of Amabel. Annabel has been used as a first name in Scotland since the Middle Ages. It was the name of the mother of King James

I of Scotland, Annabel Drummond. The name has become used in other English-speaking countries since the 19th century although the spelling Annabelle has only been in use since the mid-20th century.

ANNABELLA Form of Annabel.

ANWEN (Welsh) 'Very fair'.

APHRODITE (Greek) Name given to the goddess of love in Greek mythology. The name is also given to 'continent' on the surface of the planet Venus.

ARABELLA Form of Annabel. The name was borne by Lady Arabella Stuart, a cousin of King James VI of Scotland. The name was popular in England in the 18th century.

ARAMINTA (Latin) 'Loving'. Possibly a combination of Arabella and Aminta.

AROHA (Maori) 'Love'.

ASTRID (Old Norse) 'Divine beauty'.

AXELLE (Old German) 'Mother of peace'. Feminine form of Axel.

AYLWEN (Welsh) 'Fair'.

BEL, BELL, BELLE Shortened forms of Annabelle. Also associated with the French belle, meaning 'beautiful'.

BELINDA (Latin) 'Wise beauty'. The name has been in use in English-speaking countries since the 18th century.

BELLA Shortened form of Annabella. Also associated with the Italian word *bella* meaning 'beautiful'.

BO (French) Phonetic form of Beau, meaning 'beautiful'.

BRANWEN Name of a goddess of love and death in Welsh Druid mythology.

CALDORA (Greek) 'Beautiful gift'.

CALISTA, CALLISTA, CALISE (Greek) 'Of extraordinary beauty'.

CALLA (Greek) 'Beautiful'.

CANACE (Latin) 'The daughter of the wind'. Libra is an air sign.

CARA, KARA (Italian) 'Dearest friend'. The name has been in use since the the early part of the 20th century and became increasingly fashionable in the 1970s.

CAREL, CARELLA, CARELLE (Old English) 'Dear' or 'carer'.

CARINA, KARINA (Latin) 'Beloved'. Carina is also the name given to a star

CARITA Form of Carina or Cara.

CAROMY (Celtic) 'Friend'.

CARON, CARRON (Welsh) 'To love'.

CARREN Variant of Caron.

CARYL Form of Carys.

CARYS (Welsh) 'Love'.

CERI (Welsh) 'To love' or 'loved one'.

CERIA Derived from Ceri.

CERIAL Derived from Ceri.

CERYS Derived from Ceri.

CHARITY (Latin) 'Affectionate'. The name was adopted by the Puritans but is not so commonly found today.

CHATTIE Pet form of Charity.

CHER, CHERE, CHERIE, CHERRIE, CHERI (French) 'Dear one'.

CHERIDA (Spanish) 'Beloved one'. Form of Querida.

CHERINE, CHERISE, CHERISSA, CHERITA Variants of Cherie.

CHERITH (Latin) 'Hold dear', 'cherish'.

CHERRY Pet form of Charity, sometimes used as a name in its own right.

CHERYL Form of Carys.

COLINE, COLUMBINA, COLUMBINE, COLUMBIA, COLOMBE, COLLY Variations of Columba.

COLUMBA (Latin) 'The dove'. One of peaceful disposition.

CONCORD (Latin) 'Harmony'.

COPPER Copper is a lucky metal for Libra.

COSINA, COSIMA (Greek) 'World harmony'.

DARLA (Middle English) 'Loved one'.

DARLENE, DARLEEN (Old English) 'Dearly beloved'. From the English word darling. Used occasionally as a first name, particularly in the USA and Canada, in the mid-20th century.

DARLIN, DARLINE (Old English) 'Loved one'.

DARYL, DAREL, DARELLE, DARRELLE (Old English) 'Loved one' or 'dearly beloved'. Forms of Darlene.

DARYN Derived from Darlin.

DAVIDA 'Beloved'. Scottish feminine form of David.

DAVINA Scottish feminine form of David.

DAVINIA Scottish feminine form of David.

DINAH (Hebrew) 'Judgement'. The name occurs in the Old Testament. It was regularly used by the Puritans who introduced it into the USA where it became particularly fashionable.

EASTER Form of Ester.

EDWINA (Old English) 'Friend'. Feminine form of Edwin.

ELVINA (Old English) 'Noble friend'. Feminine form of Elvin.

ELVIRA (Spanish form of German origin) 'True'. The name was popular in Spain during the Middle Ages and spread to English-speaking countries in the 19th century.

EMERALD (Greek) After the name of the gemstone. Emerald is a lucky gemstone for Libra.

ESME (Old French) 'Loved or 'esteemed'.

ESMERELDA (Spanish) 'Emerald'. Emerald is a lucky gem for Libra. The name has been in occasional use in English-speaking countries since the 19th century.

ESTER, ESTHER (Persian) 'Star', in particular reference to the planet Venus. It is also a form of Ishtar, the name borne by the Babylonian goddess of love. The name was in regular use in English-speaking countries until the mid-20th century.

FONDA (English) 'Affectionate'.

FREDA (Old German) 'Peace'. One who is calm and unhurried.

FRIEDA, FREIDA, FRIDA, FRIEDA, FREDDIE Forms of Freda.

FREYA (Old Norse) Goddess of love in Scandinavian mythology. The name has been in occasional use in English-speaking countries since the beginning of the 20th century.

GALBANUM Lucky perfume for Libra.

GALINA (Greek) 'Peace'.

GRANIA (Irish) 'Love'. The name was borne by a character of Gaelic legend who eloped with Diamuid. The name is rarely found outside Ireland.

HARMONEL A modern name meaning 'harmony of the elves'.

HARMONIA (Greek) 'Unifying'.

HARMONY (Greek) 'Concord'.

HATHOR Name of a goddess of love in Egyptian mythology. Hathor was also known as a moon goddess and as a water goddess.

HAVIVA (Hebrew) 'Beloved'.

HERTHA (Old German) 'Earth Mother'.

HESTER Form of Esther.

HYACINTH (Greek) A flower-name meaning 'blue gem or sapphire'. In Greek mythology, the Hyacinth flower grew out of the blood of the youth Hyacinthus, who was accidently killed by Apollo. The name Hyacinth was originally used as a boys' name. Its use as a girls' name is a fairly recent adoption.

INARET (Welsh) 'Much loved'.

INGA, INGE (Old Norse) Pet form of Ingeborg 'the protection of Ing'. In Norse mythology Ing is the god of peace.

INGRID Scandinavian form of Inga.

IONA (Greek) Purple-coloured jewel. Purple is a lucky colour for Libra.

IONE Form of Iona.

IORWEN (Welsh) 'Beautiful'.

IRANA Form of Irene.

IRENA Polish form of Irene.

IRENE (Greek) 'Peace'. In Greek mythology Irene is the name of a minor goddess of peace. The name was also borne by an early Christian martyr and several Byzantine empresses. The name has been in use in English-speaking countries since the 19th century and became particularly popular in the early 20th century.

IRINA Form of Irene.

ISHTAR (Mesopotamian) Name of the Babylonian goddess of love. Ishtar Terra is also the name of a 'continent' on the surface of the planet Venus.

ISOLDA, ISOLDE (Celtic) 'The fair one'. The name was borne in Arthurian legend by the tragic lover of Tristan.

JAHOLA (Hebrew) 'Dove'.

JAMEELA, JAMELLA (Arabic) 'Beautiful'.

JAMIL (Arabic) 'Beautiful'.

JEMIE, JEMMIE Pet forms of Jemima.

JEMIMA (Hebrew) 'Dove'. The dove is a symbol of peace. The name is found in the Old Testament, being the name of one of the three beautiful daughters of Job. The name was used by the Puritans in the 17th century and has been in use since that time.

JEMINA (Hebrew) 'Peace'. Form of Jemima.

JEMIRA Blend of Jemima and Mira. Mira is from the Greek for myrrh, a sweet-smelling oil.

JEMITA A blend of Jemima and Rita. Rita is an Italian or Spanish variation of Margaret, meaning 'pearl'.

JEMMA Form of Jemima.

JUSTINA 'Just'. Latin feminine form of Justin.

JUSTINE 'Just'. French feminine form of Justin.

KALILA (Arabic) 'Beloved'.

KALYCA (Greek) 'Rosebud'. The rose is a lucky plant for Libra.

KANAKA, KANAKE 'The daughter of the wind'. Forms of Canace.

KANANI (Hawaiian) 'A beauty'.

KARENZAZA (Cornish) 'Love and affection'.

KASHIMA Form of Kasmira.

KASMIRA (Slavonic) 'Commander of peace'.

KASOTA (Native American) 'Clear sky'. Libra is an air sign.

KAYNA (Cornish) 'Beautiful'.

KERANZA (Cornish) 'Love', 'affection'.

KIRI (Maori) 'Fair'.

KOREN, KORE (Greek) 'Beautiful maiden'.

KORENZA Italian from of Koren.

LAILA, LAYLA, LILA Forms of Leila.

LAIS (Greek) 'Adored'.

LANI, LANIE (Hawaiian) 'Sky'. Libra is an air sign.

LEALA (French) 'The true one'. One who is true to home, family and friends.

LEEBA (Yiddish) 'Beloved'.

LEILA (Arabic) 'Dark beauty'. The name has been in use in English-speaking countries since the 19th century.

LENE Form of Lenis.

LENIS (Latin) 'Smooth and white as a lily'. The lily is the symbol of peace, an important attribute of Libra.

LENITA, LENETA Form of Lenis.

LENOS Form of Lenis.

LENTA Form of Lenis.

LILIAN, LILLIAN (Latin) 'Lily'. The lily is a symbol of peace. The name has been used in Britain since the 16th century and was particularly popular at the turn of the 20th century.

LILIAS, LILLIAS Scottish forms of Lilian.

LILLA, LILLAH Forms of Lily.

LILY, LILLIE (Latin) 'Lily'. The symbol of peace.

LYNWEN (Welsh) 'Fair image'.

MABEL (French) 'My beautiful one' or 'loveable'. Form of Amabel. The name has been used as a name in its own right since the 12th century. It was a popular name in the late-19th and early-20th centuries.

MABELINE Form of Mabel.

MABELLE, MAYBELLE, MAYBEL
Forms of Mabel.

MAHALA, MAHALAH, MAHALIA
(Hebrew) 'Tenderness'. The name has
been in occasional use in English-
speaking countries since the 17th
century.

MALU (Hawaiian) 'Peace'.

MALVA (Greek) 'Tender'.

MAUVE (Latin) From the name of a
purple-coloured mallow plant. Purple
is a lucky colour for Libra.

MEHALA, MEHALAH, MEHALIA
Forms of Mahala.

MELWYN (Cornish) 'Fair as honey'.

MERTICE Form of Myrtle.

MERTLE Form of Myrtle.

MERNA, MIRNA (Gaelic) 'Beloved'.

MILDRED (Old English) 'Gentle
strength'.

MIMA Shortened form of Jemima.

MINA Shortened form of Jemina.

MIRLE Form of Myrtle.

MOCARA (Gaelic) 'My friend'.

MOINA, MOYNA Forms of Myrna.

MORENWYNA (Cornish) 'Fair
maiden'.

MORNA (Gaelic) 'Beloved', 'gentle'.
Anglicized form of Muirne.

MUIRNE (Irish Gaelic) 'Beloved'.
Pronounced 'moor-nya'.

MYRNA 'Beloved.' Anglicized form of
Muirne. This form is more usually
found than Morna.

MYRTA Form of Myrtle.

MYRTIA Form of Myrtle.

MYRTILLA Form of Myrtle.

MYRTIS Form of Myrtle.

MYRTLE (Greek) From the name of the flowering shrub. Myrtle is a lucky plant for Libra. The name means 'Victorious crown'. The name was popular in the 19th century.

NAAVA (Hebrew) 'Beautiful', 'pleasant'.

NAJINA, NAJMA (Arabic) 'Benevolent'.

NALANI (Hawaiian) 'Calmness of the heavens'.

NAMA (Hebrew) 'Pleasant', 'beautiful'.

NOELANI (Hawaiian) 'Beautiful one from heaven'.

NOYA (Hebrew) 'Beautiful'.

OLATHE (Native American) 'Beautiful'.

OLIFF Form of Olive.

OLIVE (Latin) 'Olive'. A symbol of peace. In medieval times the name occurred in a variety of forms. Olive has been in use as a first name since the 16th century and became particularly popular in the 1920s.

OLIVET Form of Olive. The name was found in medieval times.

OLIVIA An Italian form of Olive. The name became fashionable in English-speaking countries in the 18th century.

ORAN (Irish) 'Green'. Green is a lucky colour for Libra.

ORANDA A blend of Oran and Amanda. Amanda is a Latin name meaning lovable.

ORANTHA A blend of Oran and Samantha. Samantha is an Aramaic name meaning 'listener'.

PACIFA (Latin) 'Peace loving'.

PALOMA (Spanish) 'Dove', 'a gentle, tender girl'.

PALOMETA, PALOMITA Forms of Paloma.

PAMPHILA (Greek) 'All-loving'.

PATIENCE (English) 'Patience'. The name was adopted by the Puritans after the reformation and is still found in English-speaking countries today.

PAZ (Spanish) 'Peace'.

PEACE (English) 'Peace, harmony'. Adopted by the Puritans after the reformation but is rarely found today.

PHILA (Greek) 'Love'.

PHILANA A blend of Phila and Lana. Lana is a Latin name meaning 'wool'.

PHILANTHA A blend of Phila and Samantha. Samantha is an Aramaic name meaning 'listener'.

PHILENA (Greek) 'Lover of Mankind'.

PHILINA (Greek) 'Lover of Mankind'.

PHILOMENA (Latin) 'To love' and 'Strength'. The name came more frequently in use in the 19th century after the supposed discovery in 1802 of the relics of St Philomena in Rome.

PHILOMON (Greek) 'Affectionate'.

PINK Lucky colour for Libra.

PLACIDA (Latin) 'Peaceful one'.

PLACIDIA Form of Placida.

PURPLE A lucky colour for Libra.

QUERIDA (Spanish) 'Beloved one'. A term of endearment.

RABIA (Arabic) 'Fragrant breeze'. Libra is an air sign.

RATI (Indian) Goddess of love.

RAYA (Hebrew) 'Friend'.

REIKA (Japanese) 'Beautiful flower'.

RENE, RENIE Pet forms of Irene.

RHODA (Greek) 'Rose'. The rose is a lucky plant for Libra. The name Rhoda is mentioned in the New Testament and has been in general use since the 17th century.

RHODIA Form of Rhoda.

RHONWEN (Welsh) 'Fair'.

RHONA Form of Rhonwen.

ROHA (Maori) 'Rose'. The rose is a lucky plant for Libra.

ROIS (Latin) 'Rose'. The rose is a lucky plant for Libra.

ROISIN Irish form of Rose. The rose is a lucky plant for Libra.

ROLANDA (Old German) 'Land'. Feminine form of Roland.

ROSA Latinized form of Rose. The rose is a lucky plant for Libra. The name Rosa was not used as a name in its own right until the 19th century.

ROSABEL, ROSABELLE, ROSABELLA Forms of Rose, translating into 'beautiful rose'.

ROSALEE Form of Rose.

ROSALEEN Irish form of Rose.

ROSALIA, ROSALEA (Latin) 'Rose'. The name was borne by St Roselia, a 12th-century patron saint of Palermo. Occasionally found in English-speaking countries.

ROSALIE, ROSALEE (Latin) 'Rose'.

ROSALIND, ROSALYND Name of uncertain origin. It may be from Old French, meaning 'tender, soft', or from Spanish origin, meaning 'pretty rose'.

ROSALINDA (Spanish) 'Pretty rose'. The rose is a lucky flower for Libra.

ROSALINE, ROSALIN Form of Rosalind.

ROSALYN, ROSALYNN Altered forms of Rosalind.

ROSALYNNE Alternative spelling of Rosalyn.

ROSAN, ROSANN, ROSANNE Blend of Rose and Ann. Ann is a Hebrew name meaning 'graceful'.

ROSANDA Blend of Rose and Wanda. Wanda is a Slavonic name meaning 'the wanderer'.

ROSANNA Blend of Rose and Anna. Anna is a Hebrew name meaning 'grace'.

ROSANNAGH Elaborated spelling of Rosanna.

ROSANTHA Blend of Rose and Samantha. Samantha is a Aramaic name meaning 'to listen'.

ROSARIA Blend of Rose and Maria. Maria is a Latin name meaning 'drop of the sea'.

ROSE (Latin) From the flower name. The rose is a lucky plant for Libra. The name was particularly popular around the turn of the 20th century and remains in use today.

ROSEAN, ROSEANN Blends of Rose and Ann.

ROSEHANNA, ROSEHANNAH A blend of Rose and Hannah. Hannah is a Hebrew name meaning 'graceful'.

ROSELIA (Latin) 'A garland of roses'.

ROSELIE French form of Rosalia. The name has been in use in English-speaking countries since the mid-19th century.

ROSELIND Form of Rosalind.

ROSELINE, ROSELYN Forms of Rosaline.

ROSELLA, ROSELLE, ROSEL Forms of Rose.

ROSELYN A blend of Rose and Lyn. Lyn is a Celtic name meaning 'waterfall'.

ROSEN (Cornish) 'Rose'.

ROSENA, ROSENE Forms of Rose.

ROSETTA Italian form of Rose. The name has been in occasional use in English-speaking countries since the 18th century.

ROSETTE Form of Rosetta.

ROSHEEN Phonetic form of Roisin, the Irish form of Rose.

ROSIA Form of Rose.

ROSIE, ROSY, ROSI Pet forms of Rose, occasionally used as a name in their own right.

ROSILYN, ROSLYN Forms of Rosaline.

ROSINA Italian form of Rose.

ROSINDA A blend of Rose and Linda. Linda is a Spanish name meaning 'pretty'.

ROSITA Spanish form of Rose.

ROSINTHA A blend of Rose and Cynthia. Cynthia is a Greek name meaning 'moon goddess'.

ROSIRA A blend of Rose and Mira. Mira is a Latin name meaning 'admired'.

ROSLYN, ROSSLYN Form of Rosaline.

ROSSALYN, ROSSLYN Forms of Rosalind.

ROWENA 'Fair'. Form of Rhonwen.

ROZA, ROZ Forms of Rose.

ROZAN A blend of Rose and Ann.

ROZELLA Blend of Rose and Ella. Ella is an Old German name meaning 'all'.

ROZELLO Form of Rose.

ROZENA, ROZINA Forms of Rosina, Italian form of Rose.

ROZLYN A blend of Rose and Lyn.

SALEMA (Hebrew) 'Peace'.

SEPTA (Latin) 'Seven'. Libra is the seventh sign of the zodiac.

SEPTIMA (Latin) 'Seventh'. Libra is the seventh sign of the zodiac.

SHALOM (Hebrew) 'Peace, wholeness'.

SALOMA, SALOMI Forms of Salome.

SALOME (Hebrew) 'Peace'. The name was borne by the granddaughter of Herod the Great in the New Testament. The name has been in occasonal use in English-speaking countries since the 17th century.

SERENA (Latin) 'Calm'. The name has been in occasional use in English-speaking countries since the 18th century.

SHAINA (Yiddish) 'Beautiful'.

SHANTI (Sanskrit) 'Peace'.

SHARA Derivative of Sharon.

SHARON, SHARRON (Hebrew) 'A princess of exotic beauty'. Also taken from the Plain of Sharon in the Holy Land. The name was taken up as a first name in the 17th century. It spread to England from the USA in the early 20th century.

SHERRY, SHARRY SHARI, SHARRI Forms of Sharon.

SHIFRA (Hebrew) 'Beautiful'.

SHIMONEL Modern name meaning 'peace of the elves'.

SHIZU (Japanese) 'Quiet, clear'.

SHUKA Form of Shula.

SHULA, SULA, SHULIE (Arabic) 'Peace'.

SHUNA, SHUNE Forms of Shula.

SHUSHANA, SHUSHANNA Forms of Susannah. These forms have been in use in English-speaking countries since the 17th century.

SIGRID (Old German) 'Victory-peace'. Feminine form of Siegfried.

SUSAN Form of Susannah. The name has been in regular use since the 18th century. In the mid-20th century it was one of the most well-used girls' names in English-speaking countries.

SUSANNAH, SUSANNA, SUZANNA (Hebrew) 'Lily'. The lily is the symbol of peace, a characteristic of Libra. The name is found in both the Old Testament and the New Testament. The name was readopted by the Puritans after the Reformation and has been in use throughout English-speaking countries since that time.

SUSANNE, SUZANNE French form of Susannah. The name has been in frequent use throughout English-speaking countries since the early-20th century.

SUE, SUSIE, SUZY Pet forms of Susan, Susannah or Suzette.

SUZETTE French form of Susannah.

THEIA Name given to a vulcano on the surface of Venus, the ruling planet of Libra.

THEMIS In classical mythology the name was borne by the goddess of Justice.

THIRZA (Hebrew) 'Pleasantness'.

TIKA (Maori) 'Just'.

TIRZAH Form of Thirza.

TIRION (Welsh) 'Kind, gentle'. Name of modern time.

TLAZOLTEOTI (Peruvian Indian) Goddess of love.

TOYA (Sioux) 'Green'. Green is a lucky colour for Libra.

TRUGAREDD (Welsh) 'Loving kindness'.

VARDA (Hebrew) 'Rose'. The rose is a lucky plant for Libra.

VASHTI, VASSY (Persian) 'Beautiful'.

VASTI (Persian) 'Most beautiful one'.

VENITA 'The goddess of love'. Form of Venus.

VENUS (Greek) 'To love'. Name of the ruling planet of Libra. Venus is the goddess of love in Greek mythology.

VERA (Russian) 'Faith', 'truth'. Also (Latin) 'True'. The name was introduced into Britain at the beginning of the 20th century and was particularly popular for the first half of the century.

VERDA (Old French) 'Green, spring-like'.

VERENA Elaboration of Vera.

VERITY (Old French) 'Truth'. Adopted by the Puritans after the Reformation and is still occasionally found today.

VIDA, VINA Shortened forms of Davina, 'beloved' or 'friend'.

VINITA (Latin) 'Of incomparable loveliness'. Derivative of Venus.

VINNY, VINNIE Pet forms of Venus.

WAHKUNA (Native American) 'Beautiful'.

WILFREDA (Old German) 'The peacemaker'. Feminine form of Wilfred.

WILFRIEDA, WILFREIDA Forms of Wilfreda.

WINIFRED (Welsh) 'Blessed reconciliation'. The name was borne by a Welsh saint of the 7th century.

WINIFRIDA, WINIFREIDA, WINIFRIEDA Forms of Winifred.

WINNIE, WINNY Shortened forms of Winifred.

WINOLA (Old German) 'Gracious friend'.

WYANET (Native American) 'Incredibly beautiful'.

WYOMIA (Native American) 'Unusually beautiful'.

YELENA (Latin) 'Lily blossom'. The lily is a the symbol of peace, an important attribute of Libra.

YOSHE (Japanese) 'Beautiful one'.

ZEFIRA (Italian) 'Breeze'. Libra is an air sign.

ZELINDA, ZERLINDA (Hebrew/Latin) 'Beautiful dawn'.

ZERLINA (Old German) 'Serenely beautiful'.

ZUBEN 'UBI The name of a star in the constellation of Libra.

ZULEIKA (Arabic) 'Fair' or 'beautiful'.

ZULEMA (Arabic) 'Peace'.

Scorpio

m,

THE SCORPION
23 October – 21 November

RULING PLANETS — Mars and Pluto. In astrology Mars is the planet of aggressive energy and Pluto is the planet of hidden depths and magnetic forces.

ELEMENT — Water

General characteristics
- Magnetic, secretive, intense.
- Protective, compassionate.
- Displays studious concentration.
- Dynamic, passionate.
- Emotional, sensual.
- Loyal, faithful.
- Concerned with birth, re-birth, life and death.

Characteristics of young Scorpio
- Tends to be secretive.
- Is emotional and sometimes moody.
- Often understands others.
- Is a loving and loyal member of the family.
- Displays compassion.
- Can be wary of strangers.

Scorpion lucky connections
Gemstones:	ruby, turquoise, snakestone
Colours:	deep red, blue-green
Plants:	ivy, oak, cactus
Perfume:	Siamese benzoin
Metals:	iron, steel
Animals:	wolf, lizard
Tarot card:	regeneration

SCORPIO is a sign of extremes, of intense loves and hates and one of the main characteristics of a Scorpio child is her emotional intensity. Your young Scorpio will possess powerful feelings which are not always openly expressed. She may hold her feelings deep within her, often giving her a calm exterior. However from time to time the strength of her feelings can erupt with volcanic intensity.

Scorpios have a deep need to respond to their world on an emotional level. Even in babyhood you may find that, rather than grasp at a new toy she will pick it up slowly, caress it and explore it. They need to explore and to discover their world in a sensitive manner, so allow your little Scorpio time to experience new situations and objects in her own meaningful way.

Young Scorpios have a tendency to respond strongly to new stimulation. Never one to do anything by halves you may find that if she takes a dislike to a new activity she will kick and scream and refuse to participate. If she doesn't like bath time for example, it is better to introduce water to her slowly, and give her, in her own time, the opportunity to explore the new

medium in her own thorough way. You will probably discover that, in no time, she learns to love water play.

Scorpios are capable of very intense and deep love and often want to know your innermost thoughts and feelings. You may often find your young Scorpio asking you what you are thinking. Or maybe she does not need to ask – she will often instinctively know.

Scorpios love secrecy and mystery. Although they may want to know your secrets they may not be nearly so keen to divulge their own. This love of secrecy is a useful tool in dealing with your little Scorpio. If she is in a dark mood, telling her a little secret is a good way of pleasing her and boosting her sense of self-worth. The fact that you thought her trustworthy enough to share a secret will boost her confidence. She will also enjoy owning a little secret treasure box, somewhere she can hide the special little things that mean so much to her. In addition a little secret den in her bedroom or the garden will provide her with the security that she readily needs.

You may find that your young Scorpio's capacity for focused emotions leads her to be loyal but also possessive. She may want all your attention, not willing to share it with siblings or your partner. She may also display this part of her nature in the friendships she makes. She may be careful about who she makes friends. When she chooses a friend she'll be loyal and true, but again possibly possessive. If the friendship ends she may be terribly hurt, the intensity of her feelings taking her to depths as well as highs.

Ensuring that your Scorpio child has outlets for physical play will help to channel her emotions into a different energy. Imaginative play is also a useful outlet for your young Scorpio. Fairy stories, mythology and stories of magic and mystery will all fascinate her. Not only will she be interested and intrigued, but they will also provide her with an alternative outlet for all those emotions.

Your young Scorpio will also enjoy complicated or intriguing puzzles and you may be astonished at the quiet determination she displays in mastering the skills necessary to complete them. This steady determination and self-discipline is a valuable part of your young Scorpio's make up and will provide her with the building blocks of success in later life.

Scorpio ~ Boys

ACKERLEY (Old English) 'Oak tree meadow'. The oak is a lucky plant for Scorpio.

ACKLEY (Old English) 'From the oak tree meadow'. The oak is a lucky plant for Scorpio.

ACTON (Old English) 'Oak tree village'. The oak is a lucky plant for Scorpio.

ADAIR (Gaelic) 'From the oak tree near the ford'. The oak is a lucky plant for Scorpio. The name has been used as both a first name and surname for centuries.

ADOLPH, ADOLPHUS, ADOLF (Old German) 'Noble wolf'. The wolf is a lucky animal for Scorpio. Adolphus was used by German aristocracy in the 17th and 18th centuries. It was introduced into Britain in the 18th century.

ADRIAN (Latin) 'Man from the sea'. Linked to Neptune. The name in the form Hadrian was borne by a 2nd-century Roman emperor who was responsible for the building of Hadrian's Wall across northern England. The name Adrian was only in occasional use until the mid-20th century when it increased in popularity.

AEGIR Name given to the Scandinavian god of the sea.

AFON (Welsh) 'River'.

AIKEN (Old English) 'Made of oak'. The oak is a lucky plant for Scorpio.

ALTON (Old English) 'Old stream source'.

AMBROSE (Greek) 'Immortal'. The name was borne by a 4th-century saint. It is most frequently found in Ireland.

AMMON (Egyptian) 'The hidden'.

ANSCOM (Old English) 'Dweller in the secret valley'. A solitary, awe-inspiring man.

ANTARES Name given to the bright star in the constellation of Scorpio. It is a bright red star meaning 'The rival of Mars'. Antares marks the head of the 'scorpion' in the constellation of Scorpio and is easily spotted in the night sky.

ARABIA Name given to the large, heavily cratered, circular area of Mars.

ARES Name of the Roman god of war, the equivalent of Mars. Mars is the ruling planet of Scorpio.

AVON (Welsh) 'River'.

ATWATER (Old English) 'One who lives by the water'.

ATWELL (Old English) 'From the spring'. One who lives by a natural well.

BARDOLPH (Old English) 'Bright wolf'. The wolf is a lucky animal for Scorpio. The name was introduced into Britain by the Normans but is seldom found today.

BLUE Blue-green is a lucky colour for Scorpio.

BOTOLF, BOTOLPH, BOTOLPHE (Old English) 'Herald wolf'. The wolf is a lucky animal for Scorpio. The name was borne by St Botulf in the 7th century. It is seldom found today.

BOURNE, BOURN (Old English) 'A brook'.

BRAN Name of the god of war in Welsh Druid mythology. Bran was also the guardian of the land.

BURNE, BURN (Old English) 'A brook'.

BYRNE (Old English) 'A brook'.

CACTUS The cactus is a lucky plant for Scorpio.

CHENEY (French) 'Oak forest dweller'. The oak is a lucky plant for Scorpio.

CHESNEY (French) 'Oak grove'. The oak is a lucky plant for Scorpio.

CHEYNEY Form of Cheney.

CLANCY 'Red warrior'. Transferred use of Irish surname. The name is mainly found in the USA. Originally an Irish surname. Its use as a first name is confined mainly to the USA.

COBURN (Middle English) 'Small stream'.

DAROL Form of Darrel.

DARREL, DARRELL (Old English) 'Grove of oak trees'. The oak is a lucky plant for Scorpio. Originally a French surname and place name it has been in use as a first name since the 19th century.

DARWIN (Old English) 'River where oaks grow'. The oak is a lucky plant for Scorpio. In addition, water is the element of Scorpio.

DEIMOS Name of one of Mars' moons. Named after one of the two mythical horses which drew the chariot of the Greek god of war, Mars. Means 'panic'.

DELMAR (Latin) 'From the sea'.

DELMER (Latin) 'From the sea'.

DERI (Welsh) 'Oak'.

DERON (Old English) 'Water'.

DERWENT (Old English) 'River where oaks grow'.

DOUGLAS (Gaelic) 'Dark blue water'. Originally a Scottish surname and place name. As a surname it was borne by one of the most powerful Scottish families. It began to be used as a first name in the 16th century and became particularly popular in English speaking countries in the first half of the 20th century.

DYLAN (Welsh) 'Man from the sea'. In Welsh mythology the name was borne by a legendary character who became a sea god known as 'the god of the waves'. It was used mainly in Wales until the mid-20th century when its use spread to other English-speaking countries.

EDMAR, EDMER (Old English) 'Rich sea'.

ELBOURNE (Old English) 'Elf stream'.

EMRYS Form of Ambrose.

ENKI Name of a god of water and wisdom in Mesopotamian mythology.

EWART (Old French) 'One who serves water'. Originally a Scottish surname. In occasional use as a first name.

FERRANT (Old French) 'Iron grey'. Iron is a lucky metal for Scorpio.

FERRIS (Latin) 'Iron'. Iron is a lucky metal for Scorpio.

FLANN (Gaelic) 'Lad with the red hair'. Deep red is a lucky colour for Scorpio. The name is a traditional Irish name which was borne by several early Irish heroes.

FLANNAN (Irish) 'Red'. The name was borne in County Clare by an Irish saint.

FLINT (Old English) 'A stream'.

GARRICK (Old English) 'Oak spear'. The oak is a lucky plant for Scorpio. Originally a surname it has been in use as a first name since the 18th century. It is found mainly in the USA.

GERVAIS, GERVAS (Old German) 'Alert warrior'. The name was borne by an early saint. It was introduced into Britain by the Normans and is still infrequently used today.

GRAFFIAS The name of a star in the constellation of Scorpio.

GRIFFIN Form of Griffith.

GRIFFITH (Celtic) 'Fierce red-haired warrior'. The name was borne by several medieval welsh monarchs. As a first name it remains in use in Wales but is found more frequently as a surname in other parts of Britain.

GUNNAR, GUNNER, GUNAR Forms of Gunther.

GUNTER, GUNTAR (Old German) 'War' or 'battle'. The name was introduced into Britain at the time of the Norman Conquest. It remained in regular use until the 15th century. It is now regarded as a German name.

GUNTHER , GUNTHAR (Old German) 'Bold warrior'. The name was introduced into Britain at the time of the Norman Conquest but is little used today.

HY Shortened form of Hyman.

HYMAN (Hebrew) 'Life'.

HYMIE Form of Hyman.

IDRIS (Welsh) 'Ardent lord or impulsive'. The name was borne by a character in Welsh mythology. The mountain Cader Idris in Gwynedd is named after him.

JARVIS, JERVIS, JARVEY, JARV (Old German) 'Alert warrior'. Forms of Gervais.

KAI (Japanese) 'Sea'.

KANE Of uncertain origin. It may be from Celtic, meaning 'warrior' or from a French place Caen, meaning 'field of combat'. Either meaning is appropriate for Scorpio.

KELSEY (Old English) 'Victory'. Originally a surname used occasionally as a first name.

KEMP (Middle English) 'Warrior', 'champion'. Transferred use of a surname which originated from the Middle Ages.

KENELM (Old English) 'Brave helmet' or 'brave protection'. The name was popular in the Middle Ages when a 9th-century Prince of Mercia of this name was revered as a saint and martyr. The name is rarely found today.

KENWARD (Old English) 'Brave guard'.

KELSEY (Old English) 'From the water'. Originally an Old English surname. It is occasionally used as both a girls' and boys' name.

KIMBALL Of uncertain origin. It may be from Old English, meaning 'bold family' or Welsh, meaning 'chief' and 'war'. Both meanings are appropriate for Scorpio.

KUANTI Name given to the god of war in Chinese mythology. Mars, one of the ruling planets of Scorpio, is the Roman god of war.

LEMARR, LEMAR (Latin) 'Of the sea'.

LOVELL (French) 'Wolf-cub'. The wolf is a lucky animal for Scorpio. Originally a medieval surname it has been in occasional use as a first name since the 11th century.

LOWELL Form of Lovell. Lowell is used as a first name mainly in the USA.

LYNN, LYN, LIN, LINN (Welsh) 'From the pool or waterfall'.

LYSITHEA Name given to one of Jupiter's moons.

LYULF, LYULPH (Old English) 'Flame' and 'wolf'. The wolf is a lucky animal for Scorpio. It is not commonly found today.

MALIN 'Drop of the sea'. Masculine form of Mary.

MANNANAN Name given to a sea god in Irish Druid mythology, Mannanan Mac Lir.

MANNAWYDDAN Name of a god of the sea in Welsh Druid mythology.

MARCELLUS Latin pet form of Marcus. In ancient Rome the name was used as a family name. The name has been borne by several minor saints and two popes.

MARCIUS (Latin) Linked to Marcus and ultimately to Mars, the Roman god of war and ruling planet of Scorpio.

MARCUS (Latin) Connected with Mars, the Roman god of war. One of the ruling planets of Scorpio. Also means 'male, virile'. The name was popular in ancient Rome, a famous bearer of the name being Marcus Antonius, better known as Mark Antony. Marcus was little used in English-speaking countries until the 19th century and was particularly popular in the latter half of the 20th century.

MAREK (Latin) Derivative of Marcius.

MARIO Italian and Spanish form of Marius.

MARIUS (Latin) Connected with Mars. Also means 'virile'. The name was used as a Roman clan name. It is occasionally found in English-speaking countries.

MARLAND (Old English) 'Dweller in the lakeland'.

MARLEN, MARLON Forms of Merlin.

MARK (Latin) English form of Marcus. Connected with Mars, the Roman god of war. The name is found in the New Testament, St Mark was the author of the second Gospel. The name was little used in English-speaking countries until the latter half of the 20th century when it became very popular.

MARKUS See Marcus.

MARTIN, MARTYN English form of the Latin name Martinus. Derived from Mars, Roman god of war. The name was borne by St Martin, a 4th-century soldier who was converted to Christianity. His fame led to the name being very popular in the Middle Ages. It enjoyed a further revival in the latter half of the 20th century.

MARTY Short form of Martin.

MARLIN, MARLEN, MARLON 'The sea'. Forms of Merlin.

MARLOW Form of Marlin.

MARLY Form of Marlin.

MARNE (Latin) 'Sea'.

MARVIN (Old English) 'Friend of the sea'. Also a Medieval form of Mervyn. Marvin was revived in the 19th century and is found most commonly in the USA.

MAYNARD (Norman French) 'Strength, brave'. The name was introduced into Britain by the Normans. It is more frequently found today as a surname than as a first name.

MEILYR (Welsh) 'Chief ruler'. A traditional Welsh name.

MERDYDD Form of Meredith.

MEREDITH (Celtic) 'Protector of the sea'. The name was only used as a boys name in Wales until the 20th century. It is now a popular Welsh name used for both boys and girls and is found throughout English-speaking countries.

MERELLO (Latin) Derivative of Marcius.

MERIDETH, MEREDETH Forms of Meredith.

MERIDITH, MEREDYTH, MERIDYTH Alternative spellings for Meredith.

MERLIN English form of the Welsh name Myrddin. Composed of Old Celtic elements meaning 'sea' and 'hill'. In Arthurian legend the name was borne by the famous wizard and advisor to King Arthur.

MORGAN (Welsh) 'Man from the wild sea'. The name has been used in Wales for centuries. Glamorgan, a Welsh county, is named after a 10th-century bearer of the name. The name is occasionally bestowed as a girls' name. Morgan le Fay, the sister of King Arthur, is a famous feminine bearer of the name.

MORIEN (Welsh) 'Sea born'.

MORRIGAN In Irish mythology the name was borne by a goddess of war.

MOULTRIE (Gaelic) Origin is uncertain but it possibly means 'sea warrior'.

MUIRIS 'Vigorous sea'. Contracted form of the Gaelic name Muirgheas.

MURCHADH 'Sea battle'. Traditional Gaelic name. Pronounced 'moor-ha'.

MURDO (Scottish) 'Sea'.

MURDOCH Gaelic form of Murdo. The name is most commonly found in Scotland.

MURPHY (Irish) 'Of the sea'.

MURRAY, MORAY (Gaelic) 'Sea'. From the Scottish surname and place name. The name has been in regular use in the English-speaking world since the 19th century.

MURROUGH Anglicized form of Murchadh.

NEIL, NEILL, NEAL, NIALL (Irish) 'Champion' or 'passionate'. The name was borne by the Irish King Niall of the Nine Hostages, who died in the early-5th century. Neil was introduced into Britain from France and Scandinavia during the Middle Ages.

NEREID In Greek mythology a Nereid is sea nymph.

NEREUS Name given to the Greek god of the sea.

NIGEL Form of Neil. The name has been used in Britain for centuries and was particularly popular in Britain in the mid-20th century.

NINIAN (Latin) 'Alive'. Masculine form of Vivian.

NJORD Scandinavian god of the sea.

OAK The oak is a lucky plant for Scorpio.

OAKES (Old English) 'Dweller by the oak tree'. The oak is a lucky plant for Scorpio.

OAKLEY, OAKLEIGH, OAKLY (Old English) 'Field of oak trees'. The oak is a lucky plant for Scorpio.

OCEAN (Greek) 'Vast sea'.

OCTAVIUS (Latin) 'Eighth'. Scorpio is the eighth sign of the zodiac. Originally a Roman clan name.

Formerly given to the eighth-born child in Victorian times but is rarely used for this purpose today.

ODIN Alternative name of Woden, the Norse god of war.

OGDEN (Old English) 'Oak valley'. The oak is a lucky plant for Scorpio. Originally a surname and place name it has been used sporadically as a first name since the 19th century.

OKELY, OKELEY Forms of Oakley.

OLOKUN (Nigerian Yoruba) 'God of the sea'.

ORION (Greek) Name of an important character in the creation of the constellation of Scorpio.

PHELAN (Irish) 'Wolf'. The wolf is a lucky animal for Scorpio.

PHOBOS Name of one of Mars' moons. Named after one of the mythical horses that drew the chariot of the Roman god of war, Mars. Means 'fear'.

PHORCYS Greek god of the sea.

RADCLIFFE, RADCLIFF (Old English) 'Red cliff'. Deep red is a lucky colour for Scorpio. Originally a surname and place name, occasionally used as a first name.

RADOLF (Old English) 'Wolf counsel'. The wolf is a lucky animal for Scorpio.

RAFE Form of Ralph. The name was in use in Britain in the 17th century and is still found on occasion today.

RALPH, RALF (Old Norse) 'Wolf counsel'. The wolf is a lucky animal for Scorpio. The name was in use in various forms in the Middle Ages. It remains in regular use today.

RANDALL, RANDAL (Old English) 'Shield' and 'wolf'. The wolf is a lucky animal for Scorpio. The name was in regular use in Britain in the Middle Ages. It was revived in the 19th century and became especially popular in USA and Canada.

RANDOLPH, RANDOLF (Old English) 'Wolf shield'. The wolf is a lucky animal for Scorpio.

RANDY Shortened form of Randolph.

RANULF Form of Randal.

RAOUL French form of Ralph. The name was in use in medieval Britain and revived in the 20th century.

RAWLINS (French) 'Son of the wolf counsellor'. The wolf is a lucky animal for Scorpio.

REDFORD (Old English) 'Red-stone river crossing'. Deep red is a lucky colour for Scorpio.

REMUS One of the twin sons of Mars, Roman god of war.

RENÉ (French) 'Reborn'. St René Goupil was a 17th-century French missionary who was martyred in North America. The name is occasionally found in English-speaking countries.

RHYS (Welsh) 'Ardour'. The name was borne by two Welsh lords in the early Middle Ages. It is frequently found in Wales but is less common in other English-speaking countries.

ROCKWELL (Old English) 'Rook stream'.

ROGAN (Gaelic) 'Red-haired one'. Deep red is a lucky colour for Scorpio.

ROLF, ROLPH (Old German) 'Fame' and 'wolf'. The wolf is a lucky animal for Scorpio. The name was introduced into Britain at the time of the Norman Conquest. It was revived in the 19th century but is rarely found in English-speaking countries today.

ROLLO Form of Rolf. The name was borne by the first Duke of Normandy.

ROMULUS One of the twin sons of Mars, Roman god of war.

RORY, RORIE (Gaelic) 'Red'. The name was borne by a 12th-century Irish king Rory O'Connor. Rory has been frequently in use in Scotland and Ireland for centuries but is seldom found elsewhere.

ROY (Gaelic) 'Red'. Deep red is a lucky colour for Scorpio. The name Roy was originally a Scottish name. Its spread to other English-speaking countries has been attributed to its reanalysis of the Old French roy, meaning king.

RUDGE (Old French) 'Red-haired'. Deep red is a lucky colour for Scorpio.

RUDOLF, RUDY, RUDI (Old German) 'Fame-wolf'. The wolf is a lucky animal for Scorpio.

RUFUS (Latin) 'Red'. Deep red is a lucky colour for Scorpio. Rufus was given as a nickname to King William II of England. The name is occasionally found in English-speaking countries.

RUSSELL, RUSSEL (Old French) 'Red'. Deep red is a lucky colour for Scorpio. The name has been used as a first name since the 19th century and became particularly popular in the latter half of the 20th century.

SEABERT, SEBERT (Old English) 'Sea glorious'.

SEABRIGHT (Old English) 'Sea glorious'.

SEABROOKE, SEBROOK (Old English) 'Stream by the sea'.

SEWALD (Old English) 'Sea powerful'.

SEWARD (Old English) 'Sea guardian'. Originally an Old-English surname used as a first name since the 19th century.

SEWALL Form of Sewell.

SEWELL (Old English) 'Sea powerful'.

SHAULA Name given to a star in the constellation of Scorpio.

SIDWELL (Old English) 'Broad stream'.

SIWALD (Old English) Form of Sewell.

STORM (Old English) 'The tempest'. A name of recent coinage.

STROTHER (Gaelic) 'Stream'.

STRUAN (Gaelic) 'Stream'.

TARANIS Name borne in Gallic mythology by the god of thunder.

TELFORD (Latin) 'Shallow stream'.

TEMPEST (Latin) 'Violent storm'.

TEUTATES Name borne in Gaelic mythology by a god of war who the Romans connected with Mars, the Roman god of war and ruling planet of Scorpio.

THOR (Scandinavian) Norse god of thunder. 'Of thundery nature'.

TORQUIL (Scandinavian) 'Belonging to Thor'.

TRAHERN (Welsh) 'Strong as iron'. Iron is a lucky metal for Scorpio.

TYR Name of the Scandinavian god of war.

UFFA, ULFA Forms of Ulrich.

ULRIC (Old English or Old German) 'Wolf' and 'ruler'. The name was borne by several saints including St Augsburg, a 10th-century German bishop. The name was found in Britain until the 13th century and was revived several centuries later.

ULRICH, ULRICK (Danish) 'Wolf'. The wolf is a lucky animal for Scorpio.

VIVIAN (Latin) 'Alive'. The name has been used occasionally as a boys' name since the Middle Ages.

WESTBOURNE (Old English) 'West stream'.

WESTBROOK (Old English) 'West stream'.

WINSLADE (Old English) 'Friend's stream'.

WODEN Name of the Norse god of war.

WOLF, WOLFE (Old German) 'A wolf'. A man of courage. The wolf is a lucky animal for Scorpio.

WOLFGANG (German) 'Wolf strife'. The wolf is a lucky animal for Scorpio.

WOLSEY, WOLSELEY Forms of Wolsey.

WOOLSEY (Old English) 'Victorious wolf'.

WORDSWORTH (Old English) 'From the farm of the wolf'.

YEO (Old English) 'River stream'.

Scorpio ~ Girls

ACACIA (Greek) 'The symbol of immortality and resurrection'.

ADINA, ADINE (Hebrew) 'Desire'.

ADITA (Hebrew) 'Desire'.

ADRIA (Latin) 'Dark lady from the sea'. Feminine form of Adrian.

ADRIANA, ADRIANE Feminine forms of Adrian.

ADRIENNE, ADRIENNA (Latin) 'Dark lady from the sea'. Feminine form of Adrian. The name became widespread in the English speaking world in the 20th century.

ALCINA (Greek) 'Sea maiden'.

ALCINE (Greek) 'Sea maiden'.

AMBROSINA, AMBROSINE 'Immortal'. Feminine forms of Ambrose.

ANA Shortened form of Anastasia.

ANASTASIA (Greek) 'She who will rise again'. The name was borne by a 4th-century saint and also by one of the daughters of Nicholas II, last Tsar of Russia. It has been in use in Britain since the 13th century and thereafter spread to other English-speaking countries. It remains in use today.

ANSTICE Form of Anastasia.

ANSTEY Form of Anastasia.

ANTARES Name given to a bright red star in the constellation of Scorpio. It means 'The rival of Mars'. Antares marks the head of the 'scorpion' in the constellation of Scorpio and is easily spotted in the night sky.

ARIANRHOD (Welsh) The name of a Welsh goddess of the Druids. Arianrhod ruled over birth and initiation. In addition she was known as the goddess of the stars, particularly the Corona Borealis, often known as the Northern Crown.

ATHENA (Greek) In Greek mythology Athena is the goddess of war and wisdom. Mars, the ruling planet of Scorpio is the god of war in Roman mythology. The city of Athens is named after Athena.

ATHENEA Alternative name of the Greek goddess of war and wisdom.

BENZOIN Siamese benzoin is a lucky perfume for Scorpio.

BEVERLEY, BEVERLY (Old English) 'Beaver stream'. Originally a surname derived from a place in Yorkshire. It was originally used as a boys' name in the late-19th century but is now more frequently found as a girls' name.

BRANWEN Name of a goddess of love and death in Welsh Druid mythology.

CACTUS The cactus is a lucky plant for Scorpio.

CALIDA (Spanish) 'Ardently loving'. One who is capable of great affection.

CARMENTIA (Roman) The name of the Roman goddess of water, childbirth and prophesy.

CERRIDWEN In Welsh Druid mythology, Cerridwen was the holder of the cauldron of inspiration and rebirth. She is possibly the most important goddess in Welsh legend.

CHARIS (Greek) Form of Charity.

CHARISSA A modern name and an elaboration of Charis.

CHARITA Form of Charity.

CHARITY (Latin) 'Benevolent and loving'. The name is taken from the three Christian virtues and was used as a first name by the Puritans. It is seldom found today.

CHARON Name of the moon of Pluto. Pluto is one of the ruling planets of Scorpio.

CHARRY Form of Charity.

CHERRY Form of Charity.

CORAL, CORALE (Latin) 'From the sea'.

CORALINE, CORALIE Forms of Coral.

CORDELIA (Welsh) The name was borne by the daughter King Lear. 'Jewel of the sea'.

CORDELIE, CORDIE Forms of Cordelia.

CYRENE (Greek) 'A water nymph'.

DANA Alternative form of Danu.

DANU In Irish Druid mythology the name is borne by a river goddess. She is also known as a mother goddess of the land. The name means 'sacred gift'.

DELILAH, DALILAH (Hebrew) 'Alluring', 'amorous'. The name was borne in the Old Testament by Samson's beautiful but treacherous mistress. It was popular with the Puritans and remains in occasional use today.

DELMA (Spanish) 'Of the sea'.

DELMAR, DELMARE (Spanish) 'Of the sea'.

DERORA (Hebrew) 'Flowing stream'.

DESIRÉE (French) 'Desired one'. The name was borne in the 18th century by a mistress of Napoleon Bonaparte. It is occasionally found in English speaking countries.

DODI Form of Doris.

DORIA Form of Doris.

DORICE, DORISE, DORRIS Forms of Doris.

DORIS (Greek) 'From the sea'. Name given to the daughter of Oceanus. The name became popular in the late-19th century and early-20th century.

DORITA Form of Doris.

EDLYN (Old English) 'Happy brook'.

EDNA A name of uncertain origin. Possibly from Hebrew, meaning 'rejuvenation'. The name was little used as a first name in English-speaking countries until the late-19th century, when it became popular in the USA. It was particularly fashionable in Britain in the 1920s.

ENID (Welsh) 'Life'. The name was borne by a character in Arthurian legend. It came into general use in the late-19th century following the publication of Tennyson's *Idylls of the King*, which contains the story of Geraint and Enid.

ERWINA (Old English) 'Friend from the sea'.

EVA Latin form of Eve.

EVARA A blend of Eva and Sara. Sara is a Hebrew name meaning 'princess'.

EVELIA A blend of Eve and Delia. Delia is a Latin name meaning 'from the Greek island of Delos'.

EVE (Hebrew) 'Life', 'living' or 'lively'. In the Old Testament the name was borne by Adam's wife, the 'mother of all living'. The name has been in regular use in English-speaking countries since medieval times.

EVELEEN Irish form of Eva or Eve.

EVIE Form of Eve.

FLANNA (Gaelic) 'Red-haired'. Deep red is lucky colour for Scorpio.

GARNET, GARNETTE (English) 'Deep red-haired beauty'. Red is a lucky colour for Scorpio. The name was originally a surname. It has been used as a boys' first name since the 19th century and as a girls' name since the mid-20th century.

GELASIA (Greek) 'Laughing water'.

GELASIE Form of Gelasia.

GRAFFIAS The name given to a star in the constellation of Scorpio.

HARMONIA (Greek) In Greek mythology Harmonia was the daughter of Ares, the god of war. The name also means 'unifying'.

HYACINTH (Greek) A flower name meaning blue gem or sapphire. Blue-green is a lucky colour for Scorpio. The name is borne in Greek mythology by a beautiful youth who was accidentally killed by Apollo and from whose blood sprang a hyacinth flower. The name was used as a boys' name for centuries. Its use as a girls' name is a fairly recent phenomenon.

HYACINTHA, HYACINTHIA Forms of Hyacinth.

IVY (Middle English) From the plant name. It is linked to 'faithfulness'. Ivy is a sacred plant of ancient religions. It is a lucky plant for Scorpio.

JACINTHA, JACINTHIA Forms of Hyacinth.

KAIYA (Japanese) 'Sea'. Feminine form of Kai.

KELLY, KELLIE (Irish) 'War'. Originally from an Irish surname. The name has only become popular as a first name since the mid-20th century and was particularly popular in Britain in the 1980s.

LAKAIYA Kaiya with a La- prefix.

LEUCOTHEA Name of a Greek sea goddess.

LILAC (Persian) 'Dark blue or purple flower'. Blue-green is a lucky colour for Scorpio.

LILITH The name of a female demon in Jewish folklore. It has the meaning 'storm goddess'. Despite its connotations it has been occasionally used as a first name in the 20th century.

LORELEI (Old German) 'Fascinating and alluring woman'.

LUCINA The name borne by the Roman goddess of childbirth. The name is occasionally given in English-speaking countries.

LYNN, LYNNE (Celtic) 'A waterfall'. The name has been in regular use in English-speaking countries since the mid-20th century.

LYN, LIN, LINN (Welsh) 'From the pool or waterfall'.

MAE Form of May. This form of the spelling became particularly popular in the USA in the 20th century due to the fame of actress Mae West.

MAIR 'Drop of the sea.' Welsh form of Mary.

MAIRE Irish Gaelic form of Mary.

MAIRENN (Irish) 'Fair sea'.

MAIRI Scottish Gaelic form of Mary.

MAMIE Short form of Mary.

MARA Form of Mary.

MARCELLA (Latin) Feminine form of Marcellus, a Latin pet form of Marcus, which in turn is derived from Mars, the Roman god of war.

MARCELLE Feminine form of Marcel.

MARCIA Feminine form of Marcus. The name originates from a Roman clan name Marcius, which is connected to Mars, the Roman god of war. Marcia came into use in English-speaking countries in the 19th century and became particularly popular in the mid-20th century.

MAREA Alternative spelling of Maria.

MARE (Latin) 'Sea'.

MAREETHA, MARITHA. Blends of Mary and Aretha. Aretha is a Greek name meaning 'virtue'.

MARELLA, MARELLE A blend of Mare and Ella. Ella is an Old German name meaning 'all'.

MARI Welsh form of Mary.

MARIA Latin form of Mary.

MARIABELLA Combination of Maria and Bella. Interpreted as 'beautiful Mary', therefore 'beautiful drop of the sea'. The name has been in occasional use in English-speaking countries since the 17th century.

MARIAH Elaborated spelling of Maria.

MARIAN Combination of Mary and Ann. Ann is a Hebrew name meaning 'graceful'.

MARIANNE Alternative spelling of Marian.

MARIE French form of Maria.

MARIELLA Italian pet form of Maria.

MARIETTA Italian pet form of Maria.

MARILEE A combination of Mary and Lee. Lee is an Old English name meaning 'meadow' or 'wood'.

MARILENE Variant of Marilyn.

MARILYN Elaboration of Mary with the addition of Lyn.

MARILYNN, MARYLYN, MARILENE Alternative spellings of Marilyn.

MARIMNE 'Drop of the sea'. Form of Miriam.

MARINA The name is from Latin meaning 'of the sea'. The name was borne by an early saint. It was first used in Britain in medieval times and was revived in the 20th century following the marriage of Princess Marina of Greece to Prince George, Duke of Kent, in 1934.

MARINER Name of the space craft sent to explore Mars, the ruling planet of Scorpio.

MARION French form of Marie.

MARIS (Latin) 'The sea'.

MARISA, MARISSA Elaboration of Maria.

MARISE Form of Marisa.

MARISELLA, MARISELA 'The sea'. Spanish form of Maris.

MARISKA Russian form of Maria.

MARITA Blend of Mary and Rita.

MARITZA Hungarian form of Mary.

MARIWIN A blend of Mary and Winifred.

MARNA Swedish form of Marina.

MARNIA 'The sea'. A form of Marina.

MAROLA (Latin) 'Sea'.

MARSHA Phonetic spelling of Marcia.

MARTI Short form of Martina.

MARTIA Derived from Marcia.

MARTINA Feminine form of Martin. Derived from Mars the Roman god of war. Mars is the ruling planet of Scorpio.

MARTINE French form of Martina.

MARY An anglicized form of the French Marie, or the Latin Maria. It is a form of Miriam, from the Latin phrase meaning 'drop of the sea' or 'star of the sea'.

MAURA (Celtic) Form of Mary.

MAY Pet form of Mary. Often used as an independent name. It became popular in the 20th century and is still occasionally found today.

MAYA Latin variation of May. Also an alternative spelling of the Roman goddess Maia, influenced by the English name May.

MEREL Form of Muriel.

MERIEL Form of Muriel.

MERIS Form of Merrie.

MERISSA, MERRISSA Blends of Meryl and Clarissa. Clarissa is a form of Clare, a Latin name meaning 'clear, bright'.

MERLYN, MERLINE Feminine forms of Merlin.

MERRIEL, MERRIELLE Forms of Merrie.

MERRILL, MERRIL, MERIL Forms of Meryl.

MERRY, MERRIE, MERRYN (Old English) 'Joyful', 'pleasant'.

MERYL A recent form of Muriel. It has been popularized by the US actress Meryl Streep.

MIA Danish and Swedish form of Maria.

MIMI Italian form of Maria. The name has been in use as an independent name since the 19th century.

MIMOSA (Latin) 'Imitative', 'sensitive'.

MINERVA Name borne by the Roman goddess of war and wisdom. It is occasionally found as a first name in English-speaking countries.

MIO (Japanese) 'Waterway'.

MIRIAM 'Drop of the sea.' Old Testament form of Maryam. The name was borne in the Old Testament by the elder sister of Moses. The name was popular in the 17th century and remains in regular use throughout English-speaking countries.

MITA A form of Mitzi.

MITZI 'Drop of the sea'. German form of Maria.

MOANA (Maori) 'Sea'.

MOIRA Anglicized form of the Irish Gaelic Maire, a form of Mary.

MOLLY Pet from of Mary.

MORGAN (Welsh) 'Man from the wild sea'. The name has been used in Wales for centuries as a boys' name. Glamorgan, a Welsh county, is named after a 10th-century bearer of the name. The name is occasionally bestowed as a girls' name. Morgan le Fay, the sister of King Arthur, is a famous feminine bearer of the name.

MORGANA Feminine form of Morgan.

MORRIGAN (Irish/Celtic) Goddess of war.

MORVOREN, MORVA (Cornish) 'Maid of the sea', 'mermaid'.

MOYA Derived from Moyra.

MOYRA Alternative spelling of Moira.

MUIREALL (Scottish Gaelic) 'White sea'. Pronounced mwir-an.

MUIREANN, MUIRINN (Irish Gaelic) 'White sea'.

MURIEL, MERIEL, MURIAL (Irish) 'Sea-bright'. The name has been used in its many forms throughout Britain since medieval times. It was revived throughout English-speaking countries in the 19th century.

MYSTIQUE (Old French) 'Atmosphere of mystery'.

NARA (English) 'Nearest and dearest'.

NERICE (Greek) 'From the sea'.

NERIMA (Greek) 'From the sea'.

NERINA Form of Nerissa.

NERINE (Greek) 'From the sea'. It is also the name given to a sea nymph in Greek mythology.

NERISSA (Greek) 'From the sea' or 'sea-nymph'. The name was borne by a minor character in Shakespeare's *The Merchant of Venice*. The name is found occasionally in English-speaking countries.

NERITA (Greek) 'From the sea'.

NERYS (Greek) 'Of the sea'.

NIA Welsh form of Niamh.

NIAMH (Irish Gaelic) 'Brightness or beauty'. Pronounced 'Nee-uv'. In Irish mythology, this is the name given to the daughter of the sea god.

NOVA (Latin) 'New'.

NOVENDA Modern invention taken from the name of the month November, a time when many Scorpios are born.

NYREE (Maori) 'Wave'.

OAK The oak is a lucky plant for Scorpio.

OCTAVIA (Latin) 'Eighth'. Scorpio is the eighth sign of the zodiac. Feminine form of 'Octavius'. The name was borne by the sister of Octavian. She was the wife of Mark Antony. It is occasionally used today.

OCTOBER Name of the month in which many Scorpios are born.

ONDINE (Latin) 'From the sea waves'. Form of Undine.

OOLA (Celtic) 'Sea jewel'. Form of Ulla.

ORA (Maori) 'Life'.

ORAN (Irish) 'Green'. Blue-green is a lucky colour for Scorpio.

ORANDA A blend of Oran and Amanda. Oran is an Irish name meaning 'green' – blue-green is a lucky colour for Scorpio. Amanda is a Latin name meaning 'loveable'.

ORANTHA A blend of Oran and Samantha. Samantha is an Aramaic name meaning 'listener'.

PELAGIE (Greek) 'Mermaid'.

RALPHINA (Old Norse) 'Wolf counsel'. Feminine form of Ralph. The wolf is a lucky animal for Scorpio.

RAN Name given to the Scandinavian goddess of the sea.

RAZA (Aramaic) 'My secret'.

RAZEEN Origin is uncertain but possibly a form of Raza.

RENATA (Latin) 'Reborn'. The name has been in use in English-speaking countries since the 17th century.

RENÉE (French) 'Reborn'. Feminine form of 'René. It has been used in English-speaking countries. Since the early-20th century.

RILLA (Old German) 'A stream or brook'.

RILLE Form of Rilla.

RILLETTE Form of Rilla.

ROSEMARY (Latin) 'Sea dew'. Did not come into use as a first name until the 19th century. It became particularly popular in the mid-20th century.

ROSEMARIE French form of Rosemary.

RUBETTA, RUBETTE Elaborated forms of Ruby.

RUBIA Form of Ruby.

RUBINA Form of Ruby.

RUBI, RUBIE Alternative spellings of Ruby.

RUBY (Latin) 'Red'. From the jewel name. The ruby is a lucky gemstone for Scorpio. Deep red is a lucky colour for Scorpio. The name was in frequent use in the late-19th century.

SABRA (Hebrew) 'Cactus'. The cactus is a lucky plant for Scorpio.

SAPPHIRA (Greek) 'Eyes of sapphire colour'. Blue-green is a lucky colour for Scorpio. The name occurs in the New Testament.

SCARLETT, SCARLET, SCARLETTA (Old French) From a surname borne by wearers or dealers in scarlet cloth. The name has been used as a first name since the publication of *Gone with the Wind* in 1936, in which the heroine's name was Scarlett O'Hara. Deep red is a lucky colour for Scorpio.

SEDNA (North American Eskimo) 'Goddess of the sea'.

SHAULA Name given to a star in the constellation of Scorpio.

SNAKESTONE Name of a lucky gemstone for Scorpio.

STORM (Old English) 'A tempest'. One of a turbulent disposition. A name of recent coinage.

SYDEL, SYDELLE (Hebrew) 'That enchantress'.

TALLULAH (Native American) 'Running water'.

TALLULA Alternative spelling of Tallulah.

TALLU, TALLA TALLIE Shortened forms of Tallulah.

TANSY (Greek) 'Immortality'. From the name of the flower. The name has been in regular use as a first name since the 20th century.

TATE, TAIT, TEYTE (Old English) 'Cheerful'.

THAISA (Greek) 'The sea'.

THIRZA (Hebrew) 'Pleasantness'. Used sporadically in English-speaking countries since the time of the Puritans.

THORA (Scandinavian). Derived from Thor, the Norse god of thunder. The name has been found in English-speaking countries from time to time.

THYRA (Scandinavian) Feminine form of Tyr, the Norse god of war.

TIRZA, TIRZAH Forms of Thirza. Tirzah is found in the bible.

TISHA (Latin) 'Joy'. Pet form of Letitia. It is occasionally found as a name in its own right.

THAISA (Greek) 'The sea'.

THALASSA (Greek) 'From the sea'.

TOYA (Sioux) 'Green'. Blue-green is a lucky colour for Scorpio.

TURQUOISE (Old French) From the name of the gemstone which originates in Turkey. It is a lucky gemstone for Scorpio.

TYRA Form of Thyra.

ULLA, ULA (Celtic) 'Jewel of the sea'.

UNDINE, UNDINA (Latin) 'From the sea waves'. In mythology, a female water spirit.

ULRICA (Old English) 'Wolf' and 'ruler'. Feminine form of Ulric. The wolf is a lucky animal for Scorpio.

VERDA (Old French) 'Green', 'spring-like'. Blue-green is a lucky colour for Scorpio.

VITA (Latin) 'Life'. The name was borne by the 20th-century English writer Vita Sackville-West.

VITIA, VETA Forms of Vita.

VIVA (Latin) 'Alive'.

VIVIA Form of Viva or Vivian.

VIVIAN, VIVIEN, VYVYAN (Latin) 'Alive'. The name became popular in the late-19th century, due in part to Tennyson's story of Merlin and Vivien, his name for *The Lady of the Lake*. The name enjoyed a further increase in popularity in the 20th century by the British actress Vivien Leigh.

VIVIANA Form of Vivian which was used as far back as the Middle Ages.

VIVIENNE French form of Vivian.

WILLA (Old English) 'Desirable'.

YEMANJÁ (Afro Brazilian) 'Goddess of the sea'.

YOKO (Japanese) 'Ocean child'.

ZELIE (Greek) 'Ardent'.

ZEVA (Hebrew) 'Wolf'. The wolf is a lucky animal for Scorpio.

ZOE, ZOË (Greek) 'Life'. The name was borne by St Zoë, a 3rd-century Roman martyr and also by a 11th-century Byzantine empress. The name was often used by early Christians in regard for their beliefs of eternal life. It came into use in English-speaking countries in the 19th century and was particularly popular in the 1970s.

Sagittarius

THE ARCHER
22 November – 21 December

RULING PLANET   Jupiter. In astrology Jupiter is the planet of joviality, benevolence and wisdom. It is also considered to be the guide to the psyche.

ELEMENT   Fire

General characteristics
- Optimistic, enthusiastic, joyful.
- Loves to travel and the outdoors, enjoys sport.
- Generous, honest, has high morals.
- Vivid imagination, intuitive.
- Inspirational, loves life.
- Intellectual, witty, good-humoured.
- Idealistic, spiritually aware.

Characteristics of young Sagittarians
- Is warm and friendly.
- Can be impulsive.
- Is happy-go-lucky.
- Displays an inquiring mind.
- Tends to adventurous and high-spirited.
- Enjoys the company of others.
- Likes to play the clown.

Sagittarian lucky connections
Gemstones: jacinth, lapis lazuli
Colours: white, blue and purple
Plants: oak, rush, fig, hyssop
Metal: tin
Perfume: lignaloes
Animals: horse, dog
Tarot card: temperance

SAGITTARIANS are outgoing, exuberant characters who are always on the go. They possess an abundance of physical, mental and emotional energy and are often keen on sports, being usually well co-ordinated and active individuals.

Naturally outgoing, Sagittarians often have a warm self-assurance that helps them to make friends easily. They are high-spirited characters, good-humoured, friendly and possess a good sense of fun.

Sagittarians love to explore and to experience new situations. They also enjoy experimenting and trying out new activities and are always keen to learn something interesting from the experience.

You may find that your Sagittarian baby will feel claustrophobic if you try to cuddle him too often. Instead, take him on outdoor trips whenever possible. A new environment will fascinate and entertain him and he will thrive in the open air.

You may also discover that your little Sagittarian will crawl and walk early as he will be keen to get going and explore his environment. He will always be on the look out for new experiences and stimulation. So give him plenty of fresh toys and safe playthings and allow your little adventurer as much freedom as possible. Do watch out however that he is not experimenting with your new CDs and trying to discover if he can post them through the cat flap...

Your little Sagittarian will usually be a happy soul who is playful and optimistic. He will learn to talk at an early age, so prepare to be bombarded with endless questions from your inquisitive Sagittarian. He will be eager to know everything there is to know about everything. Indeed you may find that once he starts school, rather than resenting the routine that will restrict his more energetic outbursts, he will readily devour all the new information and experiences offered to him. You may well discover that your energetic child will channel some of his boundless enthusiasm into his studies. Sagittarians can often become intellectual individuals who enjoy mental challenges as much as physical ones.

The young Sagittarian's love of freedom and his boundless energy can sometimes lead to problems if limits are not sometimes imposed. When limits are necessary, try to enforce them with humour. With young children, distraction is often the key. Show him something amusing or silly and hopefully he will forget all about whatever it was that he absolutely had to do.

In their readiness to experience new challenges Sagittarians can often be too impatient to take time to think things through properly. They may make a marvellous invention out of marbles, cardboard and string, but if it all falls apart because they have not tied the ends of the string together properly, they can become frustrated. However he will frequently show little interest in trying to discover how or why it went wrong. Try to help your little Sagittarian to see the reasons for his problems and show him how he can overcome them. Teach him patience. If he can learn these lessons and channel his extraordinary energy into positive directions your little Sagittarian will be an extremely capable individual.

Sagittarius ~ Boys

ADEEL (Arabic) 'Just, honest'.

ADIL (Arabic) 'Just, honest'.

AIDAN, AIDEN (Irish Gaelic) 'Fiery one'. The name was borne by several early Irish saints including a famous 7th-century monk. The name enjoyed a revival in the early 19th century and remains in regular use today.

ALAN (Celtic) 'Cheerful harmony'. The name entered Britain at the time of the Norman invasion. It was popular in medieval times and remains in regular use.

ALAIN French form of Alan.

ALAND, AILEAN, AILIN Forms of Alan.

ALBAN (Latin) 'White'. White is a lucky colour for Sagittarius. St Alban was the first British martyr. The name was revived in the 19th century and has been in occasional use since then.

ALBANY Form of Alban.

ALBIN Form of Alban.

ALLAN, ALLEN, ALLYN, Forms of Alan.

ALMALTHEA Name of one of the moons of Jupiter.

ALPIN, ALPINA (Latin) 'White'.

ALVA (Latin) 'White'. In medieval times the name was used as a boys name but in its revival it is used mainly as a girls' name.

ARANKE Name of one of Jupiter's moons.

ARCHER (Old English) 'The bowman'. Originally a medieval surname which has been in used infrequently as a first name for over a hundred years.

ARVAD (Hebrew) 'The wanderer'.

ARPAD (Hebrew) 'The wanderer'.

ASHER (Hebrew) 'The laughing one'. A happy lad. The name is found in the Old Testament, borne by one of the sons of Jacob. The name was revived in the 17th century and has been in occasional use since then.

AUBIN (Latin) 'White'.

BAIN (Gaelic) 'White'.

BETA Name given to a multiple star in the constellation of Sagittarius.

BIRCH (Old English) From the tree name meaning 'white'.

BLISS (Old English) 'Gladness', 'joy'.

BLUE Lucky colour for Sagittarians.

BLYTHE, BLYTH (Old English) 'Joyful and happy'.

BRENDAN (Gaelic) 'Fiery one' or 'prince'. The name was borne by two 6th-century Irish saints. Legend has it that one, Brendan the Voyager, was the first European to set foot on North American soil.

CAI (Latin) 'To rejoice'. Welsh form of Caius.

CAIUS 'To rejoice'. Variant of Gaius.

CALEB (Hebrew) 'A dog' hence 'bold' and 'faithful'. The dog is a lucky animal for Sagittarians. The name occurs in the Old Testament where it was borne by a follower of Moses. It was in frequent use by the Puritans who introduced the name into America, where it remains in use today.

CALLISTO Name given to one of Jupiter's moons.

CARME Name given to one of Jupiter's moons.

CHIRON In Greek mythology Chiron is an important character in the story of how the constellation of Sagittarius was formed.

CHU-JUNG Name given to the spirit of fire in Chinese mythology.

COLBRAN (Old German) 'Man of fire'.

DARIUS (Greek) 'The wealthy man'. From daraya 'possess' and vahu 'good'. It was the name given to several Persian kings.

DWIGHT (Old English) 'White, fair'. White is a lucky colour for Sagittarius. The name is originally from a surname. Its use as a first name is more frequently found in the USA, possibly due to the popularity of Timothy Dwight (1752-1817) an early president of Yale University, and of the 20th-century US president Dwight D Eisenhower.

EDAN (Celtic) 'Flame'. Scottish and Irish form of Aidan. The name was borne by St Edan, an Irish disciple of St David of Wales.

EDWARD (Old English) 'Happy guardian' or 'rich guardian'. The name has been in regular use since the early middle ages. Its association with the British royal families began in the 9th century when it was borne by the son of Alfred the Great. The name is still in widespread use today.

EDWIN, EDWYN (Old English) 'Happy or rich friend'. The name was borne by King Edwin of Northumbria, after whom it is believed the city of Edinburgh was named. The name was little used after the 12th century until its revival in the 19th century. It remained in regular use until the mid-20th century.

EGAN (Gaelic) 'Fiery'.

ERROL A name of uncertain origin. Possibly a Latin name meaning 'A wanderer'. Also a Scottish surname and place name. Alternatively a form of 'Earl'. A famous bearer of the name was the Australian actor Errol Flynn.

ESRA Alternative spelling of Ezra.

EUROPA Name given to one of Jupiter's moons.

EZ Shortened version of Ezra.

EZRA (Hebrew) 'The one who helps'. The name was borne in the Old Testament by a prophet. A book in the Bible bears his name. It was used by the Puritans in the 17th century.

FAGAN, FAGIN (Gaelic) 'Little fiery one'.

FANE (Old English) 'Glad', 'joyful'.

FARMAN (Old English) 'Long distance traveller'.

FAROLD (Old English) 'Mighty traveller'.

FARR (Old English) 'The traveller'.

FELIX (Latin) 'Happy', 'fortunate'. The name was borne by several early saints and has been in occasional use in English-speaking countries since the Middle Ages.

FIG Lucky plant for Sagittarians.

FINBAR (Irish) 'White, fair'. White is a lucky colour for Sagittarius.

FINDLAY (Gaelic) 'Fair hero'.

FINGAL, FINGALL (Scottish) 'White, fair'.

FINLAY (Scottish) 'White or fair hero'. The name was borne by the father of Macbeth. The name has been popular in Scotland for centuries, used both as a first name and surname, and remains in use today.

FINN (Irish) 'White, fair'.

FINNIAN (Irish) 'White, fair'.

FINTAN (Irish) 'White, fire'.

FIONN Modern Gaelic form of Finn.

FIRMAN (Old English) 'Long distance traveller'.

FLETCHER (French) 'The arrow maker'. Originally a surname now in occasional use as a first name.

FU Symbol of happiness in Chinese mythology.

FU-HSING Name given to the god of happiness in Chinese mythology.

GAIUS (Latin) 'To rejoice'. Name given to Gaius Julius Caesar. The name also occurs in the New Testament.

GALILEO First name of the Italian astronomer Galileo Galilei who discovered Jupiter's moons. The four largest moons are named the Galilean moons in his honour.

GANYMEDE Name given to one of Jupiter's moons. Ganymede is the largest moon in the Solar System.

GUIDO 'A guide'. Italian form of Guy. The name has been in use since medieval times.

GUY (Old German) 'A guide'. The name was introduced into England by the Normans. It was in common use until the 17th century after which it declined in popularity. It was revived in the 19th century and is still in occasional use in English-speaking countries.

HESKETH (Old Norse) 'Horse track'. The horse is a lucky animal for Sagittarius.

HEW, HUW Welsh spelling of Hugh, derived from a Celtic word for 'fire' or 'inspiration'.

HIMALIA Name given to one of Jupiter's moons.

HYSSOP Lucky plant for Sagittarians.

IDRIS (Welsh) 'Fiery lord' or 'implusive'. The name was borne by a character in Welsh mythology. The mountain Cader Idris in Gwynedd is named after him.

IFOR Form of Ivor.

IGNACE, IGNATE Forms of Ignatius.

IGNACIO (Latin) ' The fiery one'.

IGNATIUS (Latin) 'The ardent and fiery one', 'A fiery patriot'. The name was borne by St Ignatius of Antioch, a 2nd-century martyr and also by St Ignatius Loyolla, the founder of the Jesuits (1491-1556).

IKE Diminutive of Issac.

INACHUS In Roman mythology the name was borne by a river god.

INIGO Form of Ignatius.

IO Name given to one of Jupiter's moons.

IOBHAR Irish form of Ivor.

ÍOMHAR Gaelic spelling of Ivor which has been revived in Scotland.

ION (Greek) 'Purple-coloured jewel'. Purple is a lucky colour for Sagittarians.

ISSAC, IZAAK (Hebrew) 'Laughter'. The name is borne in the Old Testament by the son of Abraham. It was popular with the Puritans in the 17th century and was in regular use until the end of the 19th century.

IVAR (Norse) 'Battle archer'. The warrior with a long bow. The name has been in occasional use in Britain for centuries but is in little use in other parts of the English-speaking world.

IVEN Derivative of Ivar.

IVER Derivative of Ivar.

IVES Derivative of Ivar or 'Son of the archer'.

IVIN, IVEN, IVON 'Archer'. Forms of Ivar.

IVO Form of Ivar.

IVON Derivative of Ivar.

IVOR 'Archer'. Form of Ivar.

JACINTH Lucky gemstone for Sagittarians.

JAY 'To rejoice'. Derived from the Latin name Gaius.

JODA (Latin) 'Playful'.

JOVE Another name for the Roman god of Jupiter.

JOVIAN 'Jupiter-like'. Name given to planets like Jupiter.

JUPITER Name given to the ruling planet of Sagittarians. In astrology Jupiter is the planet of beneficence: doing good or being actively kind. In psychological terms Jupiter is the guide to the psyche and is also linked to wisdom.

JUSTIN, JUSTYN (Latin) 'Just'. The name was used mainly in Ireland until the mid-20th century when it became popular in other English-speaking countries.

JUSTUS (Latin) 'Fair and just'. The name has been in occasional use as a first name throughout English-speaking countries and Europe.

KAY (Latin) 'To rejoice.' Shortened form of Gaius. Also taken to be an alternative spelling of Cai. In Arthurian legend the name was borne by a Sir Kay, one of the knights of the round table. In modern times it is more commonly used as a girls' name.

KENWYN (Cornish) 'White chief' or 'white ridge'.

KEYE (Gaelic) 'Son of the fiery one'.

LABAN (Hebrew) 'White'. White is a lucky colour for Sagittarius. The name Laban is found in the Old Testament. It was used in the 17th century by the Puritans but is little used today.

LAGOON Name given to a nebula in the constellation of Sagittarius.

LAPIS LAZULI Name of lucky gemstone for Sagittarians.

LEDA Name given to one of Jupiter's moons.

LIGNALOES Lucky perfume for Sagittarians.

LYSITHEA Name given to one of Jupiter's moons.

LYULF, LYULPH (Old English) 'Flame' and 'wolf'. The name is little used today.

MARSHALL (Old English) 'Horse'. The horse is a lucky animal for Sagittarians. Originally a surname it has been occasionally used as a first name since the 19th century.

NIBIRU Name given to the planet Jupiter in Mesopotamian mythology.

NOAM (Hebrew) 'Joy and delight'.

NUNKI Name given to a star in the constellation of Sagittarius.

OAK Lucky plant for Sagittarians.

OMEGA Name given to a cluster of stars in the constellation of Sagittarius.

PAXTON (Old German) 'Traveller from a distant land'.

PEREGRINE (Latin) 'Wanderer'. The name was borne by a Greek philosopher of the 2nd century and by several saints.

PERRY Shortened form of Peregrine.

PHILIP (Greek) 'Lover of horses'. The horse is a lucky animal for Sagittarians. In the 4th century the name was borne by King Philip of Macedon, the father of Alexander the Great. It was also the name of one of Christ's apostles. It was popular in medieval Britain and was revived in the mid-20th century.

PHILLIP, PHIL, PIP Variations of Philip.

PURPLE Lucky colour for Sagittarians.

RADMAN (Slavonic) 'Joy'.

RANGER (Middle English) 'Wanderer'.

RANON, RANEN (Hebrew) 'Be joyful'.

REDINKA (Slavonic) 'Alive and joyful'.

ROHAN Name given to a kingdom in *The Lord of the Rings*. Its meaning is 'horse land'. The horse is a lucky animal for Sagittarians.

ROMERO (Latin) 'A traveller'.

ROSEDALE (Old Norse) 'Valley of horses'. The horse is a lucky animal for Sagittarians.

RUSH Lucky plant for Sagittarians.

SAETHYDD (Welsh) 'Archer'.

SINOPE Name given to one of Jupiter's moons.

TEMPERANCE Lucky tarot card for Sagittarians.

TIN Lucky metal for Sagittarians.

TRIFID Name given to a nebula in the constellation of Sagittarius.

TRIPP (Old English) 'The traveller'.

UYHIMALIA Name given to one of Jupiter's moons.

VERRELL (French) 'The honest one'.

VERRALL, VERRILL, VERILL Forms of Verrell.

WADE (Old English) 'A traveller'. According to legend the name was borne by a sea giant. It has been in occasional use since the 19th century.

WALLACE, WALLIS (German) 'Foreign'. Originally a surname. First used as a Christian name in Scotland in the 14th century in honour of Sir William Wallace. The name has been in occasional use in other English speaking countries since the 19th century. The name Wallis is used as both a boys' and girls' name.

WENDELL (Old German) 'A wanderer' or 'white'. White is a lucky colour for Sagittarians. Originally a medieval surname it has been in use as a first name since the 19th century. It is found most commonly in the USA.

WYNFORD, WENFORD (Welsh) 'White torrent'. Originally a surname and place name, it has been in use as a fist name since the early 20th century.

WYNNE, WYNN (Welsh) 'White', 'pure'. Originally a Welsh surname, now occasionally found as a first name.

YI In Chinese mythology Yi was known as the 'Good Archer' who saved the world from destruction.

YUL (Mongolian) 'Beyond the horizon'.

YVES 'Son of the archer'. French form of Ivor.

ZACK, ZAK (Hebrew) 'Laughter'. Shortened forms of Izaak.

ZITO (Greek) 'To seek'.

Sagittarius ~ Girls

ABBEY, ABBIE, ABBY Shortened forms of Abigail.

ABIGAIL (Hebrew) 'Father rejoiced' or 'father's joy'. In the Old Testament Abigail was the name of King David's wife. The name became popular in the 16th century and again in the 20th century.

ADA (Old English) 'Happy'. The name was introduced into Britain from Germany in the 18th century and it became fairly popular.

ADABEL Form of Adabelle.

ADABELA, ADABELLA Forms of Adabelle.

ADABELLE Combination of Ada and Belle. Belle means 'Joyous and beautiful'.

ADAR (Hebrew) 'Fire'.

AIDEEN (Gaelic) 'Fire'. Feminine form of Aidan.

AILITH 'Truth'. Form of Alitha.

AINE (Gaelic) 'Fire'. Feminine form of Aidan.

AISHA (Persian) 'Happy'.

AITHNE (Irish) 'Little fire'. The name has been popular in Ireland for centuries.

ALAIN, ALAYNE (Celtic) 'Cheerful harmony'. Feminine forms of Alan.

ALANA, ALANNA Feminine forms of Alan.

ALINA, ALLENE, ALLYN Feminine forms of Alan.

ALETHEA (Greek) 'Truth'. Alternative spelling of Althea.

ALETHIA , ALITHA, ALITHEA Forms of Alethea.

ALITHENE Form of Alethea.

ALLEGRA (Latin) 'Cheerful'. The name has been in occasional use in English-speaking countries since the 19th century.

ALMALTHEA The name given to one of the moons of Jupiter, the ruling planet of Sagittarius. In Greek mythology the name is given to the mother of Bacchus.

ALTHEA (Greek) 'Truth' or 'to heal'. The name is borne in Greek mythology by the mother of Meleager, a hero in Homer's *Iliad*.

ALTHIA Alternative spelling of Althea.

ALWEN (Welsh) 'White path'.

AMENA (Celtic) 'Honest'. One of incorruptible truth.

AMERA A blend of Amy and Vera. 'Love' and 'truth'.

AMINA Derivative of Amena.

AMINE Derivative of Amena.

ANDEANA (Spanish) 'Traveller'.

ANONA (Latin) 'Ninth born'. Sagittarius is the ninth sign of the Zodiac.

ARANKE Name of one of Jupiter's moons.

AYESHA (Persian) 'Happy'.

BEA, BEE Shortened form of Beatrice.

BEAT Shortened form of Beatrice or Beatrix.

BEATA (Latin) 'Happy'. The name was used occasionally in Britain until the 18th century, but is rarely used today.

BEATRICE (Latin) 'Bringer of happiness' or 'bringer of joy'. The name is a more common form of Beatrix. The name has been in occasional use since medieval times and was revived in the 19th century when it became very popular.

BEATRIX (Latin) 'Bringer of joy' or 'bringer of happiness'. It has been in use since 1086 when it was mentioned in the Doomsday book. It was in regular use in the Middle Ages and was revived again in the late-19th century.

BEATTIE, BEATY Shortened forms of Beatrice or Beatrix.

BEIBHINN (Irish Gaelic) 'White lady', 'fair lady'. Pronounced 'bay-vin'.

BEITRIS Form of Beatrice.

BETA Name given to a multiple star in the constellation of Sagittarius.

BETTRYS A form of Beatrix.

BIANCA (Italian) 'White'. White is a lucky colour for Sagittarius. The name was used in two of Shakespeare's plays but is little used in English-speaking countries today.

BLANCHE, BLANCH (French) 'White'. White is a lucky colour for Sagittarius. It has been in occasional use in Britain since the 13th century. It was particularly popular in the USA in the late-19th century.

BLISS (Old English) 'Perfect joy'.

BLITA (Old English) 'Perfect joy'.

BLITH, BLITHE Alternative spellings of Blythe.

BLITHA (Old English) 'Perfect joy'.

BLODWEN (Welsh) 'White flower'. The name was fairly common in the Middle Ages and has recently been revived.

BLUE Lucky colour for Sagittarius.

BLYSS (Old English) 'Perfect joy'.

BLYTH (Old English) 'Joyous and friendly'.

BLYTHE (Old English) 'Joyous and friendly'.

BRONESSA (Welsh) 'White'.

BRONWEN, BRONWYN (Welsh) 'White breast'. White is a lucky colour for Sagittarius. The name has been in regular use throughout the last century.

CAIETTA 'To rejoice'. Feminine form of Cai.

CALANDRA (Greek) 'Happy as a lark'.

CALLISTO Name of one of the moons of Jupiter, the ruling planet of Sagittarius.

CANDACE (Greek) 'Fire white'. Particularly relevant to Sagittarians as they are a fire sign and white is one of their lucky colours. The name was borne by several Ethiopian queens, one of whom is mentioned in the New Testament. The name has been in occasional throughout English-speaking countries since the 17th century. In the mid-20th century the name was particularly popular in the USA and Canada.

CANI, CANDIE, CANDY Shortened forms of Candace.

CANDICE, CANDIS, CANDYCE Forms of Candace.

CANDIDA (Latin) 'White'. A form of Candace.

CARLISS (English) 'Cheerful and kind-hearted'.

CARLISSA (English) 'Cheerful and kind-hearted'.

CARME Name of one of Jupiter's moons.

CELOSIA (Greek) 'A flame'.

CHARITY (Latin) 'Benevolent and loving'.

CHARMIAN (Greek) 'A little joy'. It was the name borne by one of Cleopatra's attendants in the Shakespearean play *Anthony and Cleopatra*. The name is still in occasional use today.

CORLISS (Old English) 'Cheerful and kind hearted'.

CORLISSA Form of Corliss.

CRESCENT (French) 'The creative one'.

CHIRON 'A centaur'. Sagittarius is represented by a centaur or 'chiron' (archer).

CYAN (Greek) 'Dark blue'. Blue is a lucky colour for Sagittarians.

CYNTHIE, CYNTHIS Shortened forms of Hyacinth.

DECHAN (Tibetan) 'Great bliss'.

DELIGHT (French) 'Pleasure'. One who brings happiness to her family.

DELICIA (Latin) 'Delight'. Only recently used as a first name.

DELISE, DELISA Forms of Delicia.

DELIZA, DELISHA Forms of Delicia.

DELWYN, DELWEN, DILWYN (Welsh) 'Pretty and white'.

DINAH (Hebrew) 'Judgement'. The name occurs in the Old Testament. It was regularly used by the Puritans who introduced it into the USA where it became particularly fashionable.

EDANA (Gaelic) 'Little fiery one'. One of a warm and loving nature. Feminine form of Edan.

EDNA EDNAH (Hebrew) 'Delight, desired'. The name occurs in the Bible and is derived from the same word as the Garden of Eden. The name became popular in the USA in the late-19th century and in Britain in the early-20th century.

EDLYN (Old English) 'Happy brook'.

EDWINA (Old English) 'Happy friend'. Feminine form of Edwin.

EIDANN Form of Edana.

EIDDWEN (Welsh) 'White and fair'.

EIRWEN (Welsh) 'White and fair'.

ELARA Name of one of Jupiter's moons. Also the name given to the granddaughter of Zeus in Greek mythology.

ELATA Form of Elara.

ELLORA (Greek) 'Happy'.

ELMIRA (Arabic) 'Truth without question'.

ELORA (Greek) 'Happy'.

ELSENA A blend of Elora and Cynthia. Cynthia is a Greek name meaning 'of Cynthus'.

ELVIRA (German) 'Foreign' and 'true'. The name was little used in English speaking countries until the 19th century and is only occasionally found today.

ENA Form of Ethne.

ERYL 'To wander'. Feminine form of Errol.

ETHNE (Irish) 'Little fire'. The name and its various forms have been popular Irish names for centuries.

EUNICE (Greek) 'Happy and victorious'. The name is found in the New Testament and has been in occasional use in English-speaking countries since the early-17th century.

EUROPA (Greek) The name is given to one of the moons of Jupiter, the ruling planet of Sagittarius. In Greek mythology Europa was the daughter of Agenor, King of Phoenicia.

FAE, FAY, FAYE Variant of Faith.

FAINE (Old English) 'Joyful'.

FAITH (Old German) 'One who is loyal and true'. 'Trusts in God'. The name came into use in the 16th century and remains in regular use today.

FARAH (Persian) 'Joy'.

FAWNIA (Old English) 'Joyous'.

FELICE, FELIS, FELISE Forms of Felicia.

FELICIA (Latin) 'Joyous one'. The name has been in use in Britain since the 12th century but is rarely found today.

FELICIDAD Form of Felicity.

FELICIE Form of Felicia.

FELICITY (Latin) 'Joyous one'. In Roman mythology the name was borne by the goddess of good luck. It was also borne by two early saints. It was regularly used by the Puritans in the 16th and 17th century and remains in use today.

FENELLA (Gaelic) 'White shoulder'.

FIG Lucky plant for Sagittarians.

FINOLA Form of Fenella.

FIONA (Gaelic) 'Fair', 'white'. The name was little used outside Scotland until the mid-20th century. Since then it has became popular in the rest of Britain and in Australia and Canada

GAIL, GALE, GAYLE 'Bringer of joy'. Shortened forms of Abigail.

GELASIA (Greek) 'Laughing water'.

GELASIE Form of Gelasia.

GENEVIEVE (Celtic) A name of uncertain origin. It could be derived from two Celtic words meaning 'tribal woman' or 'white wave'. The latter meaning is appropriate for Sagittarius. The name was introduced into Britain from France in the 19th century.

GILA (Hebrew) 'Joy'.

GIPSY Alternative spelling of Gypsy.

GITANA (Spanish) 'The gipsy'.

GUIDA (Latin) 'The guide'.

GUINEVERE (Celtic) 'White wave'. White is a lucky colour for Sagittarius. The name was borne by the legendary wife of King Arthur. The name is seldom used in modern times but exists in various forms such as Jennifer.

GWEN (Welsh) 'White'. White is a lucky colour for Sagittarius. It is often regarded as a shortened form of Gwendoline, although it has been in use as an independent name since the late 19th century.

GWENDOLINE, GWENDOLYN, GWENDOLEN, GUENDOLEN (Welsh) 'White circle'. In Arthurian legend the name was borne by the wife of Merlin. The name has been in fairly regular use in English-speaking countries since the latter half of the 19th century.

GWENETH, GWENYTH, GWENITH Welsh forms of Gwen.

GWENIVER Cornish form of Jennifer, meaning 'white wave'.

GWENLLIAN Form of Gwendoline.

GWYN (Celtic) 'White'.

GWYNETH (Welsh) 'Happiness'. The name became popular in Wales during the 19th century and subsequently became more widespread throughout Britain. It is occasionally found in other English-speaking countries.

GWYNNETH (Welsh) 'Happiness'.

GYPSY (Old English) 'Wandering maiden'.

HESTIA Name of a Greek goddess of fire.

HILARY (Latin) 'Cheerful' and 'merry'. The name was first used in Britain in the 12th century and was more commonly given as a boys' name. Since its revival in the 19th century the name is now more commonly given as a girls' name.

HILAIRE Form of Hilary.

HILLARY, HILLERY Alternative spellings of Hilary.

HIMALIA Name of one of Jupiter's moons.

HONESTY (Old French) 'Honour'. A name of recent coinage.

HONOR, HONORA, HONOUR, HONORIA (Old French) 'Honour'. The name has been in use in Britain for a thousand years. It was particularly popular in the 16th and 17th centuries and is still in occasional use today.

HYACINTH (Greek) A flower name meaning blue gem or sapphire. Blue is a lucky colour for Sagittarius. The name is borne in Greek mythology by a beautiful youth who was accidentally killed by Apollo and from whose blood sprang a hyacinth flower. The name was used as a boys' name for centuries. Its use as a girls' name is a fairly recent phenomenon.

HYACINTHA, HYACINTHIA Forms of Hyacinth.

HYSSOP Lucky plant for Sagittarians.

IDA (Old German) 'Happy'. The name originates from Mount Ida in Crete, where, in Greek mythology, Jupiter is supposed to have been hidden.

IDALIA, IDALINE, IDALINA Elaborated forms of Ida.

IDALLE, IDELLE Forms of Ida.

IDELEA, IDELIA Elaborated forms of Ida.

IDELLA Form of Ida.

IGNATIA (Latin) 'Fiery ardour'. Feminine form of Ignatius.

ILARIA (Latin) 'Cheerful'.

INIGA (Latin) 'Fiery ardour'.

IO Name given to one of Jupiter's moons. In Roman mythology Io was the daughter of the river god Inchus.

IOLA (Greek) 'Colour of the dawn cloud'. Elaboration of Io.

IONA (Greek) 'Purple coloured jewel'. Purple is a lucky colour for Sagittarians.

JACINTH Lucky gemstone for Sagittarians.

JACINTHA, JACINTHIA Forms of Jacinth.

JACINTA Forms of Jacinth.

JAY 'To rejoice'. Derived from the Latin name Gaius.

JENEFER Alternative spelling of Jennifer.

JENI, JENIA Shortened versions of Jennifer.

JENIFER Alternative spelling of Jennifer.

JENNA, JENA Shortened forms of Jennifer.

JENNI, JENNIE, JENNEY Shortened forms of Jennifer.

JENNIFER (Welsh) 'White wave'. White is a lucky colour for Sagittarius. Jennifer is a Cornish form of Guinevere. The name was seldom found outside Cornwall until early in the 20th century. By the mid-20th century it had become very popular throughout English-speaking countries and remains in regular use today.

JENNY Shortened version of Jennifer.

JENYTH Form of Jennifer.

JODETTE (Latin) 'Little playful one'.

JOSLIN, JOSLYN, JOSSLYN Forms of Jocelyn.

JOVIAN 'Jupiter-like'. Name given to planets like Jupiter, the ruling planet of Sagittarius.

JOVITA (Latin) 'The joyful one'.

JOY (Old English) 'Joy'. Jupiter, one of the ruling planets of Sagittarius, is known as the 'bringer of joy'. The name was popular in the 17th century and again in the late-19th century. It remains in regular use today.

JOYCE, JOICE (Latin) 'Gay and joyful'. In medieval times Joyce was used as both a boys' and girls' name. It was revived in the 19th century when it became popular only as a girls' name.

JOYCELYN Elaborated form of Joyce.

JOICELIN, JOICELYN, JOYCELIN Alternative spellings of Joycelyn.

JOYLENE A blend of Joy and Helene.

JOYLYN A blend of Joy and Lynda.

JOYOUS Form of Joyce.

JUNO (Latin) 'Heavenly being'. The wife of Jupiter, the ruling planet of Sagittarius.

JUPITER Name of the ruling planet of Sagittarius. In astrology Jupiter is the planet of beneficence, doing good or being actively kind. In psychological terms Jupiter is the guide to the psyche and is also linked to wisdom.

KAY 'To rejoice'. See Sagittarius boys' names.

KEELEY Form of Keelin.

KEELIN (Irish) 'White'. White is a lucky colour for Sagittarius.

KEELY, KEELIE, KEELEIGH and **KEIGHLEY** Forms of Keeley.

KEYA (Gaelic) 'Daughter of the fiery one'.

KORI (Maori) 'Playful'.

KUSHMA (Sanskrit) 'Always be happy'.

KUSHUMA (Sanskrit) 'Always be happy'.

LAETITIA Form of Letitia.

LAGOON Name of a Nebula in the constellation of Sagittarius.

LANA, LANE Shortened forms of Alana.

LAPIS LAZULI Name of lucky gemstone for Sagittarians.

LARA Shortened form of Larissa.

LARETTA A blend of Lara and Betty. Betty is a form of Elizabeth, a Hebrew name meaning 'god's oath.'

LARISSA (Greek) 'Cheerful maiden'. One who is happy as a lark.

LARYETTA A blend of Larissa and Marietta. Marietta is a form of Mary meaning 'wished-for child'.

LEDA Name of one of Jupiter's moons. In Greek mythology Leda was the beautiful mother of Castor and Pollux and also Helen of Troy.

LETA (Latin) 'Glad'. Form of Letitia.

LETITIA (Latin) 'Joyous gladness'. A popular name in the 18th century and the spelling Letitia is still found today.

LETIZIA Form of Letitia.

LETTICE, LETTIE Forms of Letitia. Lettice was the most common form of the name Letitia in medieval times. It was also popular in Victorian Britain.

LIGNALOES Lucky perfume for Sagittarians.

LILA 'Playful'.

LILAC (Persian) 'Dark mauve or blue flower'. Blue and purple are lucky colours for Sagittarians.

LOWENNA (Cornish) 'Joy'.

LYSITHEA Name given to one of Jupiter's moons.

MAB (Gaelic) 'Mirthful joy'.

MARGARIS Origin uncertain. Possibly derived from the Breton word which means 'stallion'. The horse is a lucky animal for Sagittarians.

MARNINA (Hebrew) 'To rejoice'.

MARNI, MARNIE, MARNEY (Hebrew) 'To rejoice'.

MAUVE (Latin) The purple-coloured mallow plant. Purple is a lucky colour for Sagittarians.

MAYU (Japanese) 'True reason'.

MERIS Form of Merrie.

MERRY, MERRI, MERRIE, MERRYN (Old English) 'Joyful' or 'pleasant'.

MERRIEL, MERRIELLE Forms of Merrie.

NAJINTA, NAJMA (Arabic) 'Benevolent'.

NANDA (Sanskrit) 'Giver of joy'.

NAOMI (Hebrew) 'Pleasantness', 'delight'. The name was borne in the Old Testament by the wise mother-in-law of Ruth. The name came into general use in the 17th century and became increasingly popular in the latter half of the 20th century.

NARA (English) 'Nearest and dearest'.

NIBIRU Name given to the planet Jupiter in Mesopotamian mythology.

NONA (Latin) 'The ninth'. Sagittarius is the ninth sign of the zodiac.

NONI Form of Nona.

NONIE 'Honour'. Pet form of Nora.

NORA 'Honour'. Short form of Honora.

NORAH Variant spelling of Nora.

NOREEN, NORENE, NORINE 'Honour'. Forms of Nora.

NOVENDA Modern invention based on the month of November.

NUALA, NULA (Irish) 'White shoulder'. Pet form of Fenella. Nuala is often used as an independent name.

NUMIDIA (Latin) 'The traveller'.

NUNKI Name given to a star in the constellation of Sagittarius.

OAK Lucky plant for Sagittarians.

ODESSA (Greek) 'A long journey'.

OLWEN, OLWYN (Welsh) 'White track' or 'white footprint'. This meaning refers to the white flowers that grew from the footsteps of Olwen, a character from Welsh legend. White is a lucky colour for Sagittarius.

OMEGA Name given to a cluster of stars in the constellation of Sagittarius.

PASIPHAE Name given to one of Jupiter's moons. In Greek mythology the name was borne by the wife of Minos, ruler of Crete.

PATRINIA Flowering plant named for the traveller M. Patrin.

PETA (Sioux) 'Fire'.

PETULA Name of uncertain origin but possibly from the Latin 'to seek'. The name was not in use before the 20th century but became fairly popular in the latter part of that century.

PHILIPPA (Greek) 'Lover of horses'. The horse is a lucky animal for Sagittarians. Feminine form of Philip.

PHILLIPA, PHILLIPPA Alternative spellings of Philipa.

PLEASANCE (Old French) 'Pleasure'. Since the Middle Ages it has been used as a first name but is rarely found today.

PURPLE Lucky colour for Sagittarians.

PYRENA (Greek) 'Fiery one'.

PYRENIA (Greek) 'Fiery one'.

RANI (Hebrew) 'Joy'.

RENA, RINA (Hebrew) 'Joy'.

RONI (Hebrew) 'My joy'.

RUSH Lucky plant for Sagittarians.

SAPPHIRA (Greek) 'Eyes of sapphire colour'. Blue and royal blue are lucky colours for Sagittarians.

SERAPHINA (Hebrew) 'Fiery' or 'winged'. Two saints of the 13th and 15th centuries bore the name but it is little used today.

SHUNA, SHUNE Forms of Sula.

SIKA 'The seeker'.

SINOPE Name given to one of Jupiter's moons.

SONA (Gaelic) 'Happy'.

SULA, SHULA, SHULIE (Icelandic) 'Of sunny disposition'.

SUNNY, SUNNIE Usually a pet name for someone with a happy disposition, but occasionally used as a first name.

TATE, TAIT, TEYTE (Old English) 'Cheerful'.

TEGWEN (Welsh) 'Lovely', 'white', 'fair'.

TEMPERANCE Lucky tarot card for Sagittarians.

THEA Derivative of Althea.

THIRZA (Hebrew) 'Pleasantness'. The name occurs in the bible. It has been found from time to time in English-speaking countries since the 17th century.

TIKA (Maori) 'Just'.

TIN Lucky metal for Sagittarians.

TIRZA, TIRZAH Forms of Thirza.

TISHA 'Joy'. Pet form of Letitia. It is occasionally found as a name in its own right.

TRIFID Name given to a nebula in the constellation of Sagittarius.

TRIS, TRISSIE 'Bringer of joy'. Shortened forms of Beatrice.

TRIX, TRIXIE 'Bringer of joy'. Shortened forms of Beatrix.

TRIXY, TRIXIE Shortened form of Beatrix.

VANORA (Celtic) 'White wave'.

VARENE Variation of Verena.

VENETIA (Welsh) 'Happiness'. A name of uncertain origin but possibly an elaborated form of Gwyneth. Has been in occasional use since medieval times.

VERA (Latin) 'Truth'. The name was introduced into Britain at the beginning of the 20th century and was particularly popular for the first half of the century.

VERADA (Latin) 'Truthful', 'forthright'.

VERE Variation of Vera.

VERELLA A blend of Vera and Ella. Ella is an Old-German name meaning 'all'.

VERENA (Latin) 'Truth'. The name was borne by a 3rd-century saint.

VERILA (Latin) 'Little truthful one'.

VERINA Alternative spelling of Verena.

VERINE Form of Verene.

VERITA (Latin) 'Truth'.

VERITY (Latin) 'Truth'. The name was popular amongst the Puritans and is still in occasional use today.

VERLA Form of Vera.

VERNA (Latin) 'Truth'.

VERNETTA 'Truth'. Diminutive of Verna.

VESTA Goddess of fire in Roman mythology. Only rarely found in the English-speaking world.

VON 'Archer with the yew bow'. Shortened form of Yvonne.

VONNIE Shortened form of Yvonne.

WALLIS (German) 'Foreign'. This is the usual feminine spelling of the name. See Sagittarius boys' names.

WANDA (Old German) 'A wanderer'. The name was introduced into English-speaking countries in the 19th century.

WANDIE, WANDIS Forms of Wanda.

WENDA, WENDY, WENDELINE Forms of Wanda.

WENDELIN (Old German) 'A traveller'.

WHITE Lucky colour for Sagittarians.

WINIFRED 'White', 'fair', 'blessed'. Anglicized form of the Welsh name Gwenfrewi.

WYNN, WYNNE (Welsh) 'White', 'pure'. Originally used as a surname.

YEVETTE, YEVETTA (Old German) 'The little archer'.

YVE 'Archer'. French feminine form of Ivor.

YVELDA Blend of Yvette and Velda. Velda is an Old German name meaning 'to rule'.

YVELLA Blend of Yvette and Ella. Ella is an Old-German name meaning 'all'.

YVETTE, YVETTA Forms of Yvonne.

YVINA, YVONA Variants of Yvonne.

YVONNE (French) 'Archer with the yew bow'. Feminine form of Ivor. The name has been in frequent use in English-speaking countries since the early-20th century.

ZINEVRA (Celtic) 'White wave'.

ZITA (Greek) 'To seek'. The name was borne by a 13th-century saint from Tuscany.

Capricorn

THE GOAT
22 December – 19 January

RULING PLANET Saturn. In astrology Saturn is the planet of fate, caution and wisdom.

ELEMENT Earth

General characteristics
- Determined, conscientious.
- Loyal, wise, dependable.
- Hard-working, sets high standards.
- Traditional, conventional.
- Good organisers and managers.
- Caring and considerate.

Characteristics of young Capricorn
- Can appear quite serious.
- Possesses an even temperament.
- Enjoys routine.
- Is practical and sensible.
- Enjoys pretending to be grown up.
- Loves reading.
- Often has a good sense of humour.
- Has one or two special friends.

Capricorn lucky connections
Gemstones:	ruby, black diamond, jet, onyx
Colours:	green, violet, indigo, black, grey
Plants:	ash, yew, weeping willow, hemp
Perfume:	musk
Metal:	lead
Animals:	goat, ass
Tarot card:	the devil

CAPRICORNS are steady and wise characters who may display quiet determination when pursuing their goals. They may appear quite serious, even as babies. They will look and listen carefully, taking in the world around them, before attempting new skills or venturing forth to explore. Young Capricorns need security, warmth and regular routines in their daily lives.

Capricorns are often achievers in life. Even as babies they may be among the first to hold a spoon, to talk, or to master the shape sorter. They have a determined streak which will assist them in mastering new skills, and in so doing will satisfy their need to achieve practical results. Be sure to praise your Capricorn child for their efforts and achievements, as they thrive on your approval, even if they may not always show it.

Even as young children Capricorns may appear mature and wise beyond their years. They often feel more comfortable with adults than with other children, and enjoy pretending to be grown up. They also like being given useful household chores to do such as putting laundry in the machine or putting the shopping away. Encourage this fantasy play by giving your child her own baking set or car cleaning equipment. Make-believe stories or fairy tales may not interest her but this type of 'real life' fantasy will.

As your Capricorn matures she will learn to enjoy the company of other children but may tend to have just one or two close friends. As with all other things she does the Capricorn child will choose her friends with great care.

Capricorn children usually enjoy reading, mastering reading at an early age to become little bookworms. They often enjoy school life because it offers them the opportunity of learning new skills. This, along with the structured routine on which Capricorns thrive, can often make school a place where they excel.

At home many young Capricorns enjoy the challenge of puzzles and may spend hours mastering the skills required to complete these tasks. They also usually enjoy music. So play music to your child, sing to her, and you may find her tapping and singing along with you. Such activities will help to relax your serious Capricorn baby and put a smile on her face.

Although Capricorn children can sometimes seem too sensible and serious for one so young, they often possess a wry wit and sense of humour which serves to lighten their character. Capricorns, with their love of mimicking adults, will often pick up your own mood. If you show tolerance and a relaxed view of life then this will encourage her to follow suit, maybe making her smile just a little more often.

Provide your Capricorn child with encouragement, security and laughter and you will bring out the 'kid' in her, the little mountain goat that longs to frolic on the hillside.

Capricorn ~ Boys

ADAM (Hebrew) 'Of the red earth'. Adam of the Old Testament, the father of the human race, was said to be created from the red earth. The name was particularly popular in the 13th century, the mid-19th century and again in the 1960s.

ADAMNAN 'Little Adam'. The name was borne by St Adamnan, an Irish 7th-century saint.

ADDIS Form of Adam.

ADDISON (Old English) 'Earth'. Son of Adam.

AIKEN (Old English) 'Earth'. Little Adam.

AIKIN, AICKIN Forms of Aiken.

ALDO (Old German) 'Steady and wise'. The name was borne by a 8th-century saint. The name has been popular in Italy for many years and is still used in English-speaking countries by families of Italian descent.

ALFRED (Old English) 'Wise counsel'. The name was fairly common in England before the Norman conquest. It was borne in the 9th century by King Alfred the Great. After the Norman conquest the name was little used for centuries until it was revived in the 18th century.

ALIM (Arabic) 'Wise'.

ALPHA Name given to a double star in the constellation of Capricorn.

ARVAL (Latin) 'Cultivated land'.

ASH The ash is a lucky plant for Capricorn.

ASHBURN (Old English) 'The brook by the ash tree'.

ASHBY (Old English) 'Farm by ash trees'.

ASHCROFT (Old English) 'Small farm by ash trees'.

ASHFORD (Old English) 'Ford near ash trees'.

ASLEY, ASHLEIGH, ASHLEA, ASHLEE (Old English) 'Ash wood'. The name was originally a surname and place name. The name became popular as a boys' name partly due to a character in the successful novel *Gone with the Wind* which was published in 1936. The name is used both as a boys' and girls' name.

ASHTON (Old English) 'Ash tree village'. The name is found mainly in the USA. It was originally a surname and place name but is now used both as a boys' and girls' first name.

ASTLEY (Old English) 'Ash tree glade'.

AVERY 'Wise counsel'. A variant of Alfred.

BRAN In Welsh Druid mythology, the name is borne by a guardian of the land. He was also known as a god of war, who defended British lands.

CALYPSO Name given to one of Saturn's moons.

CASSINI Last name of the astronomer Giovanni Cassini who discovered the gap in Saturn's rings in 1675. The gap is named the Cassini division in his honour.

CATO (Latin) 'The wise one'.

CHRISTMAS From the name of the Christian festival. It has occasionally been given to a child who was born on Christmas Day. The name has been in use since the Middle Ages both as a first name and as a surname.

CIARÁN (Irish Gaelic) 'Black'. Black is a lucky colour for Capricorn. The name was borne by two Irish saints of the 5th and 6th centuries.

CLEARY (Gaelic) 'Scholar'.

CONSTANT (Latin) 'Steadfast'. Medieval form of the name Constantine. The name Constant was used by the Puritans and revived in the 19th century.

CONSTANTINE (Latin) 'Steadfast'. The name was borne by the Roman emperor Constantine the Great, the first Christian emperor. It was also borne by three medieval Scottish kings. Although the name has been in occasional use in Britain since the Dark Ages it is seldom found in English-speaking countries.

CONWAY (Celtic) 'One who takes a wise course'.

COSTIN A form of Constantine.

DANTE An Italian form of Durand. The name was borne by the Italian poet Dante Alighieri and also by the British poet and painter, Dante Gabriel Rossetti, who was of Italian descent.

DARIUS (Greek) 'Good' and 'wealthy'. The name was borne by several Persian kings.

DASHIEL, DASHIELL (Old French/Old English) 'Ash tree of the elves'. The ash is a lucky tree for Capricorn.

DASHWOOD (Old French) 'The ash wood'.

DENEB ALGEDI Name given to the brightest star in the constellation of Capricorn.

DILLON (Celtic) 'Faithful, loyal'.

DREW (Celtic) 'The wise one'. Also a shortened form of Andrew.

DRUCE (Celtic) 'Wise man'.

DUANE, DWAYNE (Irish) 'Black'. Black is a lucky colour for Capricorn. The name became popular in the 1950s due to the fame of the guitarist Duane Eddy.

DURAND Form of Durant. Introduced into Britain from France during the time of the Norman Conquest. During the Middle Ages the name was in regular use but it is rarely found today.

DURANT (Latin) 'Enduring'. 'One who gives lasting friendship'.

EAMON, EAMONN Forms of Edmund.

EARTHAN (Old English) 'Of the earth'.

EDDIE, EDDIE, ED, EDD Shortened forms of Edward or Edmund.

EDLIN Form of Edwin.

EDMOND French spelling of Edmund, introduced into Britain in the Middle Ages.

EDMUND 'Rich or prosperous guardian'. The name was borne by St Edmunds, a 9th-century martyr who was also King of East Anglia. The Suffolk town of Bury St Edmunds is named in his honour. The name is also borne by two English kings in the 10th and 11th century and by another saint, Edmund Rich, who was a 13th-century Archbishop of Canterbury.

EDUARD Alternative spelling of Edward.

EDWARD 'Rich or prosperous guardian'. The name has been in regular use since the early Middle Ages. Its association with the British royal families began in the 9th century when it was borne by King Edward the Elder, son of Alfred the Great. Perhaps the most influential bearer of the name was Edward the Confessor who reigned in the 11th century.

EDWIN (Old English) 'Rich or prosperous friend'. The name was borne by King Edwin of Northumbria after whom, it is believed, the city of Edinburgh was named. The name was little used after the 12th century until its revival in the 19th century. It remained in regular use until the mid-20th century.

ELDRIDGE (Old English) 'Wise advisor'.

ELLESWORTH (Old English) 'A farmer, lover of the earth'.

ELVIS (Norse) 'All wise'. The prince of wisdom. The most famous bearer of this name was the US singer Elvis Presley.

EMIL (German) 'Industrious and hard-working'. The name originates from a Roman clan name Aemilius.

EMILE French form of Emil.

EMILIO Form of Emil.

EMLYN Form of Emil.

EMMETT, EMMET (Latin)
'Industrious and hard-working'.

EMMIT Alternative spelling of Emmet.

EMMOT, EMMOTT Form of Emmett.

EMMY Shortened form of Emmett.

ENKI Name of a Mesopotamian god of wisdom and water. Saturn, the ruling planet of Capricorn, is the planet of applied wisdom.

ENOCH (Hebrew) 'Dedicated'. The name was borne by the father of Methuselah in the Old Testament. In the 17th century the name was used by the Puritans. The most famous recent bearer of the name is the 20th-century British politician Enoch Powell.

ERNEST, EARNEST (Old German) 'Resolute, sincere'. The name was introduced into Britain in the 18th century but did not become well used until the latter half of the 19th century.

ERNIE, ERN Shortened forms of Ernie.

ETHAN (Hebrew) 'Steadfast, unwavering'. The name is mentioned in the Old Testament. It became popular in the USA in the latter half of the 18th century due to the influence of the soldier Ethan Allen who played a leading role in the American War of Independence.

EUNAN (Irish and Scottish) 'Earth'. Gaelic form of Adam.

FERRANT (Old French) 'Iron grey'. Grey is a lucky colour for Capricorns.

FIDEL (Latin) 'Faithful'. The name was borne by Fidel Castro, the Cuban revolutionary leader who was born in the early-20th century. The name is still in occasional use in the English-speaking countries.

GAIAN (Greek) 'Child of the earth'.

GEORGE (Greek) 'Earth, the farmer'. The name was borne by St George, the patron saint of England. The legend of St George and the Dragon is thought to be a medieval Italian invention. The name became popular in Britain after the accession of King George I in 1714. Its popularity in the USA grew with the initiation of George Washington as the first president of the USA (1732-99). The name remains popular today.

GEORGES Form of George.

GEORGIE, GEORDIE Pet forms of George.

GORDIE, GORDY Pet forms of George.

GEORGY, GEORG Pet forms of George.

GILES (Greek) 'Young goat' or (French) 'youthful'. The goat is a lucky animal for Capricorn. In the 8th century the name was borne by a hermit, St Giles, who was able to heal the lame and the crippled. The name was first used in Britain in the 12th century.

GILLES, GIL Forms of Giles.

GIOVANNI First name of Giovanni Cassini who discovered the gap in Saturn's ring.

GRAY (Old English) 'To shine'. Also the American spelling of grey, a lucky colour for Capricorns.

GREENDALE (Old English) 'Green valley'. Green is a lucky colour for Capricorns.

GREENWOOD (Old English) 'Green woodland'. Green is a lucky colour for Capricorn.

HADRIAN (Greek) 'Rich'.

HARLAND, HARLAN (Middle English) 'Strand of hemp'. Hemp is a lucky plant for Capricorn. The name is found mainly in the USA. It was originally a surname and place name. A famous bearer of the name was the American judge John Marshall Harlan who was a pioneer of civil rights.

HARLEY, HARLEIGH (Old English) 'Hemp field'. Hemp is a lucky plant for Capricorn. Originally a surname and place name. As a first name it is found mainly in the USA.

HARRINGTON (Old English) 'Place of the he-goat'. The goat is a lucky animal for Capricorn.

HEMP Lucky plant for Capricorn.

HYPERION Name given to one of Saturn's moons.

IVO (Old German) 'Yew'. Yew is a lucky plant for Capricorn. The name was in frequent use in the Middle Ages but is little used in modern times.

JADEN (Hebrew) 'Wise'.

JANUS Name given to one of Saturn's moons.

JASPER (Persian) 'Wise man'. Jasper is the anglicized form of the name Caspar. The name was first used in medieval times and is still in occasional use today.

JESSE, JESSEY, JESS, JES (Hebrew) 'Wealthy' or 'gift'. The name was borne by the father of King David. The name was popular with the Puritans and remains in occasional use today.

JET (Greek) From the name of the precious stone. Jet is a lucky gemstone for Capricorn. It is also a French name meaning 'to throw forward'.

JETHRO (Hebrew) 'Riches' or 'excellence'. The name is found in the Old Testament and was popular among the Puritans. The name has been revived since the formation of the rock group Jethro Tull in 1968.

JORGE 'Earth, the farmer'. Form of George.

JORIN Form of George.

JORIS Form of George.

JURGEN Form of George.

KEAN 'Wise', 'learned'. Alternative spelling of Keene.

KEANE 'Wise', 'learned'. Alternative spelling of Keene.

KEENAN 'Wise', 'learned'. Form of Keene.

KEENE (Old English) 'Wise, learned'.

KERRIN Form of Kieran.

KERRY Form of Kieran.

KERWIN , KIRWIN (Irish) 'Dark, black'. Black is a lucky colour for Capricorn.

KIERAN, KIERON, KYRAN (Irish) 'Dark, black'. The name was borne by two Irish saints in the 5th and 6th centuries.

KIRAN, KYRAN Forms of Kieron.

LELIO (Old German) 'Loyal'.

LICHFIELD (Welsh) 'Grey wood'. Grey is a lucky colour for Capricorn.

LLOYD (Welsh) 'Grey'. Originally a Welsh surname now also used as a first name throughout English-speaking countries.

MENDEL (Semitic) 'Wisdom'.

NEDDIE, NEDDY, NED 'Rich or prosperous friend'. Pet forms of Edward.

NESTOR (Greek) 'Ancient wisdom'.

NOEL (French) 'Christmas'. The name was in regular use in Britain during Medieval times. It was at one time given to both boys and girls but is now regarded as a masculine name.

OBERT (Old German) 'Wealthy and brilliant'.

ODELL (Old German) 'Wealthy one'.

ODIN, ODO Forms of Odell.

ODO (Old German) 'Wealth'. The name was borne by a French abbot St Odo of Cluny in the 1st century. The name occurs in the Doomsday Book in 1086 in a number of forms. It also influenced several surnames such as Oates, Oddie and Otis.

ORAN (Irish) 'Green'. A lucky colour for Capricorn. The name was borne by several early saints.

ORLAN (Old English) 'From the pointed land'.

ORLANDO 'Famous land'. Italian from of Roland.

ORTWIN (Old English) 'Wealthy friend'.

OTHO Form of Odo.

OTIS From a medieval form of Odo. Its use is mainly confined to the USA.

OTTO (Old German) 'Wealth'. The name was borne by four Holy Roman emperors of the 10th and 13th centuries. It was in regular use in Britain during the Middle Ages but is only used occasionally in modern times.

RESHAD (Sanskrit) 'Teacher'.

ROLAND, ROWLAND, ROLYND (Old German) 'Famous land'. The name was introduced into Britain at the time of the Norman Conquest. Rowland was the usual spelling of the name until the 19th century when the French form of the name Roland became more popular.

ROLEY, ROLLIN Forms of Roland.

ROLLAND, ROLLO Forms of Roland.

ROWAN From the name of the Scandinavian tree name. The Rowan is a mountain ash – a lucky plant for Capricorns.

SAGE (Old English) 'Wise one'.

SAFFORD (Old English) 'Dweller at the willow tree crossing'. Willow is a lucky plant for Capricorns.

SATURN Name of the ruling planet of Capricorn.

SAWARD (Old English) 'Fort where the sallows (willows) grow'.

SCHUYLER (Dutch) 'A scholar', 'a wise man'.

SEIKO (Japanese) 'Success'.

SELBY (Old English) 'Willow farm'. Since the 19th century the name has been found occasionally as a first name.

SHANAHAN (Gaelic) 'The wise one'.

SHANNON (Gaelic) 'Wise old one'.

SOLAMAN, SOLOMAN, SALOMON Alternative spellings of Solomon.

SOLOMON (Hebrew) 'Wise and peaceful'. King Solomon of the Old

Testament was considered to be a man of great wisdom. In the Middle Ages the name was in regular use in Britain. It was revived by the Puritans but is generally used as a Jewish name.

SOLON (Greek) 'Wise man'. Greek form of Solomon.

STERLING, STIRLING (Old German) 'Reliable, worthy'. Originally a surname and Scottish place name. Famous 20th-century bearers of the name include Stirling Moss, the British racing driver, and Sterling Hayden, the American actor.

TEDDY 'Rich or prosperous friend'. Pet form of Edward.

TETHYS Name given to one of Saturn's moons.

THU Name given to the god of the earth in Chinese mythology.

TIMON (Greek) 'Honourable, valuable'.

TITAN Name given to the largest of Saturn's moons.

TREVOR (Gaelic) 'Prudent, wise and discreet'. One who can be trusted to keep secrets. Originally a Welsh surname. It began to be used as a first name in the middle of the 19th century and became popular in the 20th century throughout English-speaking countries.

TRIGG (Scandinavian) 'Loyal, faithful'.

TSAI SHEN Name given to the god of wealth in Chinese mythology.

VARDON, VARDEN (Old English) 'Green hill'.

VERDANT (Latin) 'Green, spring-like'.

WELBY (Old English) 'Village near willow trees'.

WELDON (Old English) 'Willow trees on the hill'.

WILBER, WILBUR (Old English) 'Willow town'. It also means 'resolute and brilliant', 'a determined and clever person'. Originally used as a surname now occasionally found as a surname since the 19th century. A famous bearer of the name was the U.S. aviator Wilbur Wright.

WILBERT (Old English) 'Bright willows'. Occasionally found in English-speaking countries especially the USA.

WILBY Form of Wilber.

WILEY (Old English) 'Willow field'.

WILFORD (Old English) 'Willow trees near a fort'.

WILLARD (Old English) 'Willow yard'. Originally a surname, occasionally found as a first name, especially in the USA.

WILLOW (Old English) From the tree name. The willow is a lucky plant for Capricorn.

WILLOUGHBY (Old English) 'Farm near the willows'. Originally a surname and place name from northern England.

WILTON (Old English) 'Farm near the willow trees'.

WYTHE (Old English) 'Dweller near the willow'.

YEW Lucky plant for Capricorn.

YORICK 'Earth'. From a character in Shakespeare's *Hamlet*. A Danish form of George.

YORK (Celtic) 'Yew tree estate'. The yew is a lucky plant for Capricorn. Originally a surname and local name from the city in Yorkshire, England.

YNYR (Welsh) 'Honourable'.

YULES , YULE (Old English) 'Born at Christmas'.

YURI (Greek) 'Earth, the farmer'. Russian derivative of George.

YVES (Old German) 'Yew'. French form of Ivo. Yew is a lucky plant for Capricorn. The name was introduced into Britain from France at the time of the Norman Conquest. The name was made famous in English-speaking countries by the French couturier Yves Saint-Laurent.

ZENON (Greek) 'Gift of Zeus'.

ZEUS Name of Greek god in mythology. An important character in the story of Capricorn.

Capricorn ~ Girls

ABRA (Hebrew) 'Earth mother'.

ADAMINA (Hebrew) 'Earth'. A feminine form of Adam.

AGAVE (Greek) 'Illustrious and noble'.

ALDA (Old German) 'Wise and rich'.

ALFREDA (Old German) 'Wise counsellor'. Feminine form of Alfred.

ALLIE Shortened form of Alfreda.

ALODIE (Old English) 'Rich'.

ALPHA Name given to a double star in the constellation of Capricorn.

ALYSSA (Greek) 'Wise'.

AMALIA, AMALIE Forms of Amelia.

AMALTHEIA Name of the goat-nymph in the story of Capricorn in Greek mythology. The name means 'tender'.

AMEALIA, AMELEA Alternative spellings of Amelia.

AMEENA Possibly a form of Amelia.

AMELIA (Old German) 'Industrious'. The name was little used in Britain before the 18th century. It was then popularised by Princess Amelia, the daughter of King George III and also by the heroine of Henry Fielding's novel *Amelia*.

AMELINE Form of Amelia.

AMELIE Form of Amelia.

AMELITA Form of Amelia.

AMETHYST (Greek) 'Sober one'.

AMIRA (Greek) 'Wise'.

AO (Maori) 'Planet Earth'.

ASLEY, ASHLEIGH, ASHLEA, ASHLEE (Old English) 'Ash wood'.

Used as both a girls' and boys' name. See Capricorn boys' names.

ATHENA (Greek) 'Wisdom'.

ATHENE Name of the Greek goddess of wisdom.

BELINDA (Latin) 'Wise beauty'. The name has been in regular use in English-speaking countries since the 18th century.

BEV, BERRY Shortened forms of Beverley.

BEVERLEY, BEVERLY (Old English) 'Ambitious one'. Originally used as a boy's name in the late-19th century. It gradually became a girls' name, especially in the USA.

BEVERLIE Alternative spelling of Beverley.

BRYNA (Irish) 'Strength with virtue'.

CACHEL (French) 'Hidden wisdom'.

CACHELLA (French) 'Hidden wisdom'.

CACHELLE (French) 'Hidden wisdom'.

CHANTESUTA (Native American) 'Determined'.

CHRISTMAS From the name of the Christian festival. It has occasionally been given to a child who was born on Christmas Day. The name has been in use since the Middle Ages both as a first name and as a surname.

CONSTANCE (Latin) 'Steadfast'. The name has been in regular use in Britain since the time of the Normans, with whom it was popular. It was frequently found throughout the English-speaking countries in the early part of the 20th century but is seldom used today.

CONSTANTINA (Latin) 'Steadfast'. Feminine form of Constantine.

DANA Alternative name of Danu.

DANU Name given to the mother goddess of the land in Irish Druid mythology. Danu is also known as a river goddess.

DASHA (Old French) 'The ash tree'.

DEBORAH (Hebrew) 'The bee', hence 'an industrious person' who looks for 'what is sweet in life'. The name is found in the Old Testament. It has been found in English-speaking countries since the 17th century and was particularly popular in the mid-20th century.

DEBORA, DEBRA Alternative spellings for Deborah.

DEBBIE, DEBBY Shortened forms of Deborah.

DECIA (Latin) Possibly a form of 'Decima' meaning tenth. Capricorn is the tenth sign of the zodiac.

DENEB ALGEDI Name given to the brightest star in the constellation of Capricorn.

DIANTHA (Greek) 'Divine flower of Zeus'. The birth of Zeus surrounds the story of Capricorn in Greek mythology.

DIANTHE Form of Diantha.

DIANTHIA Form of Diantha.

DIDO (Greek) 'Teacher'.

DIELLA (Latin) 'The lord's faithful'.

DILLYS, DILYS (Welsh) 'Genuine'. In the mid-19th century the name was first found in Wales. It is now found throughout other parts of Britain.

DIONE Name given to one of Saturn's moons. It is also the Greek form of the Latin name Diana which means 'divine'.

DOCLIA (Latin) 'Gentle teacher'.

DORINA (Hebrew) 'Perfection'.

DURENE (Latin) 'The enduring one'.

DURETTA (Spanish) 'Little steadfast one'.

EADA, ELDA 'Wise and rich'. Forms of Alda.

EADWINA, EADWINE, EDWINE, EDINA Forms of Edwina.

EARTHA (Old English) 'From the earth'.

EDINA (Old English) 'Rich friend'.

EDMONDA (Old English) 'Rich protector'. Feminine form of Edmond.

EDMUNDA (Old English) 'Rich protector'. Feminine form of Edmund.

EDWARDINA (Old English) 'Rich guardian'. Feminine form of Edward.

EDWINA (Old English) 'Rich friend'. Of 19th-century coinage. A feminine form of Edwin.

ELFREDA (Old English) 'Wise counsellor'. The name was borne by the mother of Ethelred the Unready but was little used until it was revived in the 19th century.

ELFRIDA, ELFRIEDA, AELFREDA Alternative spellings of Elfreda.

ELRA (Old German) 'Elfin wisdom'.

EMALINE, EMELYNE Forms of Emily.

EMBLYN Form of Emily.

EMELIE Form of Emilia.

EMELINA 'Industrious and striving'. Form of Emilia from Amelia.

EMELINE, EMELYN Forms of Emily.

EMERE (Maori) Form of Emily.

EMILY (Latin) 'Ambitious', 'industrious'. The name was introduced into Britain in the Middle Ages. It was not common then but was revived in the 19th century and has been a popular name since then.

EMILIA 'Industrious and hard-working'. Form of Emily.

EMMELINE, EMMALINE, EMMILINE Forms of Emily.

ERDA (Old German) 'Child of the earth'.

ESWEN (Welsh) 'Strength'.

ETANA (Hebrew) 'Strong'.

EVONNE (Old German) 'Yew.' Alternative spelling of Yvonne. Form of Ivo. Yew is a lucky plant for Capricorn.

FABIOLA (Latin) 'Hard-working'. The name was born by St Fabiola the founder of the first Western hospital.

FABRIANNE (Latin) 'Young and hard-working'.

FAE Shortened form of Faith.

FAITH (Old German) 'One who is loyal and true'. The name came into use in Britain in the 16th century where it was very popular with the Puritans. It remains in use today.

FARRAH (Arabic) 'Wild ass'. The ass is a lucky animal for Capricorn.

FAY (Gaelic) 'The raven'. Symbol of great wisdom. A name of fairly recent coinage, first used in the late-19th century. Its use as a first name may have been influenced by Arthurian legend in that it was borne by Morgan le Fay, the half-sister of King Arthur, known as the Lady of the Lake.

FAYE Alternative spelling of Fay.

FAYETTE Form of Fay.

FIDELMA A blend of Fidel (Latin)

'faithful' and Mary (Greek form of Miriam) 'sea'.

FRODINE (Old German) 'Wise friend'.

GAEA (Greek) 'The earth'. Name of the goddess of the earth.

GAIA Alternative spelling of Gaea.

GEORGANA Form of Georgiana.

GEORGETTE 'Earth, farmer'. Feminine diminutive of George.

GEORGIA 'Earth'. Latin feminine form of George. Particularly popular in the USA. The American state of Georgia was named after the British King George II.

GEORGIANA Elaborated form of Georgia. The name was reasonably fashionable in the 18th and 19th century but is rarely found today.

GEORGENE, GEORGINE Feminine forms of George.

GEORGY, GEORGIE Pet forms of Georgia.

GEORGINA Latin feminine form of George. The name has been regularly found in Britain since the 18th century but is seldom found elsewhere.

GIANE (Greek) 'Child of the earth'.

GIROGIA Feminine form of George.

HELENE Name given to one of Saturn's moons.

HERMINA (Latin) Form of Hermione. 'Belonging to the earth'.

HERMIONE (Latin) 'Earthy'. In Greek mythology Hermione was the daughter of Helen of Troy. Hermione is a form of Hermes, the messenger of the gods.

HERTA 'Earth mother'. Form of Hertha.

HERTHA (Old German) 'Earth mother'.

IANTHA (Greek) 'Violet flower'. Violet is a lucky colour for Capricorn.

IANTHE (Greek) 'Violet flower'. The name was revived in the 19th century by the poet Shelley in his poem *Queen Mab*. He also bestowed this name on his first daughter.

IANTHINA (Greek) 'Violet flower'.

IDONEA Of uncertain origin. It may be from Old Norse, meaning 'work', or from Latin meaning 'suitable'. It has been in infrequent use in Britain since the 13th century.

IDYLLA (Greek) 'Perfection'.

INDIGO Name of a lucky colour for Capricorns.

IOLANA, IOLANI 'Violet flower'. Hawaiian form of Yolanda.

IOLANTA, IOLANTHE 'Violet flower'. Form of Yolande.

IVA (French) 'The yew tree'. The yew is a lucky plant for Capricorn.

IVANNA, IVANNE Forms of Iva.

JAALA (Hebrew) 'Wild she-goat'. The goat is a lucky animal for Capricorn.

JADA (Hebrew) 'Wise'.

JAEL (Hebrew) 'Mountain goat'. The name was adopted by the Puritans after the Reformation. It is rarely found in modern times.

JAELLE, JAELLA Forms of Jael.

JANTHINA , JANTHINE (Greek) 'Violet flower'. Forms of Iolanthe.

JESSALYN (Hebrew) 'Wealthy woman'.

JET (Greek) From the name of the precious stone. Jet is a lucky gemstone for Capricorn.

JETTA Form of Jet.

JOLANDA, JOLANDI 'Violet flower'. Forms of Yolande.

JOYA (Spanish) 'Treasure'.

KENDRA (English) 'Knowledge'.

KIERA (Irish) 'Dark', 'black'. Recently coined feminine form of Kieran.

KYNA (Gaelic) 'Great wisdom'.

LEE Shortened form of Leela.

LEELA Form of Leila.

LEILA (Arabic) 'Black as the night'. Black is a lucky colour for Capricorn. The name came into use throughout English speaking countries in the 19th century. It is still in occasional use today.

LEILIA Form of Leila.

LEILAH Form of Leila.

LELA Form of Leila.

LILIA Form of Leila.

LILAH Form of Leila.

LLOY (Welsh) 'Grey'. A form of Lloyd.

MADELINE (Greek) 'Tower of strength'. The name is found in the New Testament. It was introduced into Britain from France in medieval times.

MADELEINE, MADELAINE, MADALINE, MADELEINE, MADALAINE Forms of Madeline.

MADALENA, MADDALENA Forms of Madeline.

MADDALENE, MADELON, MADLIN Forms of Madeline.

MADEL, MADELIA, MADELLA Forms of Madeline.

MADELE Forms of Madeline.

MADELLE Forms of Madeline.

MAGDALA, MAGDA, MAGDALEN, MAGDALENE Forms of Madeline.

MAGDALYN, MAGDALANE Forms of Madeline.

MAHINA Origin uncertain. Possibly a form of Mahira.

MAHIRA (Hebrew) 'Industrious'.

MAHRA A form of Mahira.

MAIYA (Sanskrit) An aspect of the goddess Gaia, goddess of the earth.

MARLEEN, MARLENE, MARLINE Forms of Madeline.

MARLENA, MALINA Forms of Madeline.

MEL Pet form of Melanie.

MELANIA Form of Melanie.

MELANIE, MELLONEY (Greek) 'Black'. Black is a lucky colour for Capricorn. The name was borne by two Roman saints in the 4th and 5th centuries. The name was introduced into Britain from France in the mid-17th century. It was in use mainly in Devon and Cornwall until the 20th century when it became popular throughout English-speaking countries.

MELISANDE (Old German) 'Strong, hard-working and energetic'.

MELL, MELLIE 'Industrious and hard-working.' Forms of Amelia.

MILL, MILLIE Forms of Amelia.

MIMAS Name given to one of Saturn's moons.

MINERVA (Latin) 'Wise and purposeful'. Name of the Roman goddess of wisdom, arts and crafts and war. Occasionally given as a girls' name in English-speaking countries.

MORETTA, MORETA (Hebrew) 'Teacher'.

MUSK Name of the lucky perfume for Capricorn.

NATALIA (Latin) 'Birthday' – in reference to Christmas Day. In the 4th century it was the name borne by St Natalia, wife of the Christian martyr St Adrian. It has been in use throughout English-speaking countries for centuries.

NATALIE, NATHALIE French forms of Natalia. It has became more popular in English-speaking countries since the mid-20th century.

NATALYA Form of Natalia.

NATASHA Russian form of Natalia. It has been in regular use in English-speaking countries since the mid-20th century.

NOELLE, NOELE (French) 'Christmas'. Feminine forms of Noel.

NOELEEN, NOELINE Feminine forms of Noel.

ODELIA (Old German) 'Riches' or 'wealth'.

ODELIE Form of Odelia.

ODELLA Form of Odelia.

ODELINDA Elaborated form of Odelia.

ODETTE (Old German) 'Riches' or 'wealth'. French feminine form of masculine name Oda.

ODILE Form of Odelia.

ODILIA Form of Odelia.

ODILLA Form of Odelia.

ODILE, ODILLE (Old German) 'Riches'. French form of the medieval Germanic name Odila. The name was borne by the patron saint of Alsace, who founded a Benedictine Convent in the 8th century.

ODINA Origin uncertain. Possibly a form of Odile.

OFELIA, OFILIA, PHELIA Forms of Ophelia.

ONYX Name of a lucky gemstone for Capricorn.

OPHELIA (Greek) 'Wise lady'. The name appears in Shakespeare's *Hamlet*. It has been in occasional use as a first name since the 19th century.

ORANDA A blend of Oran and Amanda. Oran is an Irish name meaning 'green' – a lucky colour for Capricorn. Amanda is a Latin name meaning 'loveable'.

ORANTHA A blend of Oran and Samantha. Samantha is an Aramaic name meaning 'listener'.

OTHA Form of Odelia.

OTHALIE 'Wealthy'. Form of Otto.

OTHILLA Form of Odelia.

OTTILIE, OTTALIE 'Wealthy'. Swedish form of Otto.

OTTOLINE French pet form of Odile.

PANDORA Name given to one of Saturn's moons.

PHILYRIA (Greek) 'Graceful as a willow'. The willow is a lucky plant for Capricorn.

PHOEBE (Greek) 'Shining one'. Name given to one of Saturn's moons.

PRUDENCE (English) 'Prudence'. The name was first used in the 13th century and was one of many names of abstract qualities adopted by the Puritans. It is still in occasional use in English-speaking countries today.

RAYMONDE (Old German) 'Wise'. Feminine form of Raymond.

RESA Origin uncertain, possibly a form of Resha.

RESHA Origin uncertain, possibly a feminine form of Reshad, meaning 'teacher'.

RHEA Important character in the story of Capricorn in Greek mythology. It is also the name given to one of Saturn's moons; Saturn is the ruling planet of Capricorn. In Greek mythology Rhea was the mother of Zeus. It is occasionally given as a girl's name in English-speaking countries.

RHIANNON Name of a goddess of the land in Welsh druid mythology. The name is also associated with the moon in Celtic mythology. It has only been given as a first name since the 20th century.

ROLANDA, ROLANDE (Old German) 'Famous land'. Feminine forms of Roland.

ROLANTHA A blend of Roland and Samantha. Samantha means 'listener'.

ROLARA A blend of Roland and Lara. Lara means 'cheerful'.

ROLENE A blend of Roland and Ilene. Ilene means 'light'.

ROMAIRE A blend of Roland and Maire. Maire is a form of Mary meaning 'sea' or 'wished-for child'.

ROUANE A form of Rowena.

ROWANDA A blend of Rowena and Wanda. Wanda is from the Old Norse 'a young tree' or the Slavonic for 'traveller'.

ROWANTHA A blend of Rowena and Samantha. Samantha is an Aramaic name meaning 'listener'.

ROWENA Feminine form of Rowan. From the name of the Scandinavian tree, the mountain ash. The ash tree is a lucky plant for Capricorns.

RUBINA Diminutive of Ruby.

RUBY (Latin) Name of a lucky gemstone for Capricorn.

RUBI, RUBIE (Latin) From the name of the jewel.

SABELLA (Latin) 'Wise'.

SABLE (Old French) 'Black' (as in heraldry).

SADHBH, SADHBHB 'Wisdom'. Forms of Sophie.

SAGINA (Latin) 'Wise one'.

SAGUNA (Latin) 'Wise one'.

SAI (Japanese) 'Intelligence'.

SARADA (Sanskrit) 'Goddess of wisdom'.

SATURN Name of the ruling planet of Capricorn.

SEIKO (Japanese) 'Success'.

SHANNAGH (Gaelic) 'Wise'. Originally an Irish surname.

SHANNAH, SHANNA 'Wise'. Variants of Shannagh.

SIMA (Arabic) 'Treasure'.

SONIA, SONYA, SONJA 'Wisdom'. Russian and Slavonic forms of Sophia.

SOPHIA, SOFIA (Greek) 'Wisdom'. The name was borne by several saints and has been in use in Britain since the 17th century. It was particularly popular in the 18th century and remains in use today.

SOPHRONIA (Greek) 'Prudent'. The name is occasionally given as a first name in English-speaking countries.

TAKARA (Japanese) 'Treasure'.

TALIA Shortened form of Natalia.

TALYA Shortened form of Natalya.

TANIA, TANYA Shortened form of Tatiana. Name given to one of Saturn's moons.

TATIANA Feminine form of Titan, which is the name given to the largest of Saturn's moons.

TELESTO Name given to one of Saturn's moons.

TERAH (Latin) 'The earth'.

TERRENA (Latin) 'Of the earth'.

TETHYS Name given to one of Saturn's moons.

THEOPHANIA (Latin) Name given to the Christian festival of the Epiphany, meaning 'manifestation of God'. In medieval times the name was occasionally given to girls born on the Twelfth Night (January 6th).

TIERRA (Spanish) 'Land', 'Earth'.

TIFFANY French form of Theophania. In Medival times Tiffany was in regular use in Britain. It regained popularity in the latter-half of the 20th century, influenced by the famous jewellers, Tiffany's, and the film *Breakfast at Tiffany's* (1961).

TI-MU Name given to the earth mother, the maker of all creation in Chinese mythology.

TITAN Name given to the largest of Saturn's moons.

TITANIA Feminine form of Titan. The name was also borne by the legendary queen of the fairies in Shakespeare's *Midsummers' Night Dream*.

TI-YA Alternative name for Ti-mu.

TOYA (Sioux) 'Green'.

TYNA (Gaelic) 'Dark grey'.

UDELE (Old English) 'Great wealth'.

VALIDA 'Very wise'. Form of Velda.

VELDA (Old German) 'Very wise'.

VERDA (Old French) 'Green', 'spring like'.

VI Shortened form of Viola or Violet.

VIOLA (Latin) 'Violet'. The name was borne by one of the heroines in Shakespeare's *Twelfth Night*. It is occasionally found as a first name in English-speaking countries.

VIOLET (Middle English) From the flower name. Name of a lucky colour for Capricorns. The name was used mainly in Scotland until the latter-half of the 19th century when it spread to other English-speaking countries.

VIOLETTE, VIOLETTA Diminutives of Violet or Viola.

VITOULIA (Latin) Italian derivative of Violet.

WILLOW (Old English) From the tree name. The willow is a lucky plant for Capricorn.

WINNIE, WINA, WIN 'Rich and prosperous friend'. Shortened forms of Edwina.

YEW Lucky plant for Capricorn.

YOLA (Greek) 'Violet flower'.

YOLANA Form of Yolanda.

YOLANDA, YOLANDE (Greek) 'Violet flower'.

YOLANDRA Blend of Yolanda and Sandra. Sandra is the Italian form of Alexandra, meaning 'defender of men'.

YOLANTA Form of Yolanda.

YOLANTHA Blend of Yolanda and Samantha. Samantha is a Hebrew name meaning 'to listen'.

YOLARA Blend of Yolanda and Lara. Lara is a Latin name meaning 'famous'.

YOLINA Blend of Yolanda and Lina. Lina is a pet form of Carolina, a feminine form of Charles.

YOLITHA Blend of Yolanda and Talitha. Talitha is an Aramaic name meaning 'little girl'.

YOLONDA Blend of Yolanda and Londa. Londa is a blend of Lona and Wanda.

YVETTE (Old German) 'Yew'. French feminine form of Ivo. Yew is a lucky plant for Capricorn.

YVONNE (Old German) 'Yew'. French feminine form of Ivo. The name was used regularly throughout English-speaking countries since the early-20th century.

ZENAIDA From Zenobia 'Zeus gave life'. Zeus was an important god in the story of Capricorn in Greek mythology.

ZENAIDE Form of Zenaida.

ZENDA Form of Zenobia.

ZENIA Form of Zenobia.

ZENINA Form of Zenobia.

ZENNA Shortened form of Zenobia.

ZENNIE Shortened form of Zenobia.

ZENOBIA (Greek) 'Power of Zeus' or 'Zeus gave life'. Zeus is an important character in the story of Capricorn in Greek mythology. The name Zenobia was borne by a 3rd-century ruler of Palmyra.

ZENORBIE Form of Zenobia.

ZOLA (Greek) 'Duty'. Possibly derived from the surname of the French writer Emile Zola who was of Italian descent.

ZOSIMA (Greek) 'Riches'.

Aquarius

THE WATER CARRIER
20 January – 18 February

RULING PLANETS   Uranus and Saturn. Uranus is the planet of originality and the unexpected. Saturn is the planet of wisdom and forward planning.

ELEMENT   Air

General characteristics

- Friendly, calm, relaxed.
- Detached, cool, analytical.
- Original, intriguing, inventive.
- Independent.
- Often fortunate.
- Humanitarian, fair-minded.
- Enjoys fame and recognition.

Characteristics of young Aquarians

- Is sensitive and kind.
- Has a wide variety of friends.
- Can be unpredictable.
- Is an inventive and original thinker.

- Can be enquiring and analytical.
- Does not like rules or routine.
- Enjoys peace and harmony.
- Can be dreamy and poetic.

Aquarian lucky connections

Gemstones:	topaz, sapphire, onyx, glass
Colours:	light yellow, violet
Plants:	aspen, olive
Perfume:	galbanum
Metal:	lead
Animals:	eagle, peacock
Tarot card:	the star

AQUARIUS is the sign of inventiveness, the new and the unusual. Your Aquarius child will always have an unexpected and interesting way at looking at things, and it may not always be your way. Aquarians are not afraid to throw out the established order of things, be it your orderly household routines or a school timetable, in order to try to rearrange things in his own inventive way. This ability to look at things in a new way may not always mean that life with your little Aquarian runs smoothly. He may have no regard for the way in which you want things to be done and you may find him quite stubborn in insisting on doing things in his own particular way. But this originality of thought is also an Aquarian's strength. They see a new slant on the established way of things, and will open your eyes to new ways of tackling tasks. Aquarians are the original thinkers of this world.

Aquarians are very much group-orientated individuals. They possess a thoughtful, calm and caring nature and older Aquarians often possess strong beliefs in humanitarian issues. Communication is a strong point with Aquarians. They love to discuss and share their ideas with others, and can be persistently logical in their beliefs, even if they conflict with yours. So be prepared for a well thought out, logical discussion as to why bedtime should be an hour later than you wish it to be.

Your life can be thrown into disarray by the arrival of your Aquarian baby. Their unpredictability can mean that your baby wants to feed at very odd times. An Aquarian's development may also be erratic. He may make no progress at all, and then suddenly astonish you at how quickly he masters a new skill. He may for example learn to walk before he can crawl. He has never heard of the usual order of developmental milestones, and even if he had he would probably take absolutely no notice of them.

Along with their quirkiness, Aquarian babies can be calm, friendly and charming little individuals, full of smiles and bright-eyed wonder. The world is there for them to explore and they are fascinated by every new experience.

Provide your young Aquarian with plenty of opportunities to develop his inventiveness. Aquarians love to create and explore their environment in their own special way. Give him plenty of interesting toys but don't be surprised if he plays with them in a totally unexpected way.

Aquarians love to talk and as your child matures it will be useful for you to encourage him to develop this side of his nature. Discuss his ideas, encourage him to explore the ideas behind his actions. Developing the communicative side of his nature will help you to convince him that he shouldn't act out some of his crazier ideas no matter how much he may want to. For example, it may help him to realise that digging up your new flowerbeds is probably not such a good idea after all.

Aquarius ~ Boys

ADEEL (Arabic) 'Just, honest'.

ADIL (Arabic) 'Just, honest'.

AHREN (Old German) 'Eagle'. The eagle is a lucky creature for Aquarius.

ALBERT (Old German) 'Noble, bright and illustrious'. The name was introduced into Britain by the Normans. It became popular throughout English-speaking countries following the marriage of Queen Victoria to Prince Albert in 1840.

ALDWIN, ALDWYN (Old English) 'Old friend'. The name was popular in the Middle Ages and is still occasionally found today.

ALFRED (Old German) 'Wise'. The most famous bearer of the name was Alfred the Great in the 9th century. The name was in frequent use for centuries and was revived in the 19th century.

ALIM (Arabic) 'Wise'. Saturn, one of the ruling planets of Aquarius, is the planet of applied wisdom.

ALURED Form of Alfred.

ALVAN Form of Alvin.

ALVIN (Old English) 'Friend of all' or 'noble friend'. The name has been in existence since the time of the Normans and was revived in the 19th century. It is frequently found in the USA.

ALVIS (Scandinavian) 'Wise suitor'.

ALWYN, ALWIN Forms of Alvin.

ANGUS (Scottish) 'Unique'. The name has been popular both in Scotland and Ireland. In its Gaelic form the name was borne by an Irish god of love, Aonghus Og.

AQUILA, AQUILLA (Latin) 'Eagle'. The eagle is a lucky creature for Aquarius.

ARLIN (Old German) 'Eagle wood'. The eagle is a lucky creature for Aquarius.

ARLINGTON (Old German) 'Settlement at eagle wood'.

ARNEY (Old German) 'Eagle'. The eagle is a lucky creature for Aquarius.

ARNOLD (Old German) 'As strong as an eagle'. The eagle is a lucky creature for Aquarius.

ASPEN (Old German) From the name of the tree. The aspen is a lucky plant for Aquarius.

AVERY Form of Alfred.

AYLMER (Old English) 'Noble, famous, renowned'.

BELLAMY (Greek) 'Fair friend'.

BONAMY (French) 'Good friend'. The name originates from a Guersey surname. It is occasionally found as a first name in English-speaking countries.

BOYD (Scottish Gaelic) 'Yellow'. Light yellow is a lucky colour for Aquarians.

BUD, BUDDY From an informal form of address used in the USA, meaning 'friend'. It is more usually used as a nickname than a first name.

CARADOC (Welsh) 'Amiable'. The name is little used outside Wales. It was the name of a 1st-century British king, better known in the form of Caractacus.

CARADOG Form of Caradoc.

CARTHACH Irish form of Caradoc. It was the name of an Irish saint from the 7th century.

CARTHAGE Anglicized from of Carthach.

CASSADY 'Ingenious'. Found mainly in North America it is derived from an Irish Gaelic surname. It is used as both a girls' and boys' name.

CASSINI Last name of the astronomer Giovanni Cassini who discovered the gap in Saturn's rings in 1675. The gap is named the 'Cassini division' in his honour.

CATO (Latin) 'The wise one'.

CERDIC Form of Caradoc.

CHANCE (Old English) 'Lucky, fortunate'.

CHAUNCE, CHAUNCEY (Old English) 'Lucky, fortunate'.

CLARE, CLAIR (Latin) 'Famous'. Once used as both a boys' and girls' name but now rarely used as a masculine name.

CLARENCE (Latin/Old English) 'Famous', 'illustrious'. The name is derived from a 14th-century dukedom. It has been used as a first name since the 19th century.

CLEM, CLEMMY, CLIM Shortened versions of Clement.

CLEMENCE Derivative of Clement.

CLEMENS Form of Clement.

CLEMENT (Latin) 'Kind and merciful'. The name was borne by many early saints including a disciple of St Paul who was a pope in the 1st century. It was popular in Britain during the Middle Ages.

CONRAD (Old German) 'Wise counsellor'. The name has been in use from time to time in English-speaking countries since the 15th century.

CONROY (Celtic) 'Wise man'.

CONWAY (Celtic) 'One who takes a wise course'.

CORWIN, CORWEN (French) 'Friend of the heart'.

CRONAN (Greek) 'Companion'.

CURT, KURT Forms of Conrad.

DAGMAR (Scandinavian) 'Famous'. The name was introduced into Britain by the Danes.

DANTE 'Enduring'. Form of Durant.

DEMPSTER (Old English) 'The judge'.

DERMOT (Anglicized form of the Irish name Diarmait) 'Free man'.

DERWIN (Old English) 'Dearest friend'.

DERWYN Alternative spelling of Durwin.

DEVIN (Celtic) 'A poet'.

DIARMAIT, DIARMAID (Irish) 'Free man'.

DREW (Celtic) 'The wise one'.

DRUCE (Celtic) 'Wise man'.

DURAN Form of Durand.

DURAND (Latin) 'Enduring', 'one who's friendship is lasting'. The name was introduced into Britain from France at the time of the Norman Conquest. The name was popular in the Middle Ages but is little used today.

DURANT, DURRANT (Latin) 'Enduring'. 'One whose friendship is lasting'.

DURWIN (Old English) 'Dear friend'.

EAGLE Lucky creature for Aquarius.

EHREN (Old German) 'Honourable one'.

ELDRIDGE (Old English) 'Wise advisor'.

ELMER The name has been in use in the US since the 19th century. Its use as a first name has been due to the brothers Ebenezer and Jonathan Elmer, who were leading activists in the War of American independence.

ELMO (Greek) 'Friendly'.

ELVIS (Norse) 'All wise'. The prince of wisdom. The most famous bearer of this name was the US singer Elvis Presley.

ENLIL Name given to a god of air in Mesopotamian mythology. Aquarius is an air sign.

ENKI Name given to a god of wisdom and water in Mesopotamian mythology. Saturn, one of the ruling planets of Aquarius, is the planet of applied wisdom.

EWART (Old French) 'One who serves water'. Aquarius is the sign of the water bearer.

FAUST (Latin) 'Lucky', 'auspicious'.

FELICE (Latin) 'Fortunate'. Form of Felix.

FELIX (Latin) 'Fortunate'. The name was regularly given in the Middle Ages but is seldom in use today.

FFODUS (Welsh) 'Lucky'.

FILMER (Old English) 'Very famous one'.

FILMORE, FILLMORE (Old English) 'Very famous one'.

FORTUNATUS (French) 'The lucky one'. Child of many blessings. The name has been in occasional use in the English-speaking world since the Reformation.

FRAN Shortened form of Francis.

FRANCESCO, FRANCISCO Variations of Francis.

FRANCIS (Latin) 'Free man'. One of the best-known bearers of the name was St Francis of Assisi. It was introduced into England in the early-16th century.

FRANCHOISE Form of Francis.

FRANCHON (French) 'Free being'. Derivative of Françoise.

FRANCHOT Variant of Francis.

FRANK Shortened form of Francis.

FRANKIE Variation of Frank.

FRANKLIN (Medieval English) 'Free'. Originally a medieval surname, given to those who were not of noble birth but who owned their own land. In the US the name has been made more popular by the fame of the US President Franklin D. Roosevelt.

FRANZ Variation of Francis.

FREEMAN (Old English) 'Born a free man'.

GALBANUM Lucky perfume for Aquarius.

GALEN (Greek) 'Tranquil', 'the helper'.

GANYMEDE In Greek mythology Ganymede was an important character in the story surrounding the formation of the constellation of Aquarius.

GIOVANNI First name of Giovanni Cassini, the man who discovered the gap in Saturn's rings.

GLADWIN, GLADWYN (Old English) 'Glad friend'. Originally a surname, transferred use to that of a first name.

GLASS Lucky connection for Aquarius.

GODWIN (Old English) 'God's friend'. The name was popular in the Middle Ages but is little used today.

GOODWIN (Old English) 'Good friend', 'God's friend'.

GRADY (Gaelic) 'Illustrious and noble'.

GREGORY (Greek) 'The watchful one'. Someone ever vigilant. The name was commonly used by the early Christians and was borne by several saints including St Gregory the Great, of the 6th century.

GREG, GREGG Shortened versions of Gregory.

GREGOR Variant of Gregory.

GREIOGAIR, GREAGOIR Variant of Gregory.

GWYDDION In Welsh mythology the name is borne by the lord of the skies. Aquarius is an air sign. Gwyddion is also known as the god of words.

HALEY (Gaelic) 'The ingenious one'.

HAMAR, HAMMAR (Norse) 'Symbol of ingenuity'.

HELIX Name given to the cluster of stars in the constellation of Aquarius. The Helix Nebula is 450 light years away from Earth.

JADEN (Hebrew) 'Wise'.

JANUS Name given to one of Saturn's moons.

JASPER (Persian) 'Wise man'. Jasper is the anglicized form of the name Caspar. The name was first used in medieval times and is still in occasional use today.

JUSTIN (Latin) 'Just'. The name was mainly used in Ireland until the mid-20th century when it became popular in other English-speaking countries.

JUSTUS (Latin) 'Fair and just'. The name has been in occasional use as a first name throughout English-speaking countries and Europe.

KAN (Japanese) 'Sense', 'intuition'.

KEAN 'Wise', 'learned'. Alternative spelling of Keene.

KEANE 'Wise', 'learned'. Alternative spelling of Keene.

KEENAN 'Wise', 'learned'. Form of Keene.

KEENE (Old English) 'Wise, learned'.

IRA (Old Testament) 'Watchful'. The name was used by the Puritans, who took it to America. It is now more common in America than England.

LUTHER (German) 'Famous people' or 'people's army'. The most famous bearer of this name was Martin Luther King, the 20th-century civil rights leader.

MEL, MELL Shortened forms of Melvin.

MELVIN, MELVYN (Old English) 'Friendly counsellor'.

MENDEL (Semitic) 'Wisdom'.

MINGO (Gaelic) 'Amiable'.

MUNGA (Scottish) 'Dearest friend'. Gaelic form of Mungo.

MUNGO (Gaelic) 'Amiable'. The name is occasionally found in Scotland but has never been common.

NESTOR (Greek) 'Ancient wisdom'.

NOLAN (Irish) 'Famous'. Originally an Irish surname but found occasionally as a first name in the 20th century.

OBERON Name given to one of Uranus' moons.

OLIVER (Latin) 'Olive tree'. The olive is a lucky plant for Aquarians. The name was frequently used in medieval Britain. It subsequently fell out of use but was revived in the 19th century.

OLIVIER French form of Oliver.

OLLIE Shortened form of Olive.

ONYX Lucky gemstone for Aquarius.

OSCAR (Old Irish) 'Friend'. In more recent times the name has been associated with Oscar Wilde, the Irish poet and dramatist, and with the annual awards for achievement in the film industry made by the American Academy of Motion Picture Arts and Science.

PEACOCK Lucky creature for Aquarius.

PUCK Name given to one of the moons of Uranus.

QUINN From an Irish surname, meaning 'counsel.' Occasionally used as a first name.

RADMUND Form of Redmond.

RAFE Form of Ralph.

RAGHNALL (Irish Gaelic) 'Advice', 'decision'. The Gaelic form of Ranald.

RALF (Norman French) 'Counsel'.

RALPH (Norman French) 'Counsel'. The name occurred in several forms in medieval times. The spelling 'Ralph' was adopted in the 18th century.

RAMON (Spanish) Form of Raymond. Found in the USA and occasionally in other English-speaking countries.

RANALD 'Advice', 'decision'. Anglicized form of Raghnall.

RANAL RANDEL, RANDLE 'Advice', 'decision'. Variant of Raghnall.

RANDALL Variant of Raghnall.

RANULF (Old Norse) 'Advice', 'decision'.

RAOUL (French) Form of Ralph. The name was used in medieval Britain and was revived in the 20th century.

RAYMOND (Old French) 'Advice', 'decision'. The name was introduced into Britain by the Normans and became popular in the early-20th century.

RAYNER (Old French) 'Advice', 'decision'. The name was introduced into Britain by the Normans and was revived in the 19th century.

REDMAN (Old English) 'Counsellor, advice-giver'.

REDMOND, REDMUND (Old English) 'Counsellor, protector, advisor'.

REYNARD (Old French) 'Advice', 'decision'.

REYNOLD (Old French) 'Advice', 'decision'.

RHETT 'Advice'. Anglicized form of Dutch surname. The name became more frequently used as a first name following the success of the novel *Gone with the Wind* by Margaret Mitchell (1936) in which Rhett Butler was one of the main characters.

ROBERT 'Fame'. The name was introduced into Britain by the Normans. It was borne by three kings of Scotland, notably Robert the Bruce (1274-1329) who freed Scotland from English rule. Robert has been a popular name throughout English-speaking countries for several centuries.

ROYCE (Old German) 'Kind fame'.

SAGE (Old English) 'Wise one'.

SALOMON, SOLAMON, SOLOMAN Forms of Solomon.

SATURN One of the ruling planets of Aquarius. In Astrology Saturn is the planet of applied wisdom and forward planning. In addition there is a nebula called the Saturn Nebula in the constellation of Aquarius.

SCHUYLER (Dutch) 'A scholar', 'a wise man'.

SENNETT (French) 'Old and wise'.

SHANAHAN (Gaelic) 'The wise one'.

SHANNON (Gaelic) 'Wise old one'.

SHERWIN (Old English) 'A true and loyal friend'.

SOLAMAN, SOLOMAN, SALOMON Alternative spellings of Solomon.

SOLOMON (Hebrew) 'Wise and peaceful'. King Solomon of the Old Testament was considered to be a man of great wisdom. In the Middle Ages the name was in regular use in Britain.

SOLON (Greek) 'Wise man'. Greek form of Solomon.

STAR Lucky Tarot card for Aquarius.

TAD Anglicized form of Tadhg.

TADHG (Irish and Scottish Gaelic) 'Poet', 'philosopher'. Pronounced 'Teig'. The name was popular in medieval Ireland.

TANCRED (Old German) 'Think' and 'counsel'. The name was introduced into Britain at the time of the Norman Conquest.

TEAGUE (Celtic) 'The poet'. Anglicized form of the Gaelic name Tadhg.

TEIGUE 'Poet'. Anglicized form of Tedhg.

TETHYS Name given to one of Saturn's moons.

TIMON (Greek) 'Honourable', 'valuable'.

TIMOTHY (Greek) 'Honour'. The name was borne in the New Testament by St Timothy, a companion of St Paul. It has been used as a first name in English-speaking countries since the 16th century and is still in use today.

TIM Shortened form of Timothy.

TITAN Name given to one of Saturn's moons.

TRUGAREDD (Welsh) 'Kind'.

ULICK (Irish) 'Mind', 'spirit'.

ULYSSES Classicising form of Ulick. It has been in use in English-speaking countries, especially in the US since the 19th century.

URANUS One of the ruling planets of Aquarius. In Astrology Uranus is the planet of the unusual and unexpected.

VERE (Latin) 'Faithful and true'. Originally a Norman aristocratic surname which became used as a first name in the 18th century.

VERRALL, VERRILL, VERILL Forms of Verrell.

VERRELL (French) 'The honest one'.

WINFRED (Old English) 'Peaceful friend'. The name is rarely found in modern times.

YAVIN (Hebrew) 'Understand'.

ZETAN (Hebrew) 'An olive'. Masculine form of Zeta. The olive is a lucky plant for Aquarians.

Aquarius ~ Girls

ADARA (Sanskrit) 'Consideration'.

AETHNEN (Welsh) 'Aspen'. The aspen is a lucky plant for Aquarius.

AGAVE (Greek) 'Illustrious and noble'.

AIMEE (French) 'Beloved friend'.

AISLEEN (Gaelic) 'The vision'.

AISLING (Irish) 'Dream' or 'vision'. Aisling has been given as a first name since the start of the 20th century.

AISLINN Form of Aisling.

AKILINA (Latin) 'Eagle'. The eagle is a lucky creature for Aquarius.

ALETHEA (Greek) 'Truth'. First used as a given name in the 17th century and in occasional use since then.

ALFREDA (Old German) 'Wise'. Feminine form of Alfred.

ALITHEA, ALETHIA Forms of Alethea.

ALITHA, ALITHENE Forms of Alethea.

ALLIE Shortened form of Alfreda.

ALMIRA (Arabic) 'Truth without question'.

ALMEIRA Form of Almira.

ALMERIA Form of Almira

ALTHEA (Greek) 'The healer'. In Greek mythology Althea was the mother of Meleager, who was a hero in the stories of the *Iliad*.

ALVINA (Old English) 'Beloved friend'.

ALYSSA (Greek) 'Wise'.

AMATA Form of Amy.

AMENA (Celtic) 'Honest'. One of incorruptible truth.

AMIA Form of Amy.

AMICA (Latin) 'Friend'.

AMICE A name of uncertain origin. Possibly a form of Amy or a French from of Amica.

AMICIA Form of Amice.

AMINA, AMINE Variations of Amena.

AMIRA (Greek) 'Wise'.

AMY (Old French) 'Beloved friend'. Form of Aimee. The name has been in use since the 13th century. It enjoyed a revival in the 19th century but did not become popular in the USA until the late-20th century.

ANNORA Form of Honora.

ARABELLA, ARABEL (Old German/Latin) 'Beautiful eagle'. The eagle is a lucky creature for Aquarius.

ARIANRHOD In Welsh Druid mythology, Arianrhod is the goddess of the stars, especially the Corona Borealis, also known as the Northern Crown. The star is the lucky Tarot card for Aquarius.

ARIEL Name given to one of Uranus' moons.

ASPEN Lucky plant for Aquarius.

ASTA (Greek) 'Star like'. The star is a lucky Tarot card for Aquarius.

ASTRA (Greek) 'Star like' or 'of the stars'.

ALTHENA (Greek) 'Wisdom'.

ATHENE Name of the Greek goddess of wisdom. Saturn, one of the ruling planets of Aquarius, is the planet of applied wisdom.

BELINDA (Latin) 'Wise beauty'. It is also the name given to one of Uranus' moons.

BIANCA Name given to one of Uranus' moons.

CACHEL (French) 'Hidden wisdom'.

CACHELLA (French) 'Hidden wisdom'.

CACHELLE (French) 'Hidden wisdom'.

CANACE (Latin) 'The daughter of the wind.' Aquarius is an air sign.

CARA, KARA (Celtic) 'Dearest friend'. The name has been in use since the early part of the 20th century and became increasingly fashionable in the 1970's.

CAROMY (Celtic) 'Friend'.

CALTHA (Latin) 'Yellow flower'. Yellow is a lucky colour for Aquarius.

CARIAD Form of Cara.

CAREL, CARELLA, CARELLE (Old English) 'Dearest friend'.

CARINA, KARINA (Latin) 'Beloved friend'. Carina is also the name given to a star.

CARINE, KARINE Forms of Carina.

CARITA Form of Carina or Cara.

CASSIDY 'Ingenious'. The name is from an Irish Gaelic surname and is found mainly in North America.

CELANDINE (Greek) 'Yellow water flower'. Light yellow is a lucky colour for Aquarians.

CELANDON Alternative spelling of Celandine.

CERIDWEN (Welsh) 'Poetry' and 'white'. The name is borne by the Welsh goddess of poetic inspiration. It is seldom found outside Wales.

CLYMENE (Greek) 'Fame and renown'.

CLEMENCE (Latin) 'Merciful and kind'. The name was popular with the Puritans.

CLEMENCY, CLEMENTIA Forms of Clemence.

CLEMENTINA, CLEMENTINE Forms of Clemence. These names were popular in the 19th century.

CONNIE Shortened form of Consuela.

CONSUELA (Spanish) 'Consolation' or 'A friend when in need'.

CONSUELO Form of Consuelo.

CORDELIA (Latin) 'Heart'. The name is given to one of Uranus' moons.

CRESCENT (French) 'The creative one'.

CRESCENTIA, CRESCENTA Variant of Crescent.

CRESSIDA Name given to one of Uranus' moons.

CRISTAL, CRISTALLA Forms of Crystal. It has been used as a first name since the latter part of the 19th century.

CRYSTAL, KRYSTAL (Greek) 'Clear glass'. Glass is considered to be lucky for Aquarius.

CRYSTONEL A modern name meaning 'crystal of the elves'.

DANICA (Norse) 'The morning star', The star is a lucky Tarot card for Aquarius.

DARA (Hebrew) 'Charity', 'compassion' and 'wisdom'.

DESDEMONA Name given to one of Uranus' moons. The name was borne by a character in Shakespeare's play *Othello*. The meaning of the name is 'one born under an unlucky star'.

DINAH (Hebrew) 'Judgement'. The name occurs in the Old Testament. It was regularly used by the Puritans who introduced it into the USA where it became particularly fashionable.

DIONA, DIONNA Variations of Dione.

DION, DIONNE Alternative spellings of Dione.

DIONE Name given to one of Saturn's moons. It is also a Greek form of the Latin name Diana, which means 'Divine'.

DIONARA, DIONELLA, DIONETTA Variations of Dione.

DRUELLA, DRUILLA (Old German) 'Vision'.

EADA Alternative spelling of Eda.

EAGLE Lucky creature for Aquarius.

EDA (Old English) 'Poetry'.

EDDA Alternative spelling of Eda.

EFFIE (Greek) 'Famous beauty'. The name was popular in the 19th century.

EFFY Alternative spelling of Effie.

EISTER Form of Esther.

ELFREDA (Old German) 'Wise counsellor'. The name was borne by the mother of Ethelred the Unready but was little used until it was revived in the 19th century.

ELFRIDA, ELFRIEDA, AELFREDA Alternative spellings of Elfreda.

ELRA (Old German) 'Elfin wisdom'.

ELMA (Greek) 'Pleasant and amiable'.

ELMIRA (Arabic) 'Truth without question'.

ELUNED (Welsh) 'Idol'.

ELVINA Feminine form of Elvin (Old English) 'Noble friend'.

ELVIRA (Spanish of German origin) 'True'. The name was popular in medieval times but was not used in English-speaking countries until the 19th century.

EOLANDE (Latin) 'Violet flower'. Form of Yolande. Violet is a lucky colour for Aquarius.

ESPRIT (French) 'Spirit'.

ESSA Form of Esther.

ESSIE Pet form of Estella or Estelle.

ESTEL Forms of Estella.

ESTELAR (Spanish) 'Star'. The star is a lucky Tarot card for Aquarius.

ESTELLA Form of Estelle. The name was popularized in the 19th century due to a character of this name in *Great Expectations* by Charles Dickens.

ESTELLE (French) 'Bright star'. This name was seldom used in medieval times but was revived in the 19th century and remains in use today.

ESTHER (Hebrew) 'The star'. The lucky Tarot card for Aquarius is the star. In the Old Testament, Esther was a Jewish orphan who became the Queen of Persia. The name was in regular use in English-speaking countries until the mid-20th century.

ESTRELITA Form of Estelle.

ESTRELLA Form of Estelle.

ETTY, ETTIE Forms of Esther.

EVODIE (Greek) 'One of good deed and judgement'.

FAE, FAY, FAYE Variant of Faith.

FAITH (Old German) 'One who is loyal and true'. 'Trusts in God'. The name came into use in the 16th century and remains in regular use today.

FAY (Gaelic) 'The raven'. Symbol of great wisdom. Its use as a first name may have been influenced by Arthurian legend in that it was borne by Morgan le Fay, the half-sister of King Arthur, known as the Lady of the Lake.

FAYE Alternative spelling of Fay.

FAYETTE Form of Fay.

FAYME (French) 'Of high reputation'. 'Beyond reproach'.

FLAVIA (Latin) 'Yellow'. Light yellow is a lucky colour for Aquarius. The name is a feminine form of a Roman clan name Flavius. It was borne by several early saints.

FORTUNA Form of Fortune. The name was borne by the Roman goddess of luck.

FORTUNE (Latin) 'Fate' or 'good luck'. A woman of destiny. The name was used by the Puritans in the 17th century. It is seldom found today.

FRODINE (Old German) 'Wise friend'.

GALAXY (Greek) 'Star system'. The star is a lucky tarot card for Aquarius.

GALBANUM Lucky perfume for Aquarius.

GLASS Lucky connection for Aquarius.

GREGORIA (Greek) 'The watcher'. Feminine form of Gregory.

HESSY Form of Hester.

HESTER 'The star'. From Esther. The name has been in occasional use in English-speaking countries since medieval times.

HESTHER Form of Hester.

HETTY Form of Hester.

IANTHE (Greek) 'Violet flower'. Violet is a lucky colour for Aquarius. The name was revived in the 19th century.

IOLANTHE (Greek) 'Violet flower'. The name was popularized by the opera *Iolanthe*, by Gilbert and Sullivan.

IONA (Greek) 'Violet'. Violet is a lucky colour for Aquarius. It is rarely found outside Scotland. It is also the name of a small sacred island in the Hebrides where, in the 6th century, St Columba founded a monastery.

JADA (Hebrew) 'Wise'.

JAIRA (Hebrew) 'Enlightened'.

JANUARY Name of the month in which some Aquarians are born.

JULIET Name given to one of Uranus' moons. The name is an Italian form of Julia which has increased in popularity since the mid-20th century.

HELIX Name given to the cluster of stars in the constellation of Aquarius. The Helix Nebula is 450 light years away from Earth.

HONESTY (Old French) 'Honour'. A name of recent coinage.

HONOR, HONORA, HONOUR, HONORIA (Old French) 'Honour'. The name has been in use in Britain for a thousand years. It was particularly popular in the 16th and 17th centuries and is still in occasional use today.

HOSHI (Japanese) 'Star'. The star is the lucky tarot card for Aquarius.

HYACINTH (Greek) A flower name meaning 'blue gem or sapphire'. The sapphire is a lucky gemstone for Aquarius. The name was used as a boys' name for several centuries and only came into use as a girls' name in the 19th century.

HYACINTHA Form of Hyacinth.

HYONE (Greek) 'Sea dream'.

JACADA A blend of Jacinta and Ada. Means 'sapphire' and 'happy'.

JACANDA A blend of Jacinta and Amanda. Amanda (Latin) means 'loveable'.

JACANTHA A blend of Jacinta and Samantha. Samantha (Aramaic) means 'listener'.

JACINDA A blend of Jacinta and Linda. Linda (Old German) means 'serpent', hence 'wisdom'.

JACINE A form of Jacinth.

JACINTA (Greek) 'A sapphire'. The sapphire is a lucky gemstone for Aquarius.

JACINTH (Greek) 'A sapphire'.

JACINTHA (Greek) 'A sapphire'.

JUSTINA, JUSTINE Feminine forms of Justin.

KANAKA, KANAKE 'The daughter of the wind'. Forms of Canace. Aquarius is an air sign.

KARUNA (Sanskrit) 'Compassion'.

KASOTA (Native American) 'Clear sky' (air). Aquarius is an air sign.

KAVITA (Sanskrit) 'Poetry'.

KENDRA (English) 'Knowledge'.

KICHI (Japanese) 'Fortunate'.

LIVIA Italian form of Olive. From the Latin 'the olive tree'. The olive is a lucky plant for Aquarius.

MANON (Sanskrit) 'Imagine'.

MAYU (Japanese) 'True reason'.

MAZAL (Hebrew) 'Star'. Tarot card for Aquarius.

MAZANA Origin uncertain. Probably derived from 'Amazing'.

MELVA, MELVANA, MELVENE Forms of Melvina.

MELVINA (Old English) 'Friendly counsellor'. Feminine form of Melvin.

MERRY, MERRIE (Old English) 'Joyful', 'pleasant'.

MINERVA (Latin) 'Wise and purposeful'. Name of the Roman goddess of wisdom, arts and crafts and war. The name could also be derived from Latin meaning 'mind'.

MIRANDA (Latin) 'Worthy of admiration' or 'wonderful'. Name given to one of Uranus' moons. The name was used by Shakespeare for a character in his play *The Tempest*.

MOCARA (Gaelic) 'My friend'.

MONICA (Latin) 'To counsel' or 'advise'. The name was borne by a 4th-century saint but did not become a popular name in English-speaking countries until the 20th century.

MONIQUE French form of Monica.

MYSTIQUE (Old French) 'Atmosphere of mystery'.

NALANI (Hawaiian) 'Calmness of the heavens'.

NEMISSA (Native American) Name of a star maiden in native American mythology. The star is a lucky Tarot card for Aquarius.

NOLA (Irish) 'Famous'.

NONIE 'Honour'. Pet form of Nora.

NORA 'Honour'. Short form of Honora.

NORAH Variant spelling of Nora.

NOREEN, NORENE, NORINE 'Honour'. Forms of Nora.

OFELIA, OFILIA, PHELIA Forms of Ophelia.

OHANA (Hawaiian / Native American) 'Spiritual family'.

OLIVIA Italian form of Olive.

OLIVE (Latin) 'The olive tree'. The olive is a lucky plant for Aquarius. The name came into use as a given name during the 16th century and was revived again in the 19th century.

OLIVET, OLIVETTE Forms of Olive.

OLLIE Form of Olive.

ONYX Lucky gemstone for Aquarius.

OPHELIA (Greek) 'Help'. The name given to one of Uranus' moons. It is borne by a character in Shakespeare's *Hamlet*.

ORENDA (Native American) 'Magic power'. Aquarians are interested in mystery and magic.

ORNA (Irish) 'Olive-coloured'. The olive is a lucky plant for Aquarius.

PANSY (Old French) 'Thought'. The name was first used as a given name in the 19th century.

PORTIA (Latin) 'Offering to god'. Name given to one of Uranus' moons. The name was borne by two Shakespearian characters.

PSYCHE (Greek) 'Spiritual'.

QUANDA (Old English) 'Companion'.

RABIA (Arabic) 'Fragrant breeze'. Aquarius is an air sign.

RAFAELA, RAFAELLA Forms of Raphaela.

RAISSA (French) 'The believer'.

RAISSE Form of Raissa.

RAMONA Feminine form of Ramon.

RAPHAELA (Hebrew) 'Blessed healer'. Feminine form of Raphael.

RAPHAELLA Form of Raphaela.

RAYA (Hebrew) 'Friend'.

RAYMONDE (Old German) 'Wise'. Feminine form of Raymond.

REA Alternative spelling of Rhea.

RHEA Daughter of Uranus in Greek mythology. It is also the name given to one of Saturn's moons. It's origin is uncertain but is possibly a form of Raya, which is Hebrew for 'Friend'.

RHETTA Feminine form of Rhett.

ROBERTA (Old German) 'Bright fame'.

ROMONA Form of Ramona.

ROSALIND (Old German) 'Pretty rose'. The name is given to one of Uranus' moons.

RUE (Old German) From the plant name. Rue means 'fame'.

RUTH (Hebrew) 'Compassionate and beautiful'. The name was borne in the Old Testament by the daughter-in-law of Naomi. It was a popular name with the Puritans and is now in widespread use.

SABELLA (Latin) 'Wise little one'.

SADHBH, SADHBHB 'Wisdom'. Forms of Sophie.

SAGINA (Latin) 'Wise one'.

SAGUNA (Latin) 'Wise one'.

SAMANTHA (Aramaic) 'Listener'. The name has been used in the USA since the 18th century and became popular in throughout English-speaking countries in the latter-half of the 20th century.

SAPPHIRA (Hebrew) 'Sapphire'. The sapphire is the lucky gemstone for Aquarius. The name is mentioned in the New Testament.

SAPPHIRE (Hebrew) Lucky gemstone for Aquarius. The name became popular in the 19th century.

SARADA (Sanskrit) 'Goddess of wisdom'.

SATURN One of the ruling planets of Aquarius. In Astrology Saturn is the planet of applied wisdom and forward planning. In addition there is a nebula named the Saturn Nebula in the constellation of Aquarius.

SEREN (Welsh) 'Starlight'.

SHANNAGH (Gaelic) 'Wise'. Originally an Irish surname.

SHANNAH, SHANNA 'Wise'. Forms of Shannagh.

SIDRA (Latin) 'Star-like'. The Star is the lucky Tarot card for Aquarius.

SOFIA 'Wisdom'. Alternative spelling of Sophia.

SOLAIRE, SOLAYRE A modern combination of 'the sun' (Latin) and 'air', implying good health.

SONIA, SONYA, SONJA Russian forms of Sophia.

SOPHIA (Greek) 'Wisdom'. The name was borne by several saints and has been in use in Britain since the 17th century. It was particularly popular in the 18th century and remains in use today.

SOPHIE, SOPHY, SOFIE Forms of Sophia.

STAR, STARR (English) 'A star'. The star is the lucky tarot card for Aquarius.

STAR-CHILD A modern invention, meaning 'star-child'.

STARLYTE, STARLIGHT (Old Norse) 'Light of the stars'.

STELLA (Latin) 'Star'. The name became in regular use during the 19th century and became popular in the 20th century.

STELLE (Latin) 'Star'. Form of Stella.

TARA (Sanskrit) 'Sparkling', 'star'.

THETIS (Greek) 'Positive one'. One who knows her own mind.

TIMOTHEA Feminine form of Timothy.

TITANIA (Greek) 'Great one'. The name given to one of Uranus' moons.

TOPAZ (Greek) From the name of the gemstone. Topaz is a lucky gemstone for Aquarius.

TYCHE, TUCHE Name borne by the Greek goddess of luck.

UMBRIEL Name given to one of Uranus' moons.

UNITY (English) 'Unity'. One of many names of abstract qualities adopted by the Puritans. The name was in regular use among the Puritans.

URANIA (Greek) 'Heavenly divine'. From the name of the planet Uranus, one of the ruling planets of Aquarius.

URANUS Name of one of the ruling planets of Aquarius. In Astrology Uranus is the planet of the unusual and unexpected.

VALIDA 'Very wise'. Form of Velda.

VEDETTE (Sanskrit) 'Wise little one'.

VELDA (Old German) 'Very wise'.

VELLEDA (Old German) 'Most wise'.

VERA (Latin) 'One who is honest and steadfast'. The name has been used in English-speaking countries since the late-19th century.

VERADA (Latin) 'Truthful', 'forthright'.

VERE Variation of Vera.

VERENA, VERINA Forms of Vera.

VERITA (Latin) 'Truth'.

VERITY (Latin) 'Truth'. The name was popular amongst the Puritans and is still in occasional use today.

VERELLA A blend of Vera and Ella. Ella is an Old German name meaning 'all'.

VERENA (Latin) 'Truth'. The name was borne by a 3rd-century saint.

VARENE Variation of Verena.

VERINA Alternative spelling of Verena.

VERINE Form of Verene.

VERLA Form of Vera.

VERNA Form of Vera.

VERNETTA Diminutive of Verna.

VERILA (Latin) 'Little truthful one'.

VIOLA (Latin) 'Violet'. The name was borne by one of the heroines of Shakespeare's *Twelfth Night*.

VIOLET (Latin) 'Violet'. Lucky colour for Aquarians. The name was used mainly in Scotland until the mid-19th century, when it became popular in other English-speaking countries.

VIOLETTA, VIOLETTE Forms of Violet.

VIOLANTE Form of Yolanda.

WINOLA (Old German) 'Gracious friend'.

XAN (Greek) 'Yellow'.

XANTHE (Greek) 'Yellow'. Light yellow is a lucky colour for Aquarius. The name was borne by several minor characters in classical mythology.

YELLOW Light yellow is a lucky colour for Aquarians.

YOLANDA (Greek) 'Violet flower'. Violet is a lucky colour for Aquarians.

YOLANDE, YOLANTHE Forms of Yolanda.

ZADA (Arabic) 'Lucky one'.

ZEFIRA (Italian) 'Breeze'.

ZENAIDE Form of Zenaida.

ZENAIDA 'Zeus gave life'. From Zenobia. Zeus was an important god in the story of Aquarius in Greek mythology.

ZENDA Form of Zenobia.

ZENIA Form of Zenobia.

ZENINA Form of Zenobia.

ZENNA Shortened form of Zenobia.

ZENNIE Shortened form of Zenobia.

ZENOBIA (Greek) 'Zeus gave life'.

ZENORBIE Form of Zenobia.

ZETA (Hebrew) 'An olive'. The olive is a lucky plant for Aquarians.

ZETTA, ZETTE Forms of Zeta.

Pisces

⯓

THE FISHES
19 February – 20 March

RULING PLANET   Jupiter and Neptune. Jupiter is the planet of optimism and benevolence. Neptune is the planet of the unconscious and sensitivity.

ELEMENT   Water

General characteristics
- Dreamy, intuitive, creative.
- Enjoys music, art, drama, dance.
- Often possesses creative talent.
- Sensitive, kind, compassionate.
- Has a good sense of humour.
- Warm and loving.
- Good memory, possesses wisdom.

Characteristics of young Pisceans
- Can be shy.
- Possesses a vivid imagination.
- Enjoys make-believe.
- Loves fairy stories and myths.
- Is cheerful and even-tempered.
- Dislikes routine.
- Affectionate and loving.
- Enjoys most creative activities.

Piscean lucky connections

Gemstones:	pearl, aquamarine, amethyst, beryl
Colours:	blue, violet, light green
Plants:	water plants, opium poppy, lotus
Perfume:	ambergris
Metal:	tin
Animals:	fish, dolphin
Tarot card:	the moon

PISCEANS are the dreamers of this world, the ones who frequently escape from reality into a fantasy world of their own making. They are creative individuals and this make-believe world provides an outlet for their creativity. However they are also sensitive individuals, and their fantasy world can be a place to escape to when the real world becomes a little too harsh for them to handle.

You may find at times that this sensitivity makes your Piscean child a little hard to fathom. One minute she can be squirming with laughter, the next sobbing uncontrollably. These moods swings are often a result of the fact that she can pick up every nuance of discord and react strongly against it. A cross word, not necessarily directed at her, can have her plunging into gloomy silence, retreating within herself in an attempt to hide from the hurt she feels.

This can make chastizing a Piscean something of a problem. The smallest suggestion of negativity can send her into her introspective world. Try instead to give only positive comments. Rather than tell her that she's terribly untidy, which will probably ensure that she stays that way, try telling her that you're sure

that she could do a really good job of tidying her room. You could be surprised at the result.

This sensitive side of your Piscean child can make early babyhood a trying time for both of you. You may find that, even at this young age, she will respond to harsh words by crying. But similarly if she is in a happy atmosphere she will be full of smiles and will readily join in with the laughter. Indeed Pisceans babies are frequently the most cheerful and engaging of characters, and often display the most winning ways with adults.

As your baby grows into toddler-hood you'll discover an affectionate little person who is naturally kind and considerate. She will instinctively try to comfort another crying child and soothe their pain. This empathy with others is an instinctive part of Piscean nature and she will often react to another's distress by appearing just as distressed herself.

Pisceans, although inclined to be sensitive, are among the most cheerful, generous and optimistic of characters. They also possess a wonderful sense of fun with vivid imaginations, which may result in them inventing all sorts of interesting games for their friends to enjoy. They may not wish to be the leader, but they will often be the instigator of fun.

Creativity is another strong aspect of the Piscean personality. Your little daydreamer may suddenly come alive when given the chance to perform in an impromptu play or a game of make-believe. Such fantasy games are to be encouraged for they provide your child with an important outlet for that creative imagination that they often find hard to put into words.

It is likely that your young Piscean will love music, both to soothe her as a baby and as a means of self-expression as she matures. You may often catch her dancing unselfconsciously, displaying a natural sense of rhythm as she loses herself in the music.

Drawing and painting are also wonderful outlets for your creative little Piscean. Many a Piscean has developed a career in art, drama or music. So who knows in what direction you may be steering your young Piscean as you play her music and pass her that laden paintbrush.

Pisces ~ Boys

ADRIAN (Latin) 'Man from the sea'. Linked to Neptune. The name in the form Hadrian was borne by a 2nd-century Roman emperor who was responsible for the building of Hadrian's Wall across northern England. The name Adrian was only in occasional use until the mid-20th century when it increased in popularity.

AEGIR Name given to the Scandinavian god of the sea.

AFON (Welsh) 'River'.

ALAIN French form of Alan.

ALAN (Gaelic) 'Cheerful harmony'. The name entered Britain at the time of the Norman invasion. It was popular in medieval times and remains in regular use.

ALAND, AILEAN, AILIN Forms of Alan.

ALLAN, ALLEN, ALLYN, Forms of Alan.

ALTON (Old English) 'Old stream source'.

ALUN Welsh form of Alan.

ARANKE Name of one of Jupiter's moons.

ARTEMAS, ARTEMUS (Greek) The name is connected with Artemis the Greek goddess of the moon. The moon is the lucky Tarot card for Pisces.

AQUAMARINE Lucky gemstone for Pisces.

ASHER (Hebrew) 'The laughing one'. A happy lad. The name is found in the Old Testament, borne by one of the sons of Jacob. The name was revived in the 17th century and has been in occasional use since then.

ATWATER (Old English) 'One who lives by the water'.

ATWELL (Old English) 'From the spring'. One who lives by a natural well.

AVON (Welsh) 'River'.

BLISS (Old English) 'Gladness', 'joy'.

BLUE Lucky colour for Pisces.

BLYTHE, BLYTH (Old English) 'Joyful and happy'.

BOURNE, BOURN (Old English) 'A brook'.

BURNE, BURN (Old English) 'A brook'.

BYRNE (Old English) 'A brook'.

CADMUS In Greek mythology Cadmus was an important character in the formation of the constellation of Pisces.

CAI (Latin) 'To rejoice'. Welsh form of Caius.

CAIUS 'To rejoice'. Variation of Gaius.

CALLISTO The name of the most distant of Jupiter's moons.

CARME Name given to one of Jupiter's moons.

CEDRIC (Old English) 'Amiable'.

CLEMENT (Latin). 'Kind, gentle, calm'.

CLYDE From the name of a Scottish river. It is occasionally used as a first name in English-speaking countries, particularly the USA.

COBURN (Middle English) 'Small stream'.

DARWIN (Old English) 'Lover of the sea'.

DELMAR (Latin) 'From the sea'.

DELMER (Latin) 'From the sea'.

DELVIN (Greek) 'Dolphin'. The dolphin is considered to be lucky for Pisces.

DELWIN Form of Delmar.

DERON (Old English) 'Water'.

DOUGLAS (Gaelic) 'Dark blue water'. Originally a Scottish surname and place name. As a surname it was borne by one of the most powerful Scottish families. It began to be used as a first name in the 16th century and became particularly popular in English-speaking countries in the first-half of the 20th century.

DOVEY (Hebrew) 'To whisper', suggesting a quiet character.

DYLAN (Welsh) 'Man from the sea'. In Welsh mythology Dylan is known as the god of the waves. It was used mainly in Wales until the mid-20th century when its use spread to other English-speaking countries.

EDMAR, EDMER (Old English) 'Rich sea'.

EDWARD (Old English) 'Happy guardian' or 'rich guardian'. The name has been in regular use since the early Middle Ages. Its association with the British royal families began in the 9th century when it was borne by the son of Alfred the Great. The name is still in widespread use today.

EDWIN, EDWYN (Old English) 'Happy or rich friend'. The name was borne by King Edwin of Northumbria, after whom it is believed the city of Edinburgh was named. The name was little used after the 12th century until its revival in the 19th century. It remained in regular use until the mid-20th century.

ELBOURNE (Old English) 'Elf stream'.

ENKI God of water and wisdom in Mesopotamian mythology.

EROS In Greek mythology Eros was an important character in the formation of the constellation of Pisces.

ESRA Alternative spelling of Ezra.

EWART (Old French) 'One who serves water'. Originally a Scottish surname. In occasional use as a first name.

EZ Shortened form of Ezra.

EZRA (Hebrew) 'The one who helps'. The name was borne by a prophet in the Old Testament. It has been in occasional use in the since the 17th century.

FANE (Old English) 'Glad', 'joyful'.

FARQUHAR (Gaelic) 'Friendly'.

FELIX (Latin) 'Happy', 'fortunate'. The name was borne by several early saints and has been in occasional use in English-speaking countries since the Middle Ages.

FLINT (Old English) 'A stream'.

GAIUS (Latin) 'To rejoice'. Name given to Gaius Julius Caesar. The name also occurs in the New Testament.

GALILEO First name of the Italian astronomer Galileo Galilei who discovered Jupiter's moons. The four largest moons are named the Galilean moons in his honour.

GANYMEDE Name given to one of Jupiter's moons. Ganymede is the largest moon in the Solar System.

GARETH (Welsh) 'Gentle'.

HIMALIA Name given to one of Jupiter's moons.

IKE Diminutive of Issac.

INACHUS In Roman mythology the name was borne by a river god.

ISSAC, IZAAK (Hebrew) 'Laughter'. The name is borne in the Old Testament by the son of Abraham. It was popular with the Puritans in the 17th century and was in regular use until the end of the 19th century.

JAY 'To rejoice'. Derived from the Latin name Gaius. The name has been in occasional use since medieval times.

JODA (Latin) 'Playful'.

JOVE Another name for the Roman god Jupiter.

JOVIAN 'Jupiter-like'. Name given to planets like Jupiter.

JUPITER Name given to the ruling planet of Pisces. In astrology Jupiter is the planet of beneficence, doing good or being actively kind. In psychological terms Jupiter is the guide to the psyche and is also linked to wisdom.

KAI (Japanese) 'Sea'.

KAY (Latin) 'To rejoice.' Shortened form of Gaius. Also taken to be an alternative spelling of Cai. In Arthurian legend the name was borne by a Sir Kay, one of the knights of the round table. In modern times it is more commonly used as a girls' name.

KELSEY (Old English) 'From the water'. Originally an Old English surname. It is occasional use as both a girls' and boys' name.

KHENSU Name of an Egyptian moon god. The lucky Tarot card for Pisces is the moon.

LEMARR, LEMAR (Latin) 'Of the sea'.

LYNN, LYN, LIN, LINN (Welsh) 'From the pool or waterfall'.

LYSITHEA Name given to one of Jupiter's moons.

MALIN 'Drop of the sea'. Masculine form of Mary.

MANNANAN Name given to a sea god in Irish Druid mythology, Mannanan Mac Lir.

MANNAWYDDAN Name of a god of the sea in Welsh Druid mythology.

MARLAND (Old English) 'Dweller in the lakeland'.

MARLIN (Latin) 'The sea'.

MARLON Form of Marlin.

MARLOW Form of Marlin.

MARLY Form of Marlin.

MARNE (Latin) 'Sea'.

MARVIN (Old English) 'Friend of the sea'. Also a medieval form of Mervyn. Marvin was revived in the 19th century and is found most commonly in the USA.

MEREDITH (Celtic) 'Protector of the sea'. The name was only used as a boys name in Wales until the 20th century. It is now a popular Welsh name used for both boys and girls and is found throughout English-speaking countries.

MERIDITH, MEREDYTH, MERIDYTH, Alternative spellings for Meredith.

MERIDETH, MEREDETH Forms of Meredith.

MERDYDD Form of Meredith.

MERLIN English form of the Welsh name Myrddin. Composed of Old Celtic elements meaning 'sea' and 'hill'. In Arthurian legend the name was borne by the famous wizard and advisor to King Arthur.

MORGAN (Welsh) 'Man from the wild sea'. The name has been used in Wales for centuries. Glamorgan, a Welsh county, is named after a 10th-century bearer of the name. The name is occasionally bestowed as a girl's name. Morgan le Fay, the sister of King Arthur, is a famous feminine bearer of the name.

MORIEN (Welsh) 'Sea born'.

MOULTRIE (Gaelic) Origin is uncertain but it possibly means 'sea warrior'.

MUIRIS 'Vigorous sea'. Contracted form of the Gaelic name Muirgheas.

MURCHADH 'Sea battle'. Traditional Gaelic name. Pronounced 'moor-ha'.

MURDO (Scottish) 'Sea'.

MURDOCH Gaelic form of Murdo. The name is most commonly found in Scotland.

MURPHY (Irish) 'Of the sea'.

MURRAY, MORAY (Gaelic) 'Sea'. From the Scottish surname and place name. The name has been in regular use in the English-speaking world since the 19th century.

MURROUGH Anglicized form of Murchadh.

NANNAR Name of a moon god in Mesopotamian mythology. The moon is the lucky Tarot card for Pisces.

NEPTUNE Name of one of the ruling planets of Pisces. In Roman mythology Neptune was the god of the sea.

NEREID Name of one of Neptune's small moons. In Greek mythology a Nereid is a sea nymph.

NEREUS Name given to the Greek god of the sea.

NJORD Scandinavian god of the sea.

NOAM (Hebrew) 'Joy', 'delight'.

OCEAN (Greek) 'Vast sea'.

OLOKUN (Nigerian Yoruba) 'God of the sea'.

OSIRIS Name of a moon god from Egyptian mythology. The lucky Tarot card for Pisces is the moon. Osiris was one of the principle figures in Egyptian mythology. In addition to being the god of the moon Osiris was

also a god of fertility and god of the harvest. He was also known as As-ar.

PASIPHAE Name given to one of Jupiter's moons.

PRIMAVERA (Spanish) 'Child of the spring'.

RADMAN (Slavonic) 'Joy'.

RANON, RANEN (Hebrew) 'Be joyful'.

RAYMOND (Old English) 'Wisdom, advice'.

REDINKA (Slavonic) 'Alive and joyful'.

ROCKWELL (Old English) 'Rook stream'.

SEABERT, SEBERT (Old English) 'Sea glorious'.

SEABRIGHT (Old English) 'Sea glorious'.

SEABROOKE (Old English) 'Stream by the sea'.

SEWALD (Old English) 'Sea powerful'.

SEWALL Form of Sewell.

SEWARD (Old English) 'Sea guardian'. Originally an Old-English surname used as a first name since the 19th century.

SEWELL (Old English) 'Sea powerful'.

SEYMOUR (Old English) 'Sea'.

SIDWELL (Old English) 'Broad stream'.

SINOPE Name given to one of Jupiter's moons.

STROTHER (Gaelic) 'Stream'.

STRUAN (Gaelic) 'Stream'.

TELFORD (Latin) 'Shallow stream'.

TRITON Name given to Neptune's giant moon. In Roman mythology Triton was the son of Neptune.

WESTBOURNE (Old English) 'West stream'.

WESTBROOK (Old English) 'West stream'.

WINSLADE (Old English) 'Friend's stream'.

YEO (Old English) 'River stream'.

YUL (Mongolian) 'Beyond the horizon'.

ZACK, ZAK (Hebrew) 'Laughter'. Shortened forms of Izaak.

Pisces ~ Girls

ABBEY, ABBIE, ABBY Shortened forms of Abigail.

ABIGAIL (Hebrew) 'Father rejoiced' or 'father's joy'. In the Old Testament Abigail was the name of King David's wife. The name became popular in the 16th century and again in the 20th century.

ADA (Old English) 'Happy'. The name was introduced into Britain from Germany in the 18th century and it became fairly popular.

ADABELLE Combination of Ada and Belle. Belle means 'Joyous and beautiful'.

ADABEL Form of Adabelle.

ADABELA, ADABELLA Forms of Adabelle.

ADRIANA Feminine form of Adrian.

ADRIANNA Feminine form of Adrian.

ADRIENNE, ADRIANE, ADRIANNE Feminine forms of Adrian.

AISHA (Persian) 'Happy'.

ALANA, ALANNA Feminine forms of Alan.

ALAIN, ALAYNE Feminine forms of Alan.

ALANDA A recent form of Alana.

ALCINA (Greek) 'Sea maiden'.

ALCINE (Greek) 'Sea maiden'.

ALINA, ALLENE, ALLYN Feminine forms of Alan.

ALLEGRA (Latin) 'Cheerful'. The name has been in occasional use in English-speaking countries since the 19th century.

ALMALTHEA The name given to one of the moons of Jupiter, the ruling planet of Pisces. In Greek mythology the name is given to the mother of Bacchus.

AMBERGRIS Lucky perfume for Pisces.

AMETHA Origin uncertain although it is possibly a form of Amethyst.

AMETHYST (Greek) The name of the semi-precious stone. It is a lucky gemstone for Pisces.

APHRODITE In Greek mythology Aphrodite, the goddess of love and beauty, was thought to be responsible for the formation of the constellation of Pisces.

AQUAMARINE Lucky gemstone for Pisces.

ARANKE Name of one of Jupiter's moons.

ARANRHOD (Celtic moon goddess). The Tarot card for Pisces is the moon.

ARTEMIS In Greek mythology Artemis is the goddess of the moon. The Tarot card for Pisces is the moon.

ARTEMISIA (Greek) 'Of Artemis'.

AYESHA (Persian) 'Happy'.

BEA, BEE Shortened form of Beatrice.

BEAT Shortened form of Beatrice or Beatrix.

BEATA (Latin) 'Happy'. The name was used occasionally in Britain until the 18th century, but is rarely used today.

BEATRICE (Latin) 'Bringer of happiness' or 'bringer of joy'. The name is a more common form of Beatrix. The name has been in occasional use since medieval times and is revived in the 19th century when it became very popular.

BEITRIS Form of Beatrice.

BEATRIX (Latin) 'Bringer of joy' or 'bringer of happiness'. The name has been in use since 1086 when it was mentioned in the Doomsday book. It was in regular use in the Middle Ages and revived again in the late-19th century.

BEATTIE, BEATY Shortened forms of Beatrice or Beatrix.

BERRI, BERRIE, BERRY Forms of Beryl.

BERYL (Greek) 'Precious jewel'. This gemstone is alleged to bring good fortune. Beryl is a lucky gemstone for Pisces. The name became popular at the turn of the 20th century.

BERYLE, BERIL Alternative spellings of Beryl.

BEVERLEY, BEVERLY (Old English) 'Beaver stream'. Originally a surname derived from a Yorkshire place name. It was originally used as a boys' name in the late 19th century but is now more frequently found as a girls' name.

BLISS (Old English) 'Perfect joy'.

BLITA (Old English) 'Perfect joy'.

BLITH, BLITHE Alternative spellings of Blythe.

BLITHA (Old English) 'Perfect joy'.

BLUE Lucky colour for Pisces.

BLYSS (Old English) 'Perfect joy'.

BLYTH, BLYTHE (Old English) 'Joyous and friendly'.

CAIETTA 'To rejoice'. Feminine form of Cai.

CALANDRA (Greek) 'Happy as a lark'.

CALLISTO Name of one of the moons of Jupiter, the ruling planet of Pisces. The name is given to a maiden in Roman mythology.

CANDRA, CANDRE (Sanskrit) 'Moon'. The moon is the lucky Tarot card for Pisces.

CANDY Shortened form of Candra.

CARLISS, CARLISSA Forms of Corliss

CARME Name of one of Jupiter's moons.

CARMENTIA (Roman) The name of the Roman goddess of water, childbirth and prophesy.

CHANDRA, CHANDRE (Sanskrit) 'The moon'. The moon is the lucky Tarot card for Pisces.

CHARIS (Greek) Form of Charity.

CHARISSA A modern name and an elaboration of Charis.

CHARITA Form of Charity.

CHARITY (Latin) 'Benevolent and loving'.

CHARMIAN (Greek) 'A little joy'. It was the name borne by one of Cleopatra's attendants in the Shakespearean play *Anthony and Cleopatra*. The name is still in occasional use today.

CHARRY Form of Charity.

CHERRY Form of Charity.

CHIA (Columbian Indian) 'The goddess of the moon'. The moon is the lucky Tarot card for Pisces.

CINDY Shortened form of Cynthia.

CORAL, CORALE (Latin) 'From the sea'.

CORALINE, CORALIE Forms of Coral.

CORDELIA (Welsh) 'Jewel of the sea'. The name was borne by the daughter of King Lear.

CORDELIE, CORDIE Forms of Cordelia.

CORLISS (Old English) 'Cheerful and kind hearted'.

CORLISSA Form of Corliss.

CRESCENT (French) 'The creative one'.

CRESCENTA Form of Crescent.

CRESCENTIA Form of Crescent.

CYAN (Greek) 'Dark blue'. Blue is a lucky colour for Pisces.

CYNTHIA (Greek) Alternative name for Diana, goddess of the moon. The moon is the lucky Tarot card for Pisces.

CYNTHIE, CYNTH, CYN Forms of Cynthia.

CYRENE (Greek) 'A water nymph'.

DANA Alternative form of Danu.

DANU In Irish Druid mythology the name is borne by a river goddess. She is also known as a mother goddess of the land. The name means 'sacred gift'.

DECHAN (Tibetan) 'Great bliss'.

DELIA Shortened form of Cordelia. It is also another name for the Greek goddess of the moon.

DELICIA (Latin) 'Delight'. Only recently been in use as a first name.

DELIGHT (French) 'Pleasure'. One who brings happiness to her family.

DELISA, DELIZA Form of Delicia.

DELISE Form of Delicia.

DELISHA Form of Delicia.

DELMA (Spanish) 'Of the sea'.

DELMARE Form of Delma.

DELPHA (Greek) 'Dolphin'. The dolphin is a lucky animal for Pisces.

DELPHINE (Greek) 'Dolphin'. The dolphin is a lucky animal for Pisces. The name increased in popularity in the 19th century and is still in occasional use in English-speaking countries today.

DERORA (Hebrew) 'Flowing stream'.

DIANA Name of the Roman goddess of the moon. The moon is the lucky Tarot card for Pisces. It was not frequently in use as a first name until the late-19th century.

DIANE French form of Diana.

DIANNA Form of Diana.

DINAH, DINA Forms of Diana.

DODI Form of Doris.

DORIA Forms of Doris.

DORICE, DORISE, DORRIS Forms of Doris.

DORIS (Greek) 'From the sea'. Name given to the daughter of Oceanus. The name became popular in the late-19th century and early-20th century.

DORITA Form of Doris.

EDLYN (Old English) 'Happy brook'.

EDNA EDNAH (Hebrew) 'Delight, desired'. The name occurs in the Bible and is derived from the same word as the Garden of Eden. The name became popular in the USA in the late-19th century and in Britain in the early-20th century.

EDWINA (Old English) 'Happy or rich friend'. Feminine form of Edwin.

ELARA (Greek) Name of one of Jupiter's moons. Also the name given to the granddaughter of Zeus in Greek mythology.

ELATA Form of Elara.

ELORA (Greek) 'Happy'.

ELLORA (Greek) 'Happy'.

ELSENA A blend of Elora and Cynthia.

ERWINA (Old English) 'Friend from the sea'.

EUROPA (Greek) The name is given to one of the moons of Jupiter, the ruling planet of Pisces. In Greek mythology Europa was the daughter of Agenor, King of Phoenicia.

FAINE (Old English) 'Joyful'.

FARAH (Persian) 'Joy'.

FAWNIA (Old English) 'Joyous'.

FELICE, FELIS, FELISE Forms of Felicia.

FELICIA (Latin) 'Joyous one'. The name has been in use in Britain since the 12th century but is rarely found today.

FELICE, FELIS, FELISE Forms of Felicia.

FELICIDAD Form of Felicia.

FELICITY (Latin) 'Joyous one'. In Roman mythology the name was borne by the goddess of good luck. It was also borne by two early saints. It was regularly used by the Puritans in the 16th and 17th century and remains in use today.

GAIL, GALE, GAYLE 'Father's joy'. Shortened forms of Abigail.

GELASIA (Greek) 'Laughing water'.

GELASIE Form of Gelasia.

GILA (Hebrew) 'Joy'.

GRAYLING (Old English) From the name of the fish meaning 'small gray'. The fish is a lucky creature for Pisces. It is also the symbol given to the sign of Pisces.

GRETA German or Swedish from of Margaret. The name was little used in English-speaking countries until the late 1920s.

GRETCHEN German pet form of Margaret.

GRETEL German pet form of Margaret.

GWYNETH (Welsh) 'Happiness'. The name became popular in the late-19th century initially in Wales and then throughout Britain. It is occasionally found in other English-speaking countries.

GWYNNETH (Welsh) 'Happiness'.

HENG-O Name given to a moon goddess in Chinese mythology.

HILARY (Latin) 'Cheerful' and 'merry'. The name was first used in Britain in the 12th century and was more commonly given as a boys' name. Since its revival in the 19th century the name is now more fequently given as a girls' name.

HILAIRE Form of Hilary.

HILLARY, HILLERY Alternative spellings of Hilary.

HIMALIA Name of one of Jupiter's moons.

HYACINTH (Greek) A flower name meaning 'blue gem' or 'sapphire'. Blue is a lucky colour for Pisces. The name is borne in Greek mythology by a beautiful youth who was accidentally killed by Apollo and from whose blood sprang a hyacinth flower. The name was used as a boys' name for centuries. Its use as a girls' name is a fairly recent phenomenon.

HYACINTHA, HYACINTHIA Forms of Hyacinth.

IANTHA (Greek) 'Violet flower'. Violet is a lucky colour for Pisces.

IANTHE (Greek) 'Violet flower'. The name was revived in the 19th century. It occurred in a poem by Shelley who also bestowed the name to his daughter. It remains in occasional use today.

IANTHINA (Greek) 'Violet flower'.

IDA (Old German) 'Happy'. The name originates from Mount Ida in Crete, where, in Greek mythology, Jupiter is supposed to have been hidden.

IDALIA, IDALINE, IDALINA Elaborated forms of Ida.

IDELEA, IDELIA Elaborated forms of Ida.

IDELLA Form of Ida.

IDALLE, IDELLE Forms of Ida.

ILARIA (Latin) 'Cheerful'.

INDIRA (Sanskrit) 'Moon'.

IO Name given to one of Jupiter's moons. In Roman mythology Io was the daughter of the river god Inchus.

IOLA (Greek) 'Colour of the dawn cloud'. Extension of Io.

IOLANA, IOLANI 'Violet flower'. Hawaiian form of Yolanda.

IOLANTA, IOLANTHE 'Violet flower'. Forms of Yolande.

JACINTHA, JACINTHIA Forms of Hyacinth.

JANTHINA, JANTHINE (Greek) 'Violet flower'. Forms of Iolande.

JAY Derived from the Latin name Gaius 'to rejoice.'

JODETTE (Latin) 'Little playful one'.

JOICELIN, JOICELYN, JOYCELIN
Alternative spellings of Joycelyn.

JOLANDA, JOLANDI 'Violet flower'.
Forms of Yolande.

JOVITA (Latin) 'Full of joy'.

JOY (Old English) 'Joy'. Jupiter, one of
the ruling planets of Pisces, is known
as the 'bringer of joy'. The name Joy
was popular in the 17th century and
again in the late-19th century. It
remains in regular use today.

JOYCE, JOICE (Latin) 'Gay and
joyful'. In medieval times the name
was given to both boys and girls. It
was revived in the 19th century when
it became popular only as a girls'
name.

JOYCELYN Elaborated form of Joyce.

JOYLENE A blend of Joy and Helene.
Helene is a Greek name meaning
'sun'.

JOYLYN A blend of Joy and Lynda.
Lynda is a shortened form of Belinda,
meaning 'pretty'.

JOYOUS Form of Joyce.

JOVIAN 'Jupiter-like'. The name is
given to planets like Jupiter, the ruling
planet of Pisces.

JUPITER Name of the ruling planet of
Pisces. In astrology Jupiter is the
planet of beneficence: doing good or
being actively kind. In psychological
terms Jupiter is the guide to the
psyche and is also linked to wisdom.

KAIYA (Japanese) 'Sea'. Feminine
form of Kai.

KAY See Pisces boys' names.

KORI (Maori) 'Playful'.

KUSHMA (Sanskrit) 'Always be
happy'.

KUSHUMA (Sanskrit) 'Always be
happy'.

LAKAIYA Kaiya with a La- prefix.

LANA, LANE Shortened forms of
Alana.

LARA Shortened form of Larissa.

LARETTA A blend of Lara and Betty. Betty is a form of Elizabeth, a Hebrew name meaning 'God's oath.'

LARISSA, LARISA (Latin) 'Cheerful'.

LARYETTA A blend of Larissa and Marietta. Marietta is a form of Mary meaning 'wished-for child'.

LEDA Name of one of Jupiter's moons. In Greek mythology Leda was the beautiful mother of Castor and Pollux and also Helen of Troy.

LETA (Latin) 'Glad'.

LETITIA, LAETITIA (Latin) 'Joy'. The name was fashionable in the 18th century and the spelling Letitia is still found today.

LETIZIA Form of Letitia.

LETTICE, LETTIE Forms of Letitia. Lettice was the most common form of the name Letitia in medieval times. It was also popular in Victorian Britain.

LEUCOTHEA (Greek) Name of a sea goddess in Greek mythology.

LEVANA (Hebrew) 'Moon'. The moon is the lucky Tarot card for Pisces.

LEWANNA (Hebrew) 'As clear as the moon'. The Tarot card for Pisces is the moon.

LILA (Sanskrit) 'Playful'.

LILAC (Persian) 'Dark blue or purple flower'. Blue is a lucky colour for Pisces. The name was most frequently used around the turn of the 20th century.

LOTUS (Greek) 'Flower of the sacred Nile'. The lotus is a lucky plant for Pisces.

LOWENNA (Cornish) 'Joy'.

LUANNA Form of Lewanna.

LUNETTA (Latin) 'Little Moon'. The Tarot card for Pisces is the moon.

LYN, LYNN, LYNNE (Celtic) 'A waterfall'. The name was particularly popular during the latter half of the 20th century.

LYSITHEA Name given to one of Jupiter's moons.

MADGE Pet form of Margaret.

MAE Form of May. This form of the spelling became particularly popular in the USA in the 20th century due to the fame of actress Mae West.

MAIA Name borne by the Roman goddess of spring. Pisceans are born in the spring.

MAIR 'Drop of the sea'. Welsh form of Mary.

MAIRE Irish Gaelic form of Mary.

MAIRENN (Irish) 'Fair sea'.

MAIRI Scottish Gaelic form of Mary.

MAISIE Scottish pet form of Margaret.

MALIA Hawaiian form of Mary.

MAMIE Short form of Mary.

MARA Form of Mary.

MARAMA (Maori) 'Moon'. The moon is the lucky Tarot card for Pisces.

MARE (Latin) 'Sea'.

MAREA Alternative spelling of Maria.

MAREETHA, MARITHA Blends of Mary and Aretha. Aretha is a Greek name meaning 'virtue'.

MARELLA, MARELLE A blend of Mare and Ella. Ella is an Old German name meaning 'all'.

MARGARET (Greek) 'Pearl'. The pearl is a lucky gemstone for Pisces. The name was borne by a legendary saint of the 3rd century. It was introduced into Britain in the 11th century and became very popular in medieval times. It has remained in frequent use since that time.

MARGARETA, MARGARETTA, Hungarian of Margaret.

MARGARITA Form of Margaret.

MARGE Pet form of Marjorie.

MARGERY, MARGERIE Forms of Margaret.

MARGETHE, MARGARETHA, MAIGRGHREAD Forms of Margaret.

MARGIE Pet form of Marjorie.

MARGO, MARGOT French form of Margaret.

MARGOLAINE A blend of Margo and Elaine. Elaine is an Old French form of Helen, meaning 'the bright one'.

MARGUERITA Form of Margaret.

MARGUERITE French form of Margaret. Used as a flower name in English-speaking countries since the turn of the 20th century.

MARI Welsh form of Mary.

MARIA Latin form of Mary.

MARIABELLA Combination of Maria and Bella. Interpreted as 'beautiful Mary', therefore 'beautiful drop of the sea'. The name has been in occasional use in English-speaking countries since the 17th century.

MARIAH Elaborated spelling of Maria.

MARIAN Combination of Mary and Ann. Ann is a Hebrew name meaning 'graceful'.

MARIANNE Alternative spelling of Marian.

MARIE French form of Maria.

MARIELLA Italian pet form of Maria.

MARIETTA Italian pet form of Maria.

MARILEE A combination of Mary and Lee. Lee is an Old English name meaning 'meadow' or 'wood'.

MARILENE Variant of Marilyn.

MARILYN Elaboration of Mary with the addition of Lyn.

MARILYNN, MARYLYN, MARILENE Alternative spellings of Marilyn.

MARIMNE Form of Miriam. 'Drop of the sea'.

MARINA (Latin) 'Of the sea'. The name was introduced into Britain in medieval times and was revived in the 20th century.

MARION French form of Marie.

MARIS (Latin) 'The sea'.

MARISA, MARISSA Elaboration of Maria.

MARISE Form of Marisa.

MARISELLA, MARISELA 'The sea'. Spanish form of Maris.

MARISKA Russian form of Maria.

MARITA Blend of Mary and Rita.

MARITZA Hungarian form of Mary.

MARIWIN A blend of Mary and Winifred.

MARJORIE Form of Margaret.

MARNA Swedish form of Marina.

MARNINA (Hebrew) 'To rejoice'.

MARNI, MARNIE, MARNEY (Hebrew) 'To rejoice'.

MARNIA 'The sea'. A form of Marina.

MAROLA (Latin) 'Sea'.

MAURA (Celtic) Form of Mary.

MARY An anglicized form of the French Marie, or the Latin Maria. It is a form of Miriam, from the Latin phrase meaning 'drop of the sea' or 'star of the sea'.

MAY Pet form of Mary. Often used as an independent name. It became popular in the 20th century and is still occasionally found today.

MAYA Latin variation of May. Also an alternative spelling of the Roman goddess Maia, influenced by the English name May.

MEAGAN, MEAGHAN Forms of Megan.

MEGAN 'Pearl'. Welsh form of Margaret. The pearl is a lucky gemstone for Pisces.

MEGGIE, MEGGY Pet forms of Margaret or Megan.

MEGHAN Alternative spelling of Megan. Used more frequently in the USA.

MEREL Form of Muriel.

MERGET, MARGETTE, MARGETTA, MARGALO Forms of Margaret.

MERIEL Form of Muriel.

MERIS Form of Merrie.

MERISSA, MERRISSA Blends of Meryl and Clarissa. Clarissa is a form of Clare, a Latin name meaning 'clear, bright'.

MERLYN, MERLINE Feminine forms of Merlin.

MERRY, MERRIE, MERRYN (Old English) 'Joyful, pleasant'.

MERRIEL, MERRIELLE Forms of Merrie.

MERRILL, MERRIL, MERIL Forms of Meryl.

MERYL A recent form of Muriel. It has been popularized by the US actress Meryl Streep.

META Form of Margaret.

MIA Danish and Swedish form of Maria.

MIMI Italian form of Maria. The name has been in use as an independent name since the 19th century.

MIMOSA (Latin) 'Imitative, sensitive'.

MIO (Japanese) 'Waterway'.

MIRIAM 'Drop of the sea'. Old Testament form of Maryam. The name was borne in the Old Testament by the elder sister of Moses. The name was popular in the 17th century and remains in regular use throughout English-speaking countries.

MITA A form of Mitzi.

MITZI 'Drop of the sea'. German form of Maria.

MOANA (Maori) 'Sea'.

MOIRA Anglicized form of Irish Gaelic Maire, a form of Mary.

MOON (Old French) 'The moon'. The moon is the lucky Tarot card for Pisces.

MORGAN (Welsh) 'Man from the wild sea'. The name has been used in Wales for centuries as a boys' name. Glamorgan, a Welsh county, is named after a 10th-century bearer of the name. The name is occasionally bestowed as a girls' name. Morgan le Fay, the sister of King Arthur, is a famous feminine bearer of the name.

MORGANA Feminine form of Morgan.

MORVOREN, MORVA (Cornish) 'Maid of the sea, mermaid'.

MOYA Derived from Moyra.

MOYRA Alternative spelling of Moira.

MUIREALL (Scottish Gaelic) 'White sea'. Pronounced mwir-an.

MUIREANN, MUIRINN (Irish Gaelic) 'White sea'.

MURIEL, MERIEL, MURIAL (Irish) 'Sea-bright'. The name has been used in its many forms throughout Britain since medieval times. It was revived throughout English-speaking countries in the 19th century.

MYSIE Form of Maisie.

NAJINTA, NAJMA (Arabic) 'Benevolent'.

NALANI (Hawaiian) 'Calmness of the heavens'.

NANDA (Sanskrit) 'Giver of joy'.

NAOMI (Hebrew) 'Pleasantness, delight'. The name was borne in the Old Testament by the wise mother-in-law of Ruth. The name came into general use in the 17th century and became increasingly popular in the latter half of the 20th century.

NARA (English) 'Nearest and dearest'.

NERICE (Greek) 'From the sea'.

NERIMA (Greek) 'From the sea'.

NERINA Form of Nerissa.

NERINE (Greek) 'From the sea'. It is also the name given to a sea nymph in Greek mythology.

NERISSA (Greek) 'From the sea' or 'sea-nymph'. The name was borne by a minor character in Shakespeare's *The Merchant of Venice*. The name is found occasionally in English-speaking countries.

NERITA (Greek) 'From the sea'.

NIA Welsh form of Niamh.

NIAMH (Irish Gaelic) 'Brightness or beauty'. Pronounced 'Nee-uv'. In Irish mythology, this is the name given to the daughter of the sea god.

NIBIRU Name given to Jupiter in Babylonian mythology.

NYAME (West African Ashanti) 'The goddess of the moon'.

NYREE (Maori) 'Wave'.

ONDINE (Latin) 'From the sea waves'. Form of Undine.

OOLA (Celtic) 'Sea jewel'. Form of Ulla.

ORAN (Irish) 'Green'. Light green is a lucky colour for Pisces.

ORANDA A blend of Oran and Amanda. Oran is an Irish name meaning 'green' – light green is a lucky colour for Pisces. Amanda is a Latin name meaning 'loveable'.

ORANTHA A blend of Oran and Samantha. Samantha is an Aramaic name meaning 'listener'.

PASIPHAE Name given to one of Jupiter's moons. In Greek mythology the name was borne by the wife of Minos, ruler of Crete.

PEARL (Latin) 'Precious jewel'. The pearl is a lucky stone for Pisces. It has been in use as a first name since the mid-19th century. The name was borne by the 20th-century US novelist Pearl Buck.

PEARLE, PERLE, PERL Alternative spellings of Pearl.

PEARLIE, PERLIE Forms of Pearl.

PEARLINE A blend of Pearl and Pauline. Pauline is a French feminine form of Paul, meaning 'small'.

PEGGY, PEG Pet forms of Margaret. During the early part of the 20th century the name was often used as a name in its own right.

PELAGIE (Greek) 'Mermaid'.

PERLINE Form of Pearl.

PERLINA Form of Pearl.

PHOEBE (Latin) 'Bright'. Partly identified with Artemis, goddess of the moon. The name occurs in the New Testament. It came into general use in English-speaking countries in the 17th century, becoming widespread in the latter half of the 19th century. It remains in use today.

PLEASANCE (Old French) 'Pleasure'. In the Middle Ages the name was in occasional use, but is little used today.

POPPAEA A form of Poppy.

POPPY (Latin) 'Red flower'. The poppy is a lucky plant for Pisces. It has

been used as a first name since the late-19th century and remains in use today.

RAN Name given to the Scandinavian goddess of the sea.

RANI (Hebrew) 'Joy'.

REANNA Modern alteration of the Welsh name Rhiannon.

REANNE Variant of Reanna.

RENA, RINA (Hebrew) 'Joy'.

RHIANNON (Welsh) Name from Celtic mythology. A minor deity associated with the moon. The name did not come into use as a first name until the 20th century.

RILLA (Old German) 'A stream or brook'.

RILLE Form of Rilla.

RILLETTE Form of Rilla.

RITA Short form of Margarita, the Spanish form of Margaret. In English-speaking countries the name has been in regular use as a name in its own right since the early-20th century.

RONI (Hebrew) 'My joy'.

ROSEMARIE French form of Rosemary.

ROSEMARY (Latin) 'Sea dew'. Did not come into use as a first name until the 19th century. It became particularly popular in the mid-20th century.

SALENA, SALINA Forms of Selina.

SAPPHIRA (Greek) 'Eyes of sapphire colour'. Blue is a lucky colour for Pisces. The name occurs in the New Testament.

SEDNA (North American Eskimo) 'Goddess of the sea'.

SELIA Shortened form of Selene.

SELINA, SELENA (Greek) Name of the moon goddess in Greek mythology. The Tarot card for Pisces is the moon. The name has been in use in English-speaking countries since the 17th century. The name became particularly popular in the late-20th century.

SELINDA A blend of Selene and Linda. Linda is a Spanish name meaning 'pretty'.

SELINE (Greek) Form of Selina.

SENA, SELA (Greek) Form of Selina.

SHUNA, SHUNE Forms of Sula.

SINOPE Name given to one of Jupiter's moons.

SONA (Gaelic) 'Happy'.

SOPHIA In Celtic mythology Sophia is known as goddess of wisdom. She is considered to be a central goddess of creation and the bestower of practical and spiritual wisdom.

SPRING (Old English) 'Joyous season'. Season in which Pisceans are born.

SULA, SHULA, SHULIE (Icelandic) 'Of sunny disposition'.

SUNNY, SUNNIE Usually a pet name for someone with a happy disposition, but occasionally used as a first name.

TALLULAH (Native American) 'Running water'.

TALLULA Alternative spelling of Tallulah.

TALLU, TALLA TALLIE Shortened forms of Tallulah.

TATE, TAIT, TEYTE (Old English) 'Cheerful'.

THALASSA (Greek) 'From the sea'.

THAISA (Greek) 'The sea'.

THIRZA (Hebrew) 'Pleasantness'.

TIRZA, TIRZAH Forms of Thirza.

TISHA (Latin) 'Joy'. Pet form of Letitia. It is occasionally found as a name in its own right.

TOYA (Sioux) 'Green'. Light green is a lucky colour for Pisces.

TRIS, TRISSIE 'Bringer of joy'. Shortened forms of Beatrice.

TRIX, TRIXIE 'Bringer of joy'. Shortened forms of Beatrix.

ULLA, ULA (Celtic) 'Jewel of the sea'.

UNDINE, UNDINA (Latin) 'From the sea waves'. In mythology, a female water spirit.

VENETIA (Welsh) 'Happiness'. A name of uncertain origin but possibly an elaborated form of Gwyneth. Has been in occasional use since medieval times.

VERDA (Old French) 'Green, spring-like'. Light green is a lucky colour for Pisces. In addition Pisceans are born in the early spring.

VI Shortened form of Violet or Viola.

VIOLA (Latin) 'Violet'. The name is widespread in Italy and is in occasional use in English-speaking countries.

VIOLET (Middle English) From the flower name. Violet is a lucky colour for Pisces. The name was most frequently used in Scotland until the mid-19th century when it became more widespread throughout other English-speaking countries.

VIOLETTE, VIOLETTA Diminutives of Violet or Viola.

VITOULIA (Latin) Italian derivative of Violet.

YEMANJÁ (Afro Brazilian) 'Goddess of the sea'.

YOKO (Japanese) 'Ocean child'.

YOLANDA, YOLANDE (Greek) 'Violet flower'.

YOLA (Greek) 'Violet flower'.

YOLANDRA Blend of Yolanda and Sandra. Sandra is a variant of Alessandra, the Italian form of Alexandra, 'protector'.

YOLANTA A form of Yolanda.

YOLANTHA A blend of Yolanda and Samantha. Samantha is an Aramaic name meaning 'listener'.

YOLARA A blend of Yolanda and Lara. Lara is a form of Larissa, a Latin name meaning 'cheerful'.

YOLINA A blend of Yolanda and Lina. Lina is a shortened form of Caroline, a feminine form of Charles which means 'man'.

YOLITHA A blend of Yolanda and Talitha. Talitha is an Aramaic name meaning 'little girl'.

YOLONDA A blend of Yolanda and Londa. Londa is a form of Ilona, a Hungarian form of Helen which means 'light' or 'the shining one'.